WHERE HE STANDS

WHERE HE STANDS

Albert Shanker of the American Federation of Teachers

Dickson A. Mungazi

Westport, Connecticut
London

Library of Congress Cataloging-in-Publication Data

Mungazi, Dickson A.
    Where he stands : Albert Shanker of the American Federation of
Teachers / Dickson A. Mungazi.
        p.   cm.
    Includes bibliographical references and indexes.
    ISBN 0-275-94929-X (alk. paper)
    1. American Federation of Teachers.   2. Shanker, Albert.   3. Labor
leaders—United States—Biography.   4. Education—United States—
Philosophy.   I. Title.
LB2844.53.U6M85   1995
331.88′113711′00973—dc20   94-25964

British Library Cataloguing in Publication Data is available.

Library of Congress Catalog Card Number: 94-25964
ISBN: 0-275-94929-X

First published in 1995

Praeger Publishers, 88 Post Road West, Westport, CT 06881
An imprint of Greenwood Publishing Group, Inc.

Printed in the United States of America

The paper used in this book complies with the
Permanent Paper Standard issued by the National
Information Standards Organization (Z39.48–1984).

10 9 8 7 6 5 4 3 2 1

*To my sister, Victoria, who shared with me the
trials and pain of losing our mother early in life.*

Where one stands on issues helps to find solutions to problems of society.

Albert Shanker, 1993

Contents

Photographs follow page 106

Preface

THE PURPOSE OF THE STUDY

The purpose of this study is to present some of the important features of Albert Shanker's work in American education, both as an individual and as a well-respected leader in this field. From the moment he entered the teaching profession in 1952, through his election as president of the American Federation of Teachers (AFT) on August 20, 1974, to the present, Albert Shanker stands tall as a visionary leader. While it is not easy to separate Shanker the man from Shanker the union leader, this study is actually an attempt to present Shanker the man through what others have to say about him, what has been written regarding him, and how his record speaks for itself. That he is president of the AFT only adds an interesting dimension. Separating the professional from the individual assists in ascertaining how Shanker has influenced the development of the AFT as a national organization during his stewardship.

With this approach the study focuses upon seven specific areas of importance in order to give the reader pertinent background information about this remarkable American educational leader. These areas of import are the AFT in a historical perspective, the AFT and its legacy of educational leadership, the United States during Shanker's lifetime, Shanker and his mission, Shanker's philosophy, his viewpoints on various issues, and his relationships with other people and organizations. That the study is written primarily from original materials and records enables the author to present something novel about how Shanker has helped influence American society. Although a number of articles have been written about Shanker and teacher organizations in general, the fact that no major study of him has been undertaken is the catalyst for this study. Where appropriate, secondary sources are utilized to strengthen concepts that are important to the central argument of the study.

THE APPROACH AND THE PRESENTATION

This study begins with a discussion of some of the critical events that began to unfold at the beginning of the twentieth century and how they influenced future developments in the United States. These events include the coal miners' strike of October 1902, which was related to the students' strike that broke out in Chicago at that same time. This discussion shows that coming from the period of the Industrial Revolution, the United States, like other Western countries, entered the twentieth century under the cloud of an illusion that industrial technology would bring a panacea for all social evils.

In the midst of the excitement over the possibility of meaningful change, the American people would soon learn that no matter how advanced or good it seemed, industrial technology was no substitute for the ability to resolve problems through human cognition. The study then moves on to discuss the events that led to the formation of the American Federation of Teachers in 1916. These include the unwillingness of politicians, including members of school boards, to recognize the need to improve the conditions under which teachers worked. Although the National Education Association (NEA) was founded in 1857, coincidentally the year of the *Dred Scott* decision, it persistently refused to be involved in the political aspects of teachers' work, preferring instead to restrict its activity to the professional development of teachers. The NEA was not cognizant that by the very nature of the American system, its democratic political process was, and still is, directly and inextricably linked to professional development.

In 1916, when the United States was being slowly drawn into the war in Europe, school boards refused to do anything to eliminate the hardships that teachers were facing. This is why a group of teachers in Chicago formed the AFT. During its formative years the AFT was led by dedicated and highly persuasive women. Women were not given much respect as both teachers and members of society. They were not allowed to vote until the ratification of the Nineteenth Amendment in 1920. During that time female teachers utilized the denial of their basic human rights to demonstrate their ability to understand issues and render opinions about them. This is why, from the installation of the first AFT president, Charles Stillman, in 1916 to the end of David Selden's last term in 1974, the leaders of the AFT have provided the kind of leadership needed to ensure the growth of their organization.

The study then goes on to discuss certain major events that began to take shape in 1928, the year that Shanker was born. Naturally, these events include the Great Depression of 1929, the election of Franklin D. Roosevelt in 1932, the economic hardships that people all over the world faced, the initiation of the New Deal programs in 1933, the disaster of the Munich conference in 1938, the outbreak of war in 1939, the death of President Roosevelt in 1945, the election of Harry S. Truman in 1948, the election of Dwight D. Eisenhower in 1952, the confirmation of Earl Warren as chief justice of the U.S. Supreme Court in 1953, the landmark 1954 *Brown* decision, the Rosa Parks incident in 1955, the 1957 desegregation crisis in Little Rock, the launching of Sputnik in the same year, the enactment of the 1958 National Defense Education Act, the visit to the

United States of Nikita Khrushchev in 1959, the Gary Francis Powers incident in 1960, the election of John F. Kennedy in the same year, his tragic death in 1963, the march on Washington in the same year, and the passage of the Civil Rights Act in 1964.

These events were merely a prelude to even more dramatic events that were predetermining the direction the country was taking. These include the uprisings in major cities in 1965, the release of the Kerner Report in 1967, and the tragic death of Martin Luther King, Jr., and Robert Kennedy in 1968. These events had a profound impact on Shanker as he struggled to find his place in a troubled society. In presenting his philosophy, the study delineates his beliefs regarding society from his philosophy of education. This study concludes that Shanker has persistently integrated these two components, social and educational, in order to strike a balance in seeking improvement in society. Shanker has based his crusade to help transform society on these two components. His positions on critical national issues reflect the essential tenets of his outlook on the meaning of life.

Finally, the study discusses the kind of relationships that Shanker has had with other people and organizations. This discussion indicates that Shanker's advice has been sought by an array of people in various professions. His series of short articles entitled *Where We Stand* has been read by millions of people all over the world. His readership includes politicians, teachers, people in higher education, parents, and the general public. Chapter 6 presents insights into the kinds of issues Shanker has discussed in this column. The reader will see that Shanker diligently took his time to conduct a thorough study of all the pertinent arguments on an issue to ensure that he fully understood them before he expressed his viewpoint. One sees in this approach to national issues that Shanker is a man who embraces the principles of democracy, who listens carefully to arguments and welcomes diversity as a source of national enrichment.

SUMMARY AND IMPLICATIONS

The final chapter summarizes the preceding main features and arguments. It also draws conclusions and discusses their implications. The following are some of the conclusions the study reaches: Shanker's struggle during the early years of his life translated into struggles he undertook as a teacher, and then as a leader; Shanker's ability to comprehend issues and to articulate his own position on them has been a product of his effort to apply logic in seeking solutions to problems; Shanker has sought to understand all relevant points of view on an issue before he has tried to explain his own position. He has done this by widely reviewing the available literature. For this reason he has become a well-read and informed leader; Shanker's advice has been sought from various quarters, both nationally and internationally, because he has endeavored to review all existing knowledge about the issues in question. This is why his opinions reflect a well-rounded grasp of the issues he has discussed.

Shanker is under no illusion as he struggles to help shape the direction of the development of the AFT and education. He realizes that new problems, both social and educational, have become far more complex than in the past, with no easy solutions to them. These include the future of public education, violence and drugs in schools, teenage pregnancy, AIDS, the disintegration of the nuclear family, changes in social and moral values, pervasive disrespect toward teachers and school, declining financial resources, the need for curriculum reform, the training of teachers to meet the challenges of the new age of technology, increasing illiteracy, a growing confusion about the purpose of education, and the failure of politicians to put the educational needs of students high on the national agenda. Shanker concludes that the United States must pool its resources, people and financial, to find solutions to these problems in order to place the nation on a more solid footing as it prepares to meet the challenges of the future. This presents a new challenge to the country, to him, and to the American Federation of Teachers.

Acknowledgments

In the process of writing a book that covers important events in the life and work of a national leader, one must rely on archives, records, and materials supplied by those in a position to do so. It is for this reason that the author wishes to thank Albert Shanker himself for supporting this project and giving the author the opportunity to interview him on May 17, 1993. The author had an opportunity to meet and know this remarkable American leader and to appreciate what he has been trying to accomplish. It is worth noting that this study was initially undertaken with a somewhat skeptical attitude about Shanker's leadership of the AFT and the agenda he tried to accomplish. The results of the study have led to the dissipation of any reservations, resulting in nothing but total respect and admiration for this outstanding human being and national leader.

The author also wishes to thank Eve Sacks, Albert Shanker's secretary, and her assistant, Anna Agolli, for arranging the interview and for making available to him other important materials that enabled him to produce the study. He also wishes to thank the Archives of Labor and Urban Affairs of Wayne State University, Detroit, Michigan, for allowing him access to the voluminous and priceless materials it holds on the AFT and Shanker. The author wishes to thank Judith Schiff, chief research archivist of the Yale University Library, for materials on Jerome Davis, and Senator Ralph J. Marino, president pro tem of the New York State Senate, for materials on Clayton R. Lusk.

The author also wishes to thank several of his colleagues at Northern Arizona University for the support and the encouragement they have given him in the development of this and other projects. These include Linda K. Shadiow, Robert E. Holloway, L. Kay Walker, Sam Minner, Paul Lansing, Margaret Hatcher, Ardeth Cropper, and Jon Engelhardt, the executive director of the Center for Excellence in Education. He also wishes to thank Betty Russell, computer specialist; Ed Belunski, director of personnel; Deborrah K. Hawthorne, administrative secretary for research; and Jeannette Weatherby, director of faculty support services, for the various forms of assistance they provided in the course of producing the manuscript. He also wishes to express his special appreciation to Janice Truitt, a high school teacher in Tucson, Arizona, for materials relating to merger negotiations between the NEA, of which she is a member, and the AFT; Carla Duran, typographer; and Linda Gregonis, indexer and proofreader.

Finally, the author wishes to thank the members of his family--wife Della, daughter Marcia, and sons Alan and Gaylord--for their support and encouragement without which the study would not have been completed.

Introduction

THE PURPOSE OF THE STUDY

The formation of the American Federation of Teachers (AFT) in 1916 was an event that was destined to alter the future character of American education and the society it serves. It also ushered in a new era of interaction between teachers and the administrative structure, between teacher organizations and the government, and between the leaders of teacher organizations and the public. The purpose of this study is to present some of the important facts about the role that Albert Shanker played as an individual and as the president of the AFT. In that capacity Shanker has directed the activities of the AFT with a true understanding its purpose and functions. He has operated with a knowledge of the importance of leadership in a national climate that has placed the AFT in an environment of competing forces that have influenced the continually changing character of American society.

For Shanker, leadership of the AFT has presented both a challenge and an opportunity to influence the upgrading of education in a way that could help lead to the greatness of a nation. While he harbors no illusion about the immensity of the task at hand, he has not shied away from facing it and accepting the challenges that present themselves. This study furnishes evidence to show that in doing so, Shanker has demonstrated the importance of respecting democratic principles. Indeed, his term of office has shown that a strong and effective leader does not have to become a dictator. Rather, he encourages the offering of diverse points of view in addressing critical issues. The utilization of basic human values, common sense, and respect for differences of opinion has made Shanker the kind of person and leader he has become.

The question of educational leadership in any country must, by necessity, be discussed within the framework of historical developments that influence it. It is an accepted truth that human responses to events and efforts to plan for the future are rooted in historical developments. This is the reason why experts tell us that we must study the past in order to better understand the present and to plan the future. George Santayana (1863-1952), an American thinker, is credited with saying that if man does not learn from history, then he is bound to repeat its errors. The reality of human experience is that it is an outcome of historical developments. Without an effective knowledge of the past, human experience has limited options. Without a functional knowledge of history, it is hard to understand the present and to effectively anticipate and plan for the future.

THE INFLUENCE OF THE STUDY

Although we are reminded that the only thing we learn from history is that we do not learn from it, we can also deduce that we simply cannot ignore it if we are to make any true progress in the human endeavor on this planet. We must further learn that effective planning for the future must take account of the past. One need cite only a few examples to substantiate this conclusion. The economist who predicts an economic growth rate does so from his knowledge of similar events that have already taken place. The economic theories presented in John Locke's *On Education*, or the discussion of the rate of interest and the value of understanding finances in John Maynard Keynes's *General Theory of Employment, Interest, and Money* might serve as his or her guide.

In the same way, the biologist who studies how species can become extinct might utilize Charles Darwin's *Origin of Species* to reach his conclusions. The astronomer who explains how the universe operates might utilize his knowledge of Galileo Galilei's *A Dialogue on the Two Principal Systems of the World* to show why his explanation is accurate. In a similar vein, Arnold Toynbee and H. G. Wells echoed that one must gain a functional knowledge of the past in order to avoid errors that may thwart his need to understand the present and plan the future. Wells was particularly poignant when he suggested shortly before the outbreak of the First World War that "Human history becomes more and more a race between education and catastrophe."

In a similar fashion, a philosopher who wishes to influence the emergence of new social perceptions in his or her society might utilize Plato's *The Republic* as a basis for articulating a new theoretical position. An educator who may wish to enunciate a new theory of pedagogy might rely on his knowledge of Jean Jacques Rousseau's *Emile* to obtain fresh insights into how children learn and the kind of environment they require to maximize their success in their academic efforts. These examples suggest that history seems to provide new directions in human endeavor and enterprise and that society must at all times operate under the constraints and imperatives it provides.

A college football player who aspires to the prestigious Heisman Trophy must study what previous recipients, such as Jay Berwanger in 1935, Ernie Davis in 1961, and John Huarte in 1964, did to gain that recognition. In a similar manner, a football coach who thinks about his place in the history of the game must study what gave, for example, George Halas, Samuel Baugh, Vince Lombardi, John William Heisman, Paul "Bear" Bryant, and Joe Paterno the label of "great" that history has ascribed to them. This is why Muhammad Ali used to obtain inspiration from the success of Jack Dempsey, Joe Louis, and

Gene Tunney. These examples show that history is important to all forms of human endeavor.

THE AFT IN A HISTORICAL PERSPECTIVE

The formation of the National Education Association (NEA) in 1857 signaled the beginning of a new course of events in the profession of teaching. Since then, the NEA has operated under its traditional principle that teachers must refrain from involvement in politics because the time-honored profession of which they are members places an emphasis on the delivery of educational goods to their students. As such, they must leave the process of making decisions about the conditions under which they serve to someone else. The application of this principle by the NEA led to the continuing deterioration of conditions under which teachers worked suggests the error of adopting it as a modus operandi for members of the teaching profession. In a highly charged national political climate that intimately affects education, the fact that politically motivated persons sit on the school board in and of itself dictates a political involvement by teachers. To be apolitical is a contradiction in terms in a democracy.

By the end of the nineteenth century the image that the NEA had been trying to promote, that of teachers belonging to an exclusively professional group, was shattered by a set of political events that had a profound impact on teachers and their profession. The excitement of what Charles Dickens called the "best of times," made possible by technological advances that led to socioeconomic affluence, turned into the "worst of times," an abyss of despair, as economic decline and unemployment became the lot of most people. This dream-turned-to-nightmare precipitated an urban decay of unprecedented proportions. Teachers, who have always been on the outer edge of economic comfort, endured many of the burden and hardships from economic stagnation. The hope of a better life that President Grover Cleveland expressed at the beginning of his second term of office in 1893 was lost in the illusion of the quest for a utopia envisaged as the outcome of the Industrial Revolution. What kind of future did these events predict?

In 1902 the political involvement that the NEA had tried to avoid translated itself into an unexpected strike by students and teachers at Clarke School in Chicago. The students demanded that the school board allow their teachers to design programs that would adequately prepare them to function efficiently in a rapidly changing world. The teachers, in turn, demanded that their working conditions be greatly improved so that they could deliver to their students the educational goods they were trained to deliver.

The tragic death of President William McKinley in 1901 accentuated an already rapidly declining national morale. In these events the soul of the nation was being tested in painful ways. For NEA teachers, not only in Chicago but across the country, the professional principles they thought they were operating under were being questioned in ways that raised serious doubts about their future.

The profession that they had believed would assure the salvation of the nation was being placed perilously in the crossroads of conflicting national values.

The strike by teachers and students in Chicago was a sequel to the strike that 140,000 mine workers staged in May, only four months earlier, which suggests the conclusion that the will of the nation to shape the future much differently from the past was going through a period of crisis. The action taken by President Theodore Roosevelt in asking J. P. Morgan to mediate in the strike indicated the reality that the problems facing the nation could only be resolved within the spirit of collective action. This is the principle that the AFT later sought to make an integral component of its vision for the future. President Roosevelt knew that the mine workers had lost confidence in the ability of mine authorities to do them economic justice.

Four months later President Roosevelt also knew that teachers and students had lost confidence in the ability of the school board to render them educational justice. The combination of the outcomes of these strikes placed the country in an untenable situation. The polarization of the mining industry and the educational process, two national systems that were crucial to the future of the nation, cast a long dark shadow on its endeavor to redefine and shape its own destiny. What was so painfully disturbing about the conflict that emerged in these two national institutions is that they served as a reminder of how vulnerable the development of the country was, given the results of the labor strike of 1886.

That this conflict inflicted severe injury to national prosperity is evidenced by the fact that the decline in national productivity had a startling effect on the ability of teachers to deliver educational goods to their students. They went on working for months without pay. During the strike railroad traffic was disrupted, and trains were derailed, bringing the transportation system and the delivery of goods to a halt. The net result was social strife and labor unrest, which became the new order of things. In the process the belief in a prosperous future became derailed.

These events could not be allowed to continue without inflicting lasting damage to the nation, indicating a dire need to resolve the issues that were the precipitators of the crisis. By 1916 teachers had realized that as a result of the NEA's stated principle of refraining from political involvement, they and the educational system had been subjected to a set of debilitating conditions. The formation of the AFT resulted from the belief that teachers could and must play a constructive role in seeking solutions to the problems they were facing so that they could focus on what their profession demanded, which was teaching. Therefore, a discussion of the AFT and the role that its leadership played in shaping the course of its development must be initiated from a historical perspective.

ORGANIZATION OF THE STUDY

While this study is a discussion of the work that Albert Shanker has done as president of the AFT, it covers features and events related to American society as well. In order to give a clear picture of that work it is first necessary to trace the major developments surrounding the AFT itself from its inception up to Shanker's election. It is for this reason that Chapter 1 discusses certain events that took place in the history of the AFT. The appropriate place to start is the strikes that were staged by teachers and students in Chicago in 1902. It will be seen that as soon as the strike was settled, the political process that the NEA tried to avoid took to the center stage in interactions that took place between teachers and school boards.

It is not surprising that during its formative years the core of leadership in the teachers' movement came from women. The reason women played a crucial leadership role in teacher organizations is not hard to understand. Because women did not have any political rights or influence until the ratification of the Nineteenth Amendment some eighteen years later in 1920, they became a target of school board members who were invariably male. An example discussed in this study is the saga of the conflict that broke out at Jackson School in Chicago between teachers and the school board in 1902.

There Janie McKeon, an articulate and brilliant teacher, dismissed a student from her class for repeatedly using abusive language against another student. McKeon felt that the behavior was inconsistent with the expectations that the school had placed on all students and that the student did not even make any efforts to change his behavior. This, in turn, suggested to her that he really was not interested in education and that he should be removed from the educational environment in order to give the rest of the students an opportunity to learn.

To McKeon's surprise the board of education considered her action too severe and suspended her, arguing that she had no authority to take such an action against the student. She was even reprimanded for her refusal to allow him back in the classroom. In this environment the situation edged closer to a crisis when the board of education refused to discuss the issue with McKeon. Without an organization that could come to her aid, McKeon had no recourse to protect herself, but her students came to her rescue. One does not have to search far for the reasons that lead to the conclusion that this conflict was a product of the political process taken by the school board, that it was taking advantage of the situation in the absence of an organization that could protect teachers' rights.

This climate set in motion a chain of events that eventually led to the formation of the AFT. The principal players in this drama were, in addition to McKeon, Albert Speer, the district superintendent; John Powers, the alderman representing the district in which Jackson School was located; and Edwin G. Cooley, the superintendent of schools in Chicago. The fact that Powers and Cooley were political opponents cast the McKeon case into a political arena, rather than into an educational forum in which debate and conflict resolution would be removed from consideration of political gains to be made.

The best that the teachers in Chicago could do was to watch the conflict unfold from the side lines. Without any organization to protect them, they refrained from involving themselves in an explosive situation, fearing that they would join McKeon in an early retirement without benefits. Although Cooley won the struggle with Powers, Powers succeeded in arousing a new level of political consciousness. This later became a distinctive component of the strategy that the AFT would utilize with remarkable success.

This chapter also shows how this conflict attracted the attention of people throughout the country to a cause they believed had serious implications for the future. McKeon's cause became their cause. It brought out the best in powerful and influential women such as Catherine Beecher, Catherine Goggin, Florence Rood, Susan B. Anthony, Margaret Haley, Ella Flagg Young, Henrietta Rodman, and Nancy Cott. They concluded that the fate of Janie McKeon was, in essence, their fate. It was as a result of this crisis that women began to exercise effective leadership in the teachers' organizational movement. The awareness that the public must be informed about the plight of teachers caused the AFT at its inception to found a journal, *The American Teacher*. It has been in circulation ever since. Although the founding of the AFT occurred at the time the United States was about to enter the European conflict, it did not lose sight of its vision and intent.

Chapter 2 examines how the AFT exercised effective educational leadership as a legacy of its past. The election of Charles Stillman from Wilmette, Illinois, to serve as the first president of the AFT signaled the beginning of a new course of development in the teachers' organizational movement. Indeed, Stillman carried out his responsibility with nothing less than a total dedication to the purpose and objectives the AFT had outlined. Two of these objectives still direct the activity of the union today. The first was to seek improvement in the conditions under which teachers worked. These conditions included better salaries and benefits. The second objective was to ensure the professional competency of teachers as a necessary condition for assuring quality education in the classroom.

From the beginning of the AFT's operation quality leadership was the primary instrument with which it sought to accomplish its objectives. Stillman was assisted by a committee whose members shared his dedication to the cause. In identifying the lack of effective educational leadership as the principal factor in the decline of education, he and the committee sought ways of bringing about improvement. At the time the AFT believed that high school graduates failed to function in society because they failed to avail themselves of the tangible benefits of education. It is amazing that in the report *A Nation at Risk*, released in 1983, the Commission on Excellence in Education reached the same conclusion.

In seeking solutions to the problems of educational leadership, the AFT tried to raise to a new level of public consciousness of the need to take immediate action in key areas of the educational process. Necessary steps included eliminating large classes, introducing methodological innovation, improving teachers' academic and professional competency, introducing an effective system of public relations, and initiating an ongoing process of dialogue between teachers and administrators. By the time that Florence Rood succeeded Stillman in 1924, the AFT had been placed on a solid foundation.

Although Stillman had encountered a number of problems, which included budgetary limitations and his declining health, the executive committee had given him the support he needed to carry out his charge. When Mary C. Barker of Georgia succeeded Rood in 1926, the AFT was able to look to the future with high expectations. This was because the agenda that had been established during Rood's term of office was yielding tangible results. Membership was slowly increasing, and the financial problems that Stillman had encountered had been overcome. The result was that confidence in the future was increasing.

When Henry R. Linville, the first editor of *The American Teacher*, succeeded Barker in 1931, the AFT was examining the possibility of accomplishing other critical aspects in its objectives. Its members were increasingly becoming critical of the autocratic rule that boards of education and school administrations enjoyed in pursuing policy. Linville had faulted this practice in an editorial he wrote in *The American Teacher* in 1917. Now that he was the chief executive of the AFT, he became aggressive in seeking a resolution of this problem. Linville did so with the awareness that the organization that he led was steadily growing stronger and school administrators could not take action against him without risking adverse results.

In 1919, fearing that the AFT was gaining a measure of political influence that it had not had in the past, the New York state legislature named a committee under the chairmanship of Senator Clayton R. Lusk to investigate possible seditious activities and suggest ways of curbing its rapidly growing influence. The Lusk Committee identified two problems: (1) the declining quality of high school education due to lack of innovation in the curriculum and (2) the aggressive leadership of the AFT, which was placing more importance on political rights for teachers than on the educational benefits that they were charged with providing students. By the time Jerome Davis assumed the presidency of the AFT in 1936, the leadership role of the AFT had been fully established. From that time to the end of David Selden's term of office in 1974, which signaled the beginning of Albert Shanker's stewardship, the kind of leadership that the AFT provided could be measured in terms of its ability to be self-directive.

Chapter 3 discusses some important developments that took place in the United States beginning in 1928, the year that Shanker was born, up to the present. The first major events that took place in 1928 were the presidential nomination of Republican Herbert Hoover and his Democratic opponent, Alfred E. Smith, the powerful governor of New York. This was a pivotal year for the AFT. The announcement made by President Calvin Coolidge in 1927 that he would not seek a second term as president was followed by an announcement in February 1928 by Herbert Hoover that he would seek the nomination of the Republican party for president of the United States.

By the time that Shanker was born in September, the election campaign was heating up. The country was totally unaware that it was about to experience the most serious economic disaster in its history. Although the Wall Street crash in October 1929 was a clear indicator that the economy was in serious trouble, Hoover refused to see things from this perspective, making it impossible to design an effective strategy for dealing with the economy. Although the Republican party nominated him in 1932 for a second term as president, Hoover knew that he had little chance of being reelected. Franklin D. Roosevelt and his New Deal in 1932 rejuvenated the confidence of Americans. Roosevelt's encouraging tone in saying that the only thing Americans had to fear was fear itself inspired them to look to the future with determination.

Critical events in the United States during the next decade were closely related to events in Europe. The rise of the Third Reich in 1933, the athletic exploits and conquests of Jesse Owens in 1935 and 1936, the outbreak of the civil war in Spain in 1936, the Munich conference in 1938, and the surprise attack on the United States by Japan in 1941 had a profound effect. As soon as he was able to understand, Shanker saw these developments as being conceptualized in a global climate that produced conflicting forces that had to be appeased if the future was to be better than the past.

The introduction of the GI Bill and the publication of Gunnar Myrdal's *American Dilemma*, both in 1944, paved the way for events that would impact the development of the United States in directions that had not been anticipated. The sudden death of President Roosevelt in 1945 brought Harry S. Truman to the office of president at a time when the world was beginning to recover from the devastation of the war, raising the hope that peace would be restored for the benefit of all mankind.

The convening of the San Francisco conference in 1945 to restructure the world order as a sequel to the end of the war was marked by a collective endeavor to put the past behind them now that the threat posed by the Axis powers had finally been eliminated. However, President Truman's authorization to use the atomic bomb to end the war ushered in the period of nuclear technology, changing the way the world perceived itself and the nature of relationships that emerged among nations and individuals. The unfinished business of the war came into sharp focus as nations collectively decided to take part of the responsibility for the outbreak of the war in their individual and collective failure to articulate national and international policies consistent with the broader aspirations of people everywhere.

The fact that the hope for a better future at the end of the war was dashed by the beginning of the Cold War is evident in such events as the Korean War and the beginning of the McCarthy era. The election of Dwight Eisenhower as president of the United States in 1952, the year that Shanker began his career as a teacher, was followed in 1953 by the unexpected death of Frederick Vinson, chief justice of the U.S. Supreme Court, and the succession of Earl Warren. This set the stage for the momentous *Brown* decision in 1954, changing the character of American society. By this time Shanker was vigorously involved in teacher organizations.

Watching the drama of the civil rights movement unfold, Shanker marched with Martin Luther King, Jr. following the Rosa Parks incident in Montgomery, Alabama, in 1955. He became involved in these critical developments in the country because he believed that the plight of any ethnic group was the plight of the United States itself. He, as well as other citizens, felt that they had a responsibility in shaping the future of the country. The launching of the Sputnik in 1957, followed by the enactment of the National Defense Education Act in 1958. the 1959 visit to the United States by Nikita Khrushchev, the Gary Francis Powers incident also in 1960, and the election of John F. Kennedy in the same year all set the stage for further pressing events.

Among these events were the 1962 Cuban missile crisis, Kennedy's assassination in 1963, and the enactment of the Civil Rights Act in 1964 and the Voting Rights Act in 1965, all of which combined to make this a unique period in the U.S. history. By the time Shanker was elected president of the United Federation of Teacher (UFT) in 1964, he had been mellowed and tempered by these events. His experiences more than prepared him to assume the presidency of the AFT in 1974, a position that he continues to hold to this day.

Chapter 4 examines the major events that surrounded Shanker and his mission. It begins with a discussion of the circumstances that compelled his parents to leave Russia, the hardships they encountered in the United States and the struggles they were determined to win in order to prepare their children for a better future. Shanker's experiences would prepare him for the positions that he would later hold. His own educational adventure is a fascinating story of a man who held a vision of both self and country, cast in a national dialectic of conflicting ideals. How he set out to resolve this conflict provides sharp insights into the cognitive processes of a national leader who never gave up in bringing his mission in life to fruition.

That mission forms a major part of the discussion of Shanker as an individual and as a national leader. As soon as he assumed a position of leadership in 1964, Shanker was committed to the fulfillment of two objectives that he saw as integral components of his mission. These were the professional development of teachers and the improvement of the conditions under which teachers worked. He sought to accomplish the first objective by seeking a rigorous change in the educational system to make it consistent with other important national developments. He sought to accomplish the second objective by applying the principle of collective bargaining and ensuring its effectiveness. In this line of activity Shanker was not corrupted by the power he possessed. Rather, he remained fully committed to the observation of democratic principles. He did not become the Niccolo Machiavelli of a new era of political wisdom and action.

Chapter 5 presents Shanker's philosophy of both society and education. This discussion shows the extent of his mental prowess and the logic that he has persistently applied in seeking solutions to critical issues that the country and education have faced. In sharing his philosophy, Shanker has demonstrated that his is not a speculative philosophy. Rather, it is based on a wide reading of individuals, both historical and contemporary, who have made considerable contributions in articulating philosophical precepts that address increasingly complex human issues. The conviction that he shows, the logic that he applies, and the respect of other people that one sees in his relationships with them continue to create a graphic of an individual whose sense of self and society manifests a total dedication to the causes he believes in.

Chapter 6 presents Shanker's positions on issues, both educational and social. A discussion of the series of short articles he has been writing entitled *Where We Stand* provides a fascinating account of how Shanker goes about deciding what positions to take on issues. This chapter shows that before he takes a position on issues Shanker does an intense literature review to assure that he covers all the points of view. In this process he allows his listeners and readers an opportunity to evaluate those perceptions and beliefs for purposes of defining their own positions.

As a result of this interactive process Shanker is able to learn from others. The evidence presented in this study shows that he has refrained from being doctrinaire in his approach, and dogmatic in presenting his viewpoint. The persuasive component of where he stands on issues elevates the climate of dialogue to the level where all relevant aspects of the issue are clearly discernible. This provides an opportunity for his readers to respond by applying the same logic that he has utilized. In this manner he makes the issues much more clear and the solutions more plausible.

Chapter 7 is an account of the relationships that Shanker has had with other people and organizations. They range from ordinary to professional people, from people in high political positions to those without any position at all. Shanker treats them all with the utmost respect that they deserve. The discussion is an account of the issues that these individuals write to him about, seeking his advice. From these relationships one sees the extent of Shanker's involvement in the critical events that have had a profound effect on the United States. One can see that these relationships are also a mirror of the mind of a national leader who understands the seriousness of the problems the country faces and the effort needed to find solutions.

Chapter 8 summarizes the main features of the study, draws some conclusions, and discusses their implications. This chapter recaptures the thrust of the study and attempts to put its major components in a proper historical perspective. It also attempts to integrate in a precise manner all the forces that came into play in summarizing the critical factors that shaped the developments presented, beginning with the strike in Chicago in 1902. It will be seen that from the moment he decided to be involved in teachers' unions in 1958 to the time he was elected president of the AFT in 1974, Shanker has remained fully committed to seeking improvement and change in crucial areas of education. The author hopes that the reader will enjoy reading this study as much as he has enjoyed researching and writing it. For him it has been an enjoyable educational safari.

The AFT in a Historical Perspective: An Organization in Transition

In a simple environment the wicked man is he who thinks. But in a complex environment the wicked man is he who does not think.

The AFT, 1916

The American Federation of Teachers has passed the ten thousand mark in membership. Its prospects are better than ever.

Freeland G. Stecker, 1919

THE PURPOSE OF THE STUDY

The purpose of this study is to discuss the role that Albert E. Shanker, president of the American Federation of Teachers (AFT) since August 20, 1974, has played in bringing about educational change in the United States. The study examines critical issues that Shanker has identified as negatively impacting the course of education and what he believes must be done to counterbalance them. Among the topics presented are his philosophy on both society and education, his political views and his relationships with significant people and organizations.

In order to place Shanker's influence into proper perspective, the study will examine major developments that have occurred in the United States from the turn of the century up to the present. It begins by first discussing the working conditions that teachers found themselves in prior to the formation of the AFT. This will help shed light on what compelled Shanker and others to carry out their ongoing crusade to bring about needed changes in American education and the society it serves. The study, therefore, begins in 1902, a pivotal year in the history of education in the United States.

THE BEGINNING

When students at Clarke School in Chicago went on strike in October of 1902, neither they nor anyone associated with or affected by the event were aware that it would have such a profound impact on teacher unionization and collective-bargaining in the future. The fact that the strike ended only two days after President Theodore Roosevelt (1858-1919) settled a coal miners' strike indicates that the United States was entering the twentieth century with ominous signs of labor unrest. This, and the tragic death of President William McKinley (1843-1901) on September 14, 1901, from an assassin's bullet, cast upon the country a long and gloomy shadow of doubt about the future.

During May of 1902 nearly 140,000 members of the United Mine Workers (UMW) went on strike in Pennsylvania. Although Roosevelt had no statutory authority to intervene, he did so by calling for a conference of leaders on both sides in an effort to resolve the conflict. He was motivated to do so because the strike was harming the national economy. At Roosevelt's request, J. P. Morgan (1837-1913), the well-respected businessman, succeeded in persuading the parties to accept a mediated solution. But the strike had aroused in the workers a new mode of thinking regarding the resolution of labor problems.

The workers began to realize that their emerging consciousness demanded that they stand up for their economic interests. They became aware that if they did not, no one else would do so on their behalf. This realization, brought about by the expectations fueled by the expanding Industrial Revolution, would later have a profound impact on how workers in general, including teachers, perceived themselves and the conditions under which they worked. This was an outcome of the Industrial Revolution that no one, except perhaps Karl Marx, had anticipated. This reality was why teachers and students in Chicago lost confidence in the ability of school authorities to resolve problems in a mutually acceptable way. It seemed that, given the new climate of the Industrial Revolution, both labor and management had entered into a dialectical relationship that reflected their dichotomous best interests.[1] The catalyst for the strike was the determination by the city's health board that the water supply system in the school was unhealthy and that it must be made safe or shut-down. An outbreak of typhoid had afflicted an alarming number of students.

In an effort to calm the situation the board of education persuaded parents to have their children bring bottled water to all schools in Chicago while new arrangements were being made to resolve the problem of contaminated water being piped into the school. As is often the case in situations involving public officials, local politicians were more concerned about preserving their positions of power than they were about effectively resolving the problem. Because the city's board of health was controlled by politicians, its actions reflected the solutions they wanted implemented, which made the problem even more complicated than it already was.

---

1. Marjorie Murphy, *Blackboard Unions: The AFT and the NEA, 1900-1980* (Ithaca, N.Y.: Cornell University Press, 1990), p. 7.

While the suggestion made by the board of education to have children bring bottled water to school seemed a good solution, it carried two serious implications that had far-reaching effects on the relationship between the teachers and the board of education. The first was that the schools themselves were not responsible for the health of students. This meant that someone other than the school had an obligation to protect the health and safety of both teachers and students. The second was that the crisis caused by the water supply placed the general responsibility for students' safety squarely on the shoulders of parents. This indicated that the city's board of health did not have any real responsibility for the health of its citizens. Because many parents did not have containers for safe water, their children ran the risk of drinking tainted water from the fire hydrants that were being installed around the city.

The teachers, already dissatisfied by the denial of their request for a salary raise, decided to take on an additional responsibility by boiling water for their students. Neither the school authorities nor the board of education seemed to show any interest or concern about the health of the students or the conditions under which they attended school. This forced the teachers to reach the conclusion that they themselves had to assume the responsibility for ensuring their own and their students' welfare. The idea of teachers forming their own organization was born out of this situation. They had come to the painful conclusion that neither the board of education nor the politicians were interested in providing safe working conditions for teachers. Given this perception, they took it upon themselves to display their educational responsibilities by providing a secure learning environment for their students. The water supply crisis became the catalyst that brought to the surface the institutional conflict that had been simmering for quite some time. If the issue of the water supply had not set it off, another issue would have most certainly have ignited it.

Wishing to maintain his position of authority, Edwin G. Cooley, the Chicago Schools superintendent, reorganized the administrative structure of the schools under his charge in such a way as to eliminate five district superintendent positions that were filled by men considered sympathetic toward the plight of the teachers and reduce the role of those he kept. Cooley also tried to convince the students, teachers, members of the board of education, and general public that the reorganization was needed to improve the effectiveness of the administrative system. But what Cooley was actually doing was reducing the role that the five district superintendents played in the administrative structure of the school system.[2]

The fact that the members of the board of education, the public, the teachers, and the students readily recognized the true intent of Cooley's action only contributed to the complexity of the problem. That the members of the school board did nothing to stop it only added a tragic twist of fate to a situation that was increasingly being recognized for what it was: a conspiracy against teachers. According to the *Chicago Tribune,* the deteriorating health conditions coupled

---

2. Chicago Board of Education, *Forty-Seventh Annual Report, 1903.*

with Cooley's reorganization scheme created a restive environment for both the students and the teachers to reject what was transpiring and go on strike.[3]

It must be understood that these two strikes had as a precedent, the May 4, 1886, labor strike called to protest poor working conditions throughout Chicago. The year previous to the 1886 strike, Grover Cleveland (1837-1908) had been inaugurated as president of the United States. This was a period of time full of expectations that the Industrial Revolution would greatly improve the standard of living for all people. But the labor strike of 1886 "greatly injured business prospects. In many instances, railroad traffic was suspended, trains were derailed, and valuable property was destroyed. The police attempted to scatter a body of anarchists to whom a bomb was thrown resulting in the death of seven policemen and the injury of many others."[4]

Coming out of the era of Charles Dickens (1812-1870) and his great proclamation of the best of times, this state of affairs raised serious doubt about the claimed benefits of the Industrial Revolution. What had happened to the humanistic belief that the creation of a social utopia was within man's grasp? What had happened to the belief that the benefits of the Industrial Revolution would transform a life of hard toil into a new era of comfort for all? What had happened to the belief that cooperation rather than conflict, hope rather than despair would bring all of humanity closer together? Although Dickens's novel *A Tale of Two Cities* (1859) was addressing social conditions that existed in Europe during the French Revolution its influence was felt on the United States during the nineteenth century.

The enthusiasm that had engulfed the Industrial Revolution now turned into an abyss of despair. Frustration and social conflict became the order of things. The foremost question on everyone's mind was whether the Industrial Revolution was a blessing or a curse. One thing became clear--labor relations, including those between teachers and their administration, were permanently altered. The worker, placed in a demanding environment that called for increasing productivity, suspected management of employing tactics that were designed to increase the margin of profit at his expense. Management, who often relied upon conflicting and experimental procedures intended to increase productivity, in turn, suspected the worker of operating under a veiled desire to increase his wages at the expense of the increasing costs of an expanding industrialized society. The concept of collective bargaining, mediation, or arbitration did not exist to the extent that it does today. Differences of opinion regarding labor costs and wages created a problem that had no mutually satisfying solution. The idea of win-win was decades away from being a means for conflict resolution.

---

3. Ibid.

4. Barness's Historical Series, *A Brief History of the United States* (New York: American Book Company, 1899), p. 299.

CHICAGO: THE   BIRTHPLACE   OF   A   MOVEMENT

As the drama of the teacher-student strike and conflict began to unfold, it carried with it other serious political implications that began to be painfully realized. When it appeared that the strike might be settled, Superintendent of Compulsory Education Wiliam G. Bodine ordered his truant officers to round up students from the streets closest to Clarke School and bring them to the school. About two hundred students were involved.[5] This number indicates that there was something basically wrong with the school system. The parents had came to the erroneous conclusion that because the board of health refused to accept the responsibility of ensuring the health of their children, they had the right to keep them at home.

Bodine's action, therefore, constituted what they saw as a violation of their parental responsibility, which only they could legally exercise. To their surprise Bodine and his officials discovered that they did not have the support of the parents as they had believed. Bodine also found that he was on the wrong side of the issue. He and his subordinates were caught in the middle of the emerging struggle, and their behavior only exacerbated the conflict between the school system and the community.

The turmoil in the school system took a dramatic and ominous turn when Bodine's policy and action led to a strike at another school, Jackson School. There Janie McKeon suspended from her class a student who had used foul language against another student. The male principal of the school, recently appointed to replace a female principal under the reorganization plan initiated by Cooley revoked the suspension and ordered McKeon to take the student back.[6] When McKeon refused to take the student back into her class until he apologized, the principal concluded that she had violated her duty and proceeded to charge her with insubordination. After consulting Cooley, the principal proceeded to suspend McKeon for one month without pay.[7] McKeon, now deprived of an income, was left to fend for her economic survival all by herself. Without an organizational structure to help, her fate was sealed. She alone fought a cause that would have far-reaching implications for teachers everywhere.

Unwilling to see their highly respected teacher fall prey to the power politics of the unpopular Cooley, McKeon's students persuaded students in other schools to march to the office of Alderman John Powers to demand her immediate reinstatement. When Cooley declined to honor the students' request, the number of protesters grew to four hundred. This caused the situation to become volatile, and what the police called threatening, when the students were joined by residents of the neighborhood.[8] By seeking the involvement of their alderman the people opted for a political solution to the problem. This strategy

---

5. Marjorie Murphy, *Blackboard Unions: The AFT and the NEA, 1900-1980*, p. 9.

6. Ibid. p. 11.
7. Ibid. p. 13.
8. Ibid. p. 14.

is what the AFT has utilized to this day in seeking solutions to the problems it has encountered.

At the height of his political power and influence, John Powers had acquired the reputation of a cunning and shrewd politician, whose control of the ward he represented was absolute in every way. In many ways Powers was the Richard Daley of his time. His influence was felt well beyond his ward. Even Jane Addams (1860-1935), the famous founder of Hull House,[9] failed twice to unseat this flamboyant and powerful alderman. Powers often dictated the tone of the campaign and made a career out of making his opponents look unsure of themselves and the issues. He also had the reputation of being knowledgeable about every issue and having the ability to logically articulate and demonstrate his political savvy. These skills made him the key political figure in the politics of Chicago. Slowly Powers was becoming an institution, the chief cornerstone of the political system. He had an uncanny way of capitalizing on the inability of members of the city council to express positions that reflected the will of the people in the wards they represented.

With all his power and influence Powers faced a new and formidable challenge in the students' strike in protest of McKeon's dismissal. This was the kind of problem the like of which he had never before encountered. This time his political opponent was Edwin G. Cooley, the determined and equally powerful superintendent of schools, who believed that he had a mission to clean up the educational system and curb the increasing militancy of the teachers. The escalating conflict among the students, their teachers, and the administration took a backseat to the emerging political confrontation between two men possessing big egos, Edwin G. Cooley and John Powers.

Recognizing his vulnerability to a united effort by Powers, the students, and their teachers and to the support they received from the neighborhood residents, Cooley appealed to the business community to come to his aid. He convinced them that they had an interest in the educational reforms that he was trying to initiate to assure proper education for their future workforce. Cooley remained firm in his belief that the militancy that was rapidly spreading among teachers would eventually lead to the deterioration of educational standards. Teachers would soon place more emphasis on gaining political power than on gaining professional competency.

John Powers saw Janie McKeon, the students, and the teachers in general as victims of a system that was led by a ruthless and ambitious man who was interested more in the exercise of his own political power than in the educational needs of the community. To him Cooley was nothing more than a power broker who stood to benefit from the confusion that ensued between what was political and what was educational. From this conflict between the ideal and the real, McKeon and the cause she represented became only an incidental issue in the struggle of wills between two strong and determined personalities.

---

9. In 1931 Addams shared the Nobel Peace Prize with Nicholas Murray Butler (1861-1947), president of Columbia University from 1902 to 1945, for her work in settling immigrants from Europe in Chicago. She was also recognized for her campaign to give women the right to vote. This objective was finally accomplished by the passage of the Nineteenth Amendment in 1920.

On the one hand, Powers felt that to allow a petty political person to control the system of education would carry political implications that would damage both the teaching profession and the political process he steered. On the other hand, Cooley concluded that Powers was nothing more than an ambitious, immature politician who lacked any legitimate right to make decisions regarding education. This is why he perceived Power's support for McKeon as gross interference in an area in which he was not qualified to pass judgment, let alone be involved.

Unable to resolve the conflict and unwilling to see the issue from one another's perspective, the two men entered into a deadly political dual from which emerged no clear winner. The resulting stalemate only helped to compound the problem. Even the teacher appointed to replace Janie McKeon saw herself as a pawn in the political game played by the two sides, saying that she was only being used to advance the political fortunes of the protagonists. McKeon's immediate supervisor, District Superintendent Albert Speer, supported his boss, arguing that although she was a good and efficient teacher, McKeon was guilty of insubordination and was not entitled to a formal hearing.[10] Speer had no choice but to support the system of which he was a part. But in doing so he accentuated the problem. His actions made it increasingly difficult for the educational status quo to continue. Speer became part of the burgeoning problem. He contributed nothing in the search for a solution.

Realizing that this unresolved conflict did not help their cause or improve their situation, that the stalemate between Cooley and Powers was hurting them, the teachers paused to rethink and revise their strategy. In doing so they realized that unless they did something to protect their interests, no one, especially politicians, was likely to take risks on their behalf. They, therefore, began to think of forming an organization that would promote their professional competency and protect their economic and political interests. They also concluded that political dialogue was essential to the nature of interactions that would emerge between them and the administration. Although John Powers had failed in his intent to reduce the power that Edwin G. Cooley exercised over the teachers, he succeeded in arousing in them a new level of political consciousness that has remained a distinct feature of the AFT.

In reaching this conclusion and initiating their renewed strategy, the teachers in Chicago became united in opposing both the reorganization scheme that Cooley implemented and the centralization of the administration that he introduced because both concentrated power in his hands. To coordinate only the efforts directed at their objectives, the teachers also opposed the legislation that was intended to place even more control upon them. Although John Powers emerged as a champion of teachers' causes in a way that elevated his political fortunes to newer heights, it was the teachers themselves who directed the development of the idea of forming an organization and who directed its movement.

Janie McKeon took the center stage in this struggle of political wills. Her refusal to carry out her duties under conditions imposed by Cooley's centralized

---

10. Chicago Board of Education, *Forty-Seventh Annual Report, 1903.*

power earned her the support and the respect of parents, whom she needed to continue her crusade. Janie McKeon became a household name not only in Chicago, but throughout the country. Teachers across the nation came to recognize the reality that her vision was intended to secure for them the respect of the communities of which they were members. Slowly they began to realize that the refusal of the National Education Association (NEA) to be involved in this struggle meant that they must become separately united in recognizing the reality of the impact of politics on their livelihood. They recognized the need for a balance between professional competency and political influence. They became aware that the administration was imposing its will upon them without taking their views into consideration in formulating policy. This situation had to be changed. They saw Edwin G. Cooley as a symbol of a national system of public school education that deprived them of their basic rights as professionals. John Power was viewed as a petty politician whose influence and power were limited by the political forces that controlled him.

Cooley succeeded in convincing the business community[11] that if McKeon's campaign was allowed to succeed, the result would be a deterioration of the educational administrative system. This highlights the seriousness of the conflict. Most members of the business community were also members of the men's club, a private but powerful organization that was highly influential in most aspects of life in Chicago. That Cooley was a potent member of the club was no accident. It was at the members-only club meetings that Cooley's school reform plan was first discussed, shaped, and adopted even before it was presented to the school board. This fact was not ignored by the teachers. The central question that remained in their minds was, who was running the schools in the city, the board of education or the men's club? Cooley made no effort to conceal the actual fact, and his arrogance betrayed his own cause.

In this manner alliances were slowly being formed that later accentuated discord between the two sides. Members of the business, medical, and legal communities formed a coalition with Cooley. Reflecting upon this drawing of battle lines, the *Chicago Tribune* did not think that the teachers, the students, and their parents had any chance. The *Tribune* concluded that their efforts were a "dismal burlesque."[12] William G. Bodine, recognizing that the confrontational nature of the interaction between the two sides was likely to hurt all concerned, decided to try to utilize diplomacy. He persuaded the striking students and members of the community from the South Side to engage in direct talks with Cooley and his cohorts.

In this initiative Bodine was motivated by a belief that each side should make an effort to understand the concerns of the other side. Once this understanding was established, it would lead to solutions to the conflict, which

---

11. The practice of having the business community involved in education was not new. In 1837 Edmund Dwight (1780-1849), a leader of the business community in Massachusetts, nominated Horace Mann to serve as the secretary of the newly created board of education. But during the time that Cooley was superintendent in Chicago, the practice acquired Machiavellian dimensions.

12. Marjorie Murphy, *Blackboard Unions: The AFT and the NEA, 1900-1980,* p. 16.

was paralyzing Chicago's educational process. When one student indicated that "the talk of strikes by teachers suggested the idea to their pupils,"[13] Cooley deduced that teachers were using students to promote their own political agenda and accused them of engaging in unprofessional behavior. He also argued that they were opposed to his centralization plan because they had close ties to corrupt politicians like John Powers. In going to the limits that he did in accusing the teachers, Cooley was denying Bodine a chance to succeed with his mediation. Bodine was forced to abandon his efforts. This suggests just how much support Cooley had from the members of the business and professional communities.

Expressing his complete support for Cooley, Clayton Mark, president of the board of education and a key figure in the business community and the men's club, argued in his annual report, "Political influence has been used to subvert an impartial and effective administration of the school system. The strenuous effort of friendship with teachers would cripple the school system by politicians and men of influence."[14] There is no doubt that Mark was directing his remark at John Powers, the only politician who supported the teachers. Mark's attitude was typical of the attitudes of the members of the business and professional communities and reflected the values and objectives of the members of the men's club who wanted to exert absolute influence over the character of the school and Chicago society. This is why Bodine's effort at mediation through dialogue had no chance of succeeding.

To complicate the dissent further, a law required teachers to graduate from the normal school and to hold a teaching certificate issued by the school district. They were also evaluated by the principal of the school and rehired by the vote of the board of education, which consisted of twenty-one members. Because the evaluation of teachers was done individually, there was little that those like John Powers could do to protect them from becoming victims of the power exercised by the administration. The reason most frequently used to dismiss a teacher was that of incompetence. The criteria were known only to the administration, and the teachers were not told in advance the standards by which they were evaluated. Because the teachers felt that the evaluation process entailed bias against them, they believed that they alone must assume the responsibility of protecting themselves against the action of the board of education.

In an effort to convince the business community that supported him that he was doing the right thing for Chicago, Cooley endorsed Mark's view that teaching had been subverted by teachers who were seeking to promote political goals aimed at reducing the authority of the board of education and his administration. He singled out John Powers for blame, stating that he had deceived the teachers into believing that some day they would assume the running of their school.[15] Powers, in turn, stressed that Cooley was behaving

---

13. Ibid. p. 19.
14. Chicago Board of Education, *Forty-Seventh Annual Report*, 1903.
15. Ibid.

in a manner that showed he was persuaded to carry out an educational reform plan initiated by the business community so that it could maximize profits.[16]

These extreme positions made it difficult for the antagonists to find a common ground where they could seek out solutions to a serious problem shared by all. The era of progressive education that John Dewey (1859-1952) set off in 1902 as a member of the University of Chicago fell into the background with this struggle for power and influence. The social discord precluded establishing a channel of communication in order to initiate a process of problem-solving. The damage that the rhetoric was inflicting on human feeling could only be undone through the very thing it was impeding - the process of dialogue. The refusal of the parties to initiate this remedy was a tragic turn of events that occurred at a critical time in the development of the nation. The close association that the students and their teachers shared with the community posed a threat to the power the administration wanted desperately to preserve.

What the administration seemed to grossly ignore was that a new phenomenon was emerging all over the world. People were organizing for political, social, economic, religious, and professional purposes. Labor activities began to take shape following the dictums that Karl Marx (1818-1883) and his associate Friedrich Engels (1820-1895) made in 1848 by publishing *The Communist Manifesto*. Various professional organizations began to take new directions and dimensions.

From 1892 to 1900 Susan B. Anthony (1820-1906), in her capacity as president of the Reunited Women Suffragists, galvanized women to work towards creating a powerful body to exert the influence that she felt women needed to bring about political equality in the country. The industrial revolution had the unexpected effect of impressing upon people the need to come together to promote and protect their shared interests, much like what the business community had always done. For the board of education and the school administration in Chicago to argue that the teachers were motivated by political considerations was to fail to recognize the influence of the rise of political consciousness brought about by changes in socioeconomic conditions as a result of the Industrial Revolution.

By the beginning of the twentieth century, when it was an accepted practice for women to become teachers, emphasis shifted from developing academic, intellectual, and professional skills to developing moral character and deportment as the desirable qualities that female teachers must acquire. By 1915 it was quite common for school boards to prescribe rules of conduct for female teachers far different from those prescribed for male teachers. For example, the board of education in Virginia outlined the following rules for female teachers:

---

16. Marjorie Murphy, *Blackboard Unions: The AFT and the NEA, 1900-1980*, p. 21.

1   You will not marry during the term of your contract.
2. You must be home between the hours of 8:00 p.m., and 6:00 a.m. unless you are attending a school function.
3. You may not loiter downtown in ice cream stores.
4. You may not travel beyond the city limits unless you have the permission of the chairman of the school board.
5. You may not ride in a carriage or automobile with any man unless he is your father or brother.
6. You may not smoke.
7. You may not dress in bright colors.
8. You may, under no circumstance, dye your hair.
9. You must wear at least two petticoats.
10. Your dress must not be any more than two inches above the ankle.
11. You must:

> (a) keep the school room clean
> (b) scrub the floor at least once a week with soap and water
> (c) clean the blackboard at least once a day
> (d) start the fire at 7:00 a.m. so that the room will be warm at 8:00 a.m.[17]

These rules point to the conclusion that Cooley did not take Janie McKeon's action as professional because it came from a woman and because it was incompatible with the norms of behavior expected of women. When G. Stanley Hall (1844-1924) was invited to speak on psychology in Chicago in 1902, the board of education discouraged female teachers from attending because it considered it inappropriate for women to listen to the ideas he was discussing.[18]

By 1915, however effective the action of one individual, such as that of Janie McKeon was, it was no longer considered adequate just to protect the collective interests of the members of the teaching profession. Teachers were now thinking of forming a union that would politicize the balance between professional mastery and security. The time to make such a move presented itself in 1915.

THE FORMATION OF THE AFT

Recognizing the critical nature of the political problems they faced, teachers began to formally organize themselves. Because of their education, teachers provided the core leadership needed in political undertakings such as seeking the right to vote.[19] A number of leaders in these movements for equality were women. Susan B. Anthony was a teacher whose arrest in 1872 for trying to vote created a rebellious climate for women. Anna Howard Show, Henrietta Roadman,

---

17. Board of Education, Virginia, *Rules of Conduct for Female Teachers* (1915).

18. The Chicago Board of Education Records (1902).

19. In Africa most political leaders were once teachers. They provided the leadership that was needed to direct the rise of African nationalism.

Margaret Haley, Nancy Cott, and Catherine Goggin had all distinguished themselves as excellent teachers, but were viewed as holding extreme political views because of their refusal to accept their second-class positions in the status quo. It was increasingly becoming evident that teachers must form a united organization much stronger than the association that had existed in the past in order to confront the problems they were facing.

In May 1915, afraid that teachers were about to form a union for the sole purpose of launching a political campaign to minimize the power of the board of education, Jacob Loeb (1859-1924), president of the board of education, ordered the board attorney to begin an investigation of the financial books of the teachers' association that Ella Flagg Young and Margaret Haley kept as officials of the association. Both women were misled into believing that the purported investigation was a legal and legitimate exercise that was intended to ensure their integrity and promote their ideas of running a honest organization. The real intent of the investigation, however, became apparent when Young was subpoenaed to appear before the committee. She faced a barrage of hostile questions. She was also subjected to personal attack by the committee's attorney for refusing to answer questions that could incriminate her.[20]

As the hostility from both the board of education and the business community increased, the women were subjected to higher levels of ridicule and humiliation, which had never before been see in Chicago labor relations. Newspapers carried daily reports on the three-ring circus. Their personal lives, even their religious beliefs, became the subjects of attack. Jacob Loeb launched a campaign to discredit teachers, the overwhelmingly majority of which were female. It was his hope to isolate them from other women in the mainstream of American life. He accused the teachers of promoting their own agenda at the expense of other women's issues. He also urged counseling for the women because their behavior supposedly manifested immature thinking that advocated anarchy.[21] Loeb further accused these so-called fanatical women of harassing their fellow teachers who were not supporting their campaign.

While all of this was happening, the board of education adopted the "yellow dog contract resolution," which prohibited teachers from becoming members of a union and allowed schools to refuse to rehire those teachers who were already members of the Chicago Teachers Federation. Those who joined the federation were considered either mindless followers or rebels without a cause.[22] In desperation, Young, Haley, and their small group of supporters requested the assistance of organized labor[23] in their struggle against the board. The teachers perceived the tactics employed by Jacob Loeb, Edwin G. Cooley, and the business and professional communities that they represented as a direct threat to the principle of collective bargaining and as an erosion of democratic principles in general.

---

20. Marjorie Murphy, *Blackboard Unions: The AFT and the NEA, 1900-1980*, p. 82.

21. Ibid., p. 83.

22. Jacob Loeb, Stenographic Report: Chicago Teachers Federation, February 2, 1917)

23. This explains why at its inception the AFT affiliated with AFL-CIO.

The teachers saw the personal attack on Ella Flagg Young, Margaret Haley, Henrietta Roadman, Nancy Cott, and Catherine Goggin as an assault on the profession of teaching, a profession they believed was designed to meet the needs of society as a whole. They saw this as character assassination coming from a small group of people who sought total control over an honored profession solely for their own political gain. They, therefore, concluded that if the teachers themselves failed to organize for purposes of forming a union, then they had only themselves to blame for their political exploitation. Indeed, using the Loeb rule (the "yellow dog contract resolution"), the board of education dismissed thirty-five teachers before the end of the school year in 1916, and more were targeted for dismissal before the beginning of the new school year because they had violated the Loeb rule by belonging to the federation.

Thinking that this court action gave them the legal basis for refusing to sign the yellow dog contract ,teachers began to search for further means of protecting themselves. With the injunction granted by the court, things seemed to move in favor of the teachers' union. On April 15, 1916, members of the four teacher organizations that operated in Chicago met to launch a national organization they called the American Federation of Teachers (AFT). This group quickly allied itself with the CIO in order to strengthen itself and promote its cause. The move was also intended to coordinate strategies for dealing with the board of education.

Thus, was born a national organization that, in due course, would alter permanently the nature of the relationships between the members of the teaching profession and the school administration. Although the NEA criticized the AFT for its decision to affiliate with labor instead of joining ranks with it, it must be remembered that the board of education did not think highly of the NEA either because the board did not think highly of it because it would not take positions contrary to its believes.

On May 1, 1916, just as the AFT was gaining strength, the state appellate court overturned the temporary injunction and ruled in favor of the board of education that teachers who were members of unions could be dismissed. On June 27, as teachers were preparing for the beginning of summer vacation, Loeb compiled a secret "hit list" of teachers he wanted dismissed because they had become members of the AFT.[24] Despite this retaliatory action, the AFT never lost sight of its goal to balance its political agenda with the development of professional skills. This effort was evident in two basic principles.

The first was that teachers were entitled to a life of dignity through a higher standard of professionalism that is justly demanded of the teaching profession. The second was that teachers had the right to think freely and to exercise their right to free speech without fear of retaliation. This included the right to hold views contrary to those held by the majority.[25] Since its inception the AFT has operated under these two basic principles. It has sought to maintain an effective

---

24. "The Dismissal of Chicago Teachers," *School and Society*, 4 (July 15, 1916) : 94. The names of the teachers involved are listed in this article.

25. William van Til, *Education: A Beginning* (Boston: Houghton Mifflin Company, 1974), p. 122.

balance between them in order to enhance the profession of teaching and sustain the socioeconomic position of its membership.

To assist in promoting its program, the AFT founded a journal, *The American Teacher*.[26] It immediately began to address issues the AFT considered crucial in the development of effective education. One of these issues was the fear among the members of the AFT that the board of education would continue to abuse its power and authority in dealing with teachers. An editorial in the June 1917 issue was used to inform the board of education that teachers feared the erosion of freedom of thought more than anything else. Arguing that free thinking was a critical tenet of human existence, the editorial went on to quote Bertrand Russell (1872-1970), the British social reformer, who said in 1903:

> Men fear thought as they fear nothing else on earth--more than ruin, more than death. Thought is subversive and revolutionary, destructive and terrible. Thought is merciless to privilege, established institutions, and comfortable habits. Thought is anarchic and lawless, indifferent to authority, careless of the well-tried wisdom of the ages. Thought looks into the part of hell and is not afraid. It sees man, a feeble speck, surrounded by unfathomable depths of silence, yet it bears itself proudly as if it were the lord of the universe. Thought is great and swift and free, it is the light of the world and chief glory of man.[27]

There is no question the members of the board of education feared divergent thinking and believed that if it was allowed to be the AFT's chief cornerstone, it would transform the American system of education far beyond the ability of communities to comprehend and manage it. If the board of education had thought that it was having problems with Chicago Teachers Federation (CTF), how was it going to deal with the AFT, a much stronger, nationally allied labor organization? Indications were that difficult times lay ahead as the AFT refused to be coerced in the same way the CTF was.

What was really threatening to the board of education and the business community was the AFT's philosophy of education and its insistence that the development of the curriculum must remain the primary responsibility of the teachers, using the general guidelines established by the board, not administrators. Arguing in support of this position, the AFT stressed its thinking that "teachers must be given a free hand in designing the curriculum. If we were to consult the business man we might come to some agreement as to the subject matter to be taught. But what particular stratum in the business world shall be our ideal in the inculcating of personal habit? The business man, if given a free hand in the revision of the curriculum, would remove unceremoniously the fads and frills. The remedy is not the wholesale deletion of

---

26. This study has utilized the journal to document some of its findings and conclusions.

27. The AFT, "The Marvelous Revolutionist" (editorial) *The American Teacher*, 6, no. 6 (June 1917): p. 79.

the subjects, but a careful elision of parts that are antiquated. Teachers have proved that they possess the ability to fulfill their task."[28]

At its first annual convention, held in Chicago December 29-30, 1916, the AFT adopted an impressive platform. A summary of its major planks follows:

1. We urge the enactment of laws securing to teachers tenure of position when they prove to be efficient professionals.

2. We protest against the present system of rating the efficiency of teachers based on personal caprice, bias or prejudice. We favor an objective system of rating based on scientific standards to be applied during the teachers' probationary period.

3. We condemn the appointment and promotion of teachers and school officers through political and personal influence.

4. We favor the rating of supervisory officers by teachers in accordance with the standards by which teachers themselves are rated.

5. We demand the legal establishment of self-governing schools and district councils of teachers to the purpose of utilizing the experience and initiative of the teaching body in the conduct of the schools.

6. We urge adequate pension plans for teachers.

7. We endorse all honest efforts of experimental pedagogy in seeking to establish a scientific basis for educational development.

8. We recommend the policy of releasing teachers without loss of pay to engage in educational research, the results to accrue to the public.

9. We favor the widest possible use of the school plant for social, civic, and educational purposes.

10. We demand nation-wide adult suffrage as a fundamental principle of democracy.[29]

Again, one can clearly see that the targets of this platform included both the board of education and AFT's emphasis on efforts to elevate its professional functions to a level where it would earn the respect and support of the public.

A persistent issue that was critical to the success of the AFT was the quality of its leadership.[30] Before it attempted to elect its leaders, the AFT stated the following seven principles that it believed were essential in guiding its agenda and program:

---

28. Ibid., p. 83
29. Ibid., p. 94.
30. The question of leadership is the subject of Chapter 2 of this study.

1. The leader must remember that in a simple environment the wicked man is he who thinks. But in a complex environment the wicked man is he who does not think.

2. The leader must sense poignantly the pathos of his predicament.

3. The leader must remember that to lead in a complex milieu and champion the cause of ideas suited to a simple milieu is the very miscarriage of treason itself.

4. The leader's preliminary labor is to show comprehensively the vast chaotic age in which we live.

5. Instead of representing the ancient blunder of provincialism which has attempted to ignore the world at large in order to convene its local precarious habitat, the leader must be on his guard against the trivial.

6. He who would serve mankind must know mankind. He who would cherish the state must cherish the world.

7. The leader must be conscious of the marvelous things that are recreating the world in which we live.[31]

Arguing that only teachers must be called upon to provide effective leadership of the AFT, J. Edward Mayman put it in comparative terms, saying, "When the hospitals are suspected of inefficiency the advice of expert physicians is sought. When the legal machinery is in need of change the prominent lawyers are called in. When transportation facilities are inadequate the advice of the engineer is solicited. But when the educational system is maladjusted, the advice and experience of the teachers is not only not sought, but is also in most cases actually suppressed. For this organization to succeed it needs leadership that has a vision of the future different from the past."[32]

Although the AFT had a clear set of criteria for leadership, the task of electing its first president proved to be much harder than its members had anticipated. They were looking for a leader who possessed these attributes in order to shape the character and effectiveness of the organization. It was a time of both excitement and uncertainty. As delegates began the task of selecting the AFT's first president, there emerged a strong sense that Margaret Haley[33] should be their first standard- bearer. Margaret Haley was a sixth grade teacher in Chicago. She was pure Americana, seeing things as did her father, a poorly educated man whom she deeply admired. He had given his daughter what he himself had failed to obtain, the self-esteem that educational success brings.

---

31. The AFT, "The Marvelous Revolution," p. 96.

32. J. Edward Mayman, "Business and Education," *The American Teacher* 6, no. 6 (June 1917): p. 82.

33. See Chapters 2 and 8 of this study for further reference to Margaret Haley.

An absolute believer in the principle of shared governance in education as a manifestation of modeling democratic values, Haley became active in Chicago's teacher organizations in 1895 when there was a struggle for an adequate pension for teachers. Women teachers had little to look forward to in the future because they were considered temporary employees, a practice that still exists today in some countries of the Third World, including Africa. Campaigning for teachers' input in the decision-making process in education, Haley helped raise public consciousness to a new level when she argued that the boards of education across the country were treating their housemaids better than they were treating teachers.

Margaret Haley was a well-read person. Her favorite authors included John Boyle O'Reilly, William Shakespeare, John Dewey, and Adam Smith. Smith's *Wealth of Nations* formed the basis of her socioeconomic philosophy. At the St. Louis World's Fair in 1904,[34] Haley attracted large crowds by the eloquence and logic in her oratory persuasion. In 1909, when thousands of workers in clothing factories were questioning the autocratic rule of their employers, she rose to the occasion and provided the leadership that they needed to arouse the struggle of the working class.

Margaret Haley was proud of the fact that she was the daughter of a mason whose income was so sporadic and uncertain that she was forced to seek work at the age of sixteen. She taught in rural elementary schools in Illinois, where she enjoyed the support of the community and the respect of her students. She then moved to Chicago, where schools were considered better and the opportunity for professional development through education was available. That she stayed out of the politics of education until the Pullman strike[35] of 1894 shows the delicate balance that existed between the professional life and the political activity of individuals. The strike convinced her that political activity was an integral part of the professional activity of all people. The Pullman incident also convinced her that instead of blaming workers for the strike, authorities, including President Grover Cleveland, should have blamed the management for relentlessly pursuing economic policies whose implementation resulted in exploiting workers.

There is no question that by 1916 Margaret Haley had become an institution revered by some, hated by others, and respected by many. She was obviously the most qualified candidate to be the first president of the AFT. She had become an icon in a world controlled by men who were ruthless in dealing with women. She was thorough and complete in her professionalism. She had learned from her father the importance of dedication to duty and the essence of being human and humane. Throughout her adult life Margaret Haley operated under the principles that human behavior based upon principles of justice and equality shaped the

---

34. Officially known as the Louisiana Purchase Centennial Exposition, the fair was actually held in Forest Park to stimulate trade and cultural development in the city.

35. In May 1894 workmen at the Pullman Company, founded in 1859 by George Pullman (1831-1897), went on strike in protest against low wages and poor working conditions. Violence broke out, causing damage estimated at $10 million and forcing the federal government to send troops in to stop it and restore peace.

character of institutions and that every person had a duty to contribute to the development of society.

Amidst the excitement of forming a national organization ,there was an irony in the quest for the AFT's first president. Ida Fursman, who would become the vice-president of the AFT, concluded that "she took if for granted that Miss Margaret Haley would be the natural choice for president of the new national union"[36] and that she was disappointed when Haley was not given the honor of becoming the first president of the AFT. Margaret Haley was unable to overcome   criticisms that she was too combative, that she refused to compromise, that she placed political rights for teachers above educational rights for students, and that she had serious problems accepting men as leaders of organizations involving women.

GROWTH AND PROBLEMS

The election of Charles Stillman of the Chicago Teachers Federation as the AFT's first president caught everyone by surprise. Ida Fursman protested Stillman's election because she thought that the new organization had been manipulated by the board of education and the business interests of the community. Stillman, who served until 1924, was by all accounts considered to be a moderate. However, Fursman came to understand that Stillman was elected not because Margaret Haley lacked the qualities of leadership needed to make the new organization strong and great, but because of the differences in the perception of what direction the AFT should take for the future.[37] Both Margaret Haley and Ida Fursman came to accept the reality that a consensual decision had been made and that they must support it to ensure the effectiveness of the AFT.

Now that the presidency of the new organization had been settled, focus shifted to the question of just who Charles Stillman was. Stillman had a close association with Samuel Gompers (1850-1924), the founder and first president of CIO. Gompers was known for his belief that labor organizations must not yield to the dictates of management. Throughout his life Gompers campaigned against labor restrictions and injunctions issued by the courts, arguing that the relationship between labor and management was based on political and economic considerations. However, Gompers supported legislation intended to improve conditions at the workplace and regulate the employment of children and women. He was influential in the establishment of the U.S. Department of Labor.

Stillman admired Gompers for his ability to organize as well as for his power of persuasion. In his quiet and unassuming manner, Stillman exhibited qualities that would endear him to teachers. His brilliant performance as president of the CTF showed that he could lead the AFT to new heights of accomplishment. Gompers and Stillman supported President Wilson's labor and foreign policies even though the American public did not support increasing

---

36. Marjorie Murphy, *Blackboard Unions: The AFT and the NEA, 1900-1980*, p. 84.

37. Ida Fursman, CTF Collection, Walter Reuther Archives of Labor and Urban Affairs, Wayne State University, Detroit.

American involvement in the conflict in Europe. But two years after the tragedy of the *Lusitania*,[38] Stillman responded to public outcry and joined Gompers in giving President Woodrow Wilson their unconditional support to involve the United States in the European war to make the world safe for democracy. This action enhanced the triangle of relationships that emerged among Wilson, Gompers, and Stillman.

Within a relatively short period of time Stillman's reputation as a strategist was known across the country. This setting helped give the AFT new vigor and influence. Stillman's election served notice to Edwin G. Cooley and the business community that things were about to change in favor of the teachers. The threats that had come from the board of education and the damage to reputation that both labor and teacher organizations had suffered in the aftermath of the Pullman strike were now being reversed. Under Stillman's leadership the AFT was on its way to playing a proper role in both the political activity and the educational development of the country.

In order to elevate the AFT to a position where its members would demonstrate a clear understanding of both national and international issues, Stillman moved forward without fearing any reprisals from the board of education. He was motivated only by what he considered to be in the best interests of the AFT. But his close association with Gompers, his tendency to fail to consult his associates on critical issues, and his support of President Wilson's foreign policy all created climate of conflict within the AFT.[39] This was not because Stillman was pursuing wrong policy, but because he seemed to ignore the principle of collectiveness that had always been part of labor organizations. It is not clear why Stillman followed an operating procedure different from the one he utilized as CTF president. Perhaps it was because the demands of national office placed upon him pressures that required a different approach to issues.

On April 16, 1917, ten days after the United States had entered World War I, the Chicago Teachers Federation withdrew from the city labor organization to respect the court's injunction and joined the AFT. Margaret Haley encouraged Stillman to direct the activities of the new organization in the manner that he had done to enhance the CTF. The members of the CTF, though inhibited by the action of court, now found a larger and stronger national milieu in which to promote and protect their socioeconomic and political interests. While the board of education seemed to gain from the ruling of the court, that ruling inadvertently established groundwork needed to strengthen the AFT. While the court found it easy to rule in favor of the board of education, its task proved to be much harder when dealing with a national labor union. Therefore, from its inception the AFT had advantages that the CTF could not have.

The cordial relationship that developed among Wilson, Gompers, and Stillman began to take shape as early as 1913 when the president signed a bill

---

38. A passenger ship of the Cunard Line, the *Lusitania* sank off the coast of Ireland on May 7, 1915, after it was torpedoed by a German submarine, killing 1,198 of the 1,924 passengers including 128 Americans.

39. AFT Collection, Series 13, Walter Reuther Archives of Labor and Urban Affairs, Wayne State University, Detroit.

creating an independent Department of Labor. In 1914 he signed another bill creating the Federal Trade Commission. Both laws were considered favorable to the objectives of the labor movement. Among Wilson's Fourteen Points, which he presented at the Versailles Peace Conference and for the founding of the League of Nations, was a clause calling for national development through the removal of economic barriers. The establishment of free trade conditions, based upon practices that secured the rights of workers as a fundamental principle of democracy, was strongly advocated by Wilson. Stillman did everything in his power to capitalize on this national momentum cast in an international setting. He saw it as an opportunity to give his union the strong foundations he believed it needed to build itself for the future.

While things appeared to go reasonably well for the AFT, tension soon developed between Charles Stillman and Henry Linville, the influential editor of *The American Teacher* who would serve as the AFT president from 1931 to 1934. They had a difference of opinion over the degree of the relationship between Stillman and Gompers. Linville felt that Gompers was far more conservative than Stillman and that he would exercise a retarding influence on the agenda and actions of the AFT. Arguing that the affiliation of the AFT with the CIO would weaken the AFT and strengthen the political fortunes of the board of education and the business community, Linville persuaded Stillman to bring Gompers to an understanding that women were involved in the new labor movement because they wanted to improve their professional skills more than they wanted to obtain political clout.

Linville further argued that Gompers was exploiting Stillman's limited experience in order to enhance the CIO, that he was not forceful enough in expressing the benefits of the affiliation between the two. Linville wanted the AFT to focus more on academic and professional development for teachers than on a political agenda for the union.[40] Aware that prolonged tension between the two men would hurt the AFT, Stillman and Linville decided to redirect their efforts toward the development of their organization in ways that would secure for its members the benefits they were trying to obtain. Their principal objective was to bring the AFT to a point where it would be recognized as a national institution fully capable of serving the interests of the constituency it represented: teachers and students.

When teachers in Seattle went on strike in February 1919, it provided evidence to support Linville's concern that Gompers did, indeed, have considerable influence on Stillman, who reacted to the strike by saying, "It is an illegal strike, called in defiance of the constitution and of the resolution of the AFT and of the international unions. Of course, it is not up to us to condemn our fellow teachers in Seattle, even if we think that they are mistaken."[41] Coming at a time when national attitudes were rapidly changing in favor of recognizing the rights of workers, including teachers, Stillman's reaction to the

---

40. Marjorie Murphy, *Blackboard Unions: The AFT and the NEA, 1900-1980*, p. 104.

41. Charles Stillman, "Response to a Strike by Teachers in Seattle," March 20, 1919, Linville Collection, AFT Files. See also *The American Teacher* (February 8, 1919).

strike in Seattle created doubt about the kind of strategies that he was utilizing for the AFT in order to assure its legitimacy. His reaction also showed that he was not going to sanction strikes as the only instrument in seeking broader outcomes without carefully considering other options.

Regardless of the controversial nature of Stillman's leadership, the AFT began to grow in a manner that James Earl Clarke characterized as "an avalanche-like increase in the number of local organizations. To the original eight charter locals in 1916 were added nine more in 1917, and in 1918 eighteen new locals were formed. Then in the single year 1919, one hundred and one new locals were formed."[42] At a time when Stillman's leadership was being questioned, Freeland G. Stecker, the AFT's secretary-treasurer until 1926, wrote, "The AFT has passed the ten thousand mark in membership. Its prospects are better than ever before. The increasing number of inquiries received daily indicate a great awakening among the teachers. Nor is this development confined to any one region of the country. It comes from all directions, from all states, from cities and country districts, from elementary, high, normal and college institutions."[43]

Encouraged by the growth of his organization, Stillman initiated a plan of action that, when fully implemented, would help increase its membership throughout the country. In 1918 the NEA issued a statement criticizing the AFT for adopting union strategies saying, "One need be disturbed by the fear that unionist organizations will resort to undignified and violent means to achieve their goals. Unions formed of American teachers may not be depended upon to pursue a wise, patient, and purely democratic policy."[44] From that time to this day this has remained a major area of dissension between the AFT and the NEA. In the negotiation between the two organizations for a possible merger, the question of the AFT affiliation with the CIO has inhibited their ability to reach unification.

In 1918 the membership of the NEA was 10,104 compared to only 2,000 for the AFT. But one year later, when the AFT had 11,000 members, the NEA began to suspect that the AFT was trying to persuade NEA members to join its ranks. With an increase in the number of students in high school from 1.6 million in 1915 to 2.6 million in 1920,[45] the AFT attracted more new members than the NEA. This was because it offered greater prospects for starting teachers than the NEA approach. The principle of collective bargaining had a special appeal to new members of the AFT because it represented the practice of democracy. It also gave teachers an opportunity to contribute to the development of society beyond the boundaries of the educational development of the country. For the AFT this was the best of times, and for the NEA it was the worst of times.

---

42. James Earl Clarke, "The American Federation of Teachers: Origins and History from 1870 to 1952," diss., Cornell University, 1966, p. 140.

43. Freeland G. Stecker, "The October Message," *The American Teacher* 8 (October 1919): 179.

44. The NEA, "Teachers' Salaries and Cost of Living, 1918," NEA Files, Washington, D.C..

45. Department of the Interior, *Biennial Survey of Education, 1920-24, vol.* 2, no. 44 (Washington, D.C.: Government Printing Office, 1925), p. 5.

In 1920 national development carried with it a price tag that led to an increase in taxes in order for the country to meet its fiscal objectives. In that year the average annual expenditure for education rose from $38.30 in 1913 to $65.00 per child.[46] Already faced with increasing taxes, taxpayers expressed resentment toward an increase in teachers' salaries because it meant an additional increase in their tax bill. On the surface it appeared that the United States was spending nearly twice as much per student in 1920 as it did in 1913. In actuality, purchasing power had declined in 1920 from what it was in 1913. While taxpayers experienced an increase in taxes, teachers found that because their buying power had been steadily eroding, they had experienced a declining standard of living.

Compounding this problem was the fact that deteriorating working conditions had combined with overcrowded classrooms to inhibit teachers' ability to effectively discharge their responsibility to their students. In Sacramento, California, some teachers were charged with disloyalty when they raised questions about this situation. The teachers appealed to the AFT for help in seeking a solution to the problem. The result was the formation of one of the strongest local affiliates of the AFT.[47] This development not only increased the membership of the AFT, but also strengthened and enhanced its influence all around the country.

Although Stillman was criticized for developing a close relationship with Samuel Gompers, he rose to the occasion to exert strong leadership in resolving a problem that teachers were facing: continuing accusations that the AFT was operating under principles of intimidation often associated with labor unions. In 1921, when Stillman thought that he had found a solution to this credibility problem, his stewardship was challenged once again. Representing a group of teachers who were not pleased with the Stillman-Gompers relationship, Earnest B. Collette, an influential member of the Chicago Federation of Male Teachers and an active participant in the AFT, wrote a letter on June 19, 1921, addressed to Freeland G. Stecker. In it he stated that "Gompers has been very effective in building up a machine that certainly dominates the AFL-CIO. It has also done just what every machine does under capitalist system. It controls the lives of the men, women, and children. It exercises power in great strength. It has become autocratic as it realizes that with power it has influence."[48]

Although Stecker agreed with Collette's view that Gompers was having undue influence on Stillman, he did not share Collette's opinion that the AFT should break its ties with the AFL-CIO. Recognizing that Stillman had provided positive leadership for the AFT in seeking to accomplish the objectives it had identified at its inception, Stecker believed it was now incumbent upon Collette to defend the reputation of a man who was doing a good job of promoting the needs and interests of an organization that was founded under adverse circumstances. Stecker went on to argue that Stillman was trying to forge a new

---

46. Ibid., p. 6.
47. Wellington G. Furdycee, "The Historical Background of American Teacher Unions," *American School Board Journal* (May 1946).
48. Earnest B. Collette to Freeland B. Stecker June 19, 1921, AFT Files, Washington, D.C.

vision for the development of the AFT in order to meet the challenges it was sure to face in the future. He found himself defending Stillman and Gompers, saying, "While the Gompers administration is not accompanied by as intelligent and forward looking policies as we would like to see, it has been free from graft and crookedness within it."[49]

Both Stillman and Stecker knew that Gompers had an influence on Stillman that members of the AFT considered negative. But their intuition led them to believe that the AFT needed the support and encouragement of a man who had gained considerable experience in leading labor organizations.[50] Their observation that Gompers and his associates were honest men who were trying to function in a hostile environment became the principal factor that sustained their leadership role within the AFT. This reality weighed heavily in the minds of the future leaders of the AFT, including Shanker. Indeed, honesty, decency, and loyalty became the leadership qualities that the AFT demanded in order to carry out its mission. This was the legacy that the AFT wanted to leave to its future leaders.

In 1920, when Stillman thought he had answered all concerns about him, he faced yet another spate of negativity about his administration of the AFT. In that year Lotus D. Coffman, professor of education at the University of Minnesota, told the NEA convention held in Cleveland, Ohio, that he was not opposed to teachers forming professional organizations, but that he was opposed to unions such as the AFT.

Coffman outlined a number of reasons for his criticism of the AFT. Among them were the following: that by forming a union, teachers were reducing themselves to the level of laborers; that methods for seeking solutions to problems in the teaching profession were different from those utilized to seek solutions to problems of manual labor; that teachers, as members of a profession, must never resort to strikes to resolve problems; and that the AFT's affiliation with AFL-CIO would accentuate class conflict and so lower professional standards.[51] Again, Stillman rose to the occasion to provide the effective leadership needed to address Coffman's points. As a result, Coffman's criticism helped to strengthen the AFT. Its members began to look to the future with great expectations.

SUMMARY AND CONCLUSION

The discussion thus far leads to two conclusions. The first is that the formation of the AFT in 1916 was an event destined to alter the character of both

49. Freeland G. Stecker to Earnest B. Collette, June 17, 1921, AFT Files, Washington, D.C.

50. Indeed, Gompers, who emigrated from Britain at the age of 13, served as president of the AFL-CIO from its inception in 1886 until his death in 1924, except for one year. He was considered knowledgeable about most aspects of labor relationships, and his advice was sought by those not affiliated with the AFL-CIO.

51. Lotus D. Coffman, "Address to the NEA," February 1920, AFT Files, Washington, D.C.

politics and education in the United States. With the formation of the NEA in 1857, the teaching profession glorified itself in the absoluteness of its service to society through its educational endeavors. Since the reform movement of the time of Horace Mann, teachers approached their duty with a total dedication to the educational development of their students. They believed that politics had no place in their functions and operations. But the formation of the AFT would alter that perception forever, as it operated under the principle that there must be a balance between discharging professional duty and exerting political influence on the degree of institutional control of teachers. This has remained a constant and core feature of the AFT up to this day.

The second conclusion is that from the formative days of the Chicago Teachers Federation during the time of Margaret Haley through the turbulent period that characterized the leadership of Charles Stillman, the AFT's character and the role it was trying to play were invariably determined by the quality of its leadership. This is why Janie McKeon, John Powers, Susan B. Anthony, Henrietta Rodman, Nancy Cott, Catherine Goggin, and Ella Flagg Young all made contributions that made it possible for the AFT to play a prominent role in shaping the future of both education and the country. How the AFT expanded and exercised leadership in public education is the subject of Chapter 2.

2

The AFT and Educational Leadership: The Legacy of the Past

> *Educational leadership requires a special aspect of its efficiency in promoting democracy in the kind of relationship that must develop between teachers and the school board.*
>
> Abraham Lefkowitz, 1917

> *The reasons which to us are all sufficient for the damnation of the autocratic board of education are startling evidence of the need for new forms of educational leadership.*
>
> Henry R. Linville, 1917

THE AFT AND THE QUEST FOR A ROLE IN EDUCATIONAL LEADERSHIP

When the Committee on Commercial Education of the New York Chamber of Commerce released its report in 1916, it discussed a disturbing reality about the condition of education that few people were aware of.[1] The New York Chamber of Commerce had appointed the committee to investigate the impact of commercial education on the educational development of the state. In order to fully understand the educational implications of this relatively narrow aspect of the educational process, the committee's points of reference included an examination of the much broader field of education from elementary through high school.

Concluding from the evidence before it that both elementary and high schools were in an abysmal state, the committee pointed to the lack of leadership in education as the major cause for its decline. For this reason the committee's report on commercial education received less attention than its conclusions about the condition of elementary and secondary education. The lack of effective

---

1. The AFT, Committee on Commercial Education of the New York Chamber of Commerce, *The American Teacher* 6, no. 6 (June 1916): p. 82.

leadership was also cited as the reason why "the report is largely a condemnation of general elementary education and their teachers, rather than an investigation of commercial education."2 The committee reached its conclusion as a result of extensive observations and countless meetings with teachers, principals, superintendents, members of the school board, parents, and members of the community.

After citing the lack of adequate educational leadership as a major cause of the decline in education, the committee identified four problems that it said must be resolved in order to begin the arduous task of improving education. The first was that high school graduates from typically failed to demonstrate a functional knowledge of the subjects they had studied. The second problem was that those students showed no evidence of understanding basic social and moral values so critical to building a national character. The school system failed either to impart these values to students or to have them form the foundation of the educational process. Without these values, education would lead to no real meaning in the lives of the students and of society itself.

The third obstacle was that leaders in education failed to provide positive role models for teachers to acquire professional competency. This would entail the ability to teach effectively and be skilled in recognizing the needs of individual students both as human beings and as students. The fourth was that the members of the board of education did not have a thorough understanding of the educational process and student needs because their primary concern was the political benefits that they would accrue from holding public office. The result was that many were far removed from the reality of properly understanding and resolving problems in education. Neither the school board nor the school administration discharged its leadership responsibility in a manner that would bring about quality education.

In suggesting a strategic approach to seeking solutions to the problems of educational leadership, the committee attempted to raise public consciousness to a new level so citizens would recognize the imperative for immediate action in the four key problem areas noted in the committee's report. The first was the need to design strategies for eliminating the overcrowded classrooms where teachers were already overworked. The second was how to allow teachers greater responsibility in designing a curriculum that would be utilized to motivate students to learn and be excited about the educational process in general.

The third was how to have members of the school board become accountable to the public for formulating an effective educational policy as the first step toward restoring effective educational leadership. The fourth was to initiate the process of team-building in creating an educational environment that would make possible dialogical interaction between the administration and the teachers because institutional policy cannot be imposed.

Released in 1920, four years after the founding of the AFT, the report of the Committee on Commercial Education in New York played a major role in arousing a new understanding that leadership was a critical element in the effectiveness of any educational system. The report was a sequel to

---

2. Ibid., p. 83.

developments of earlier times. Writing three years earlier in 1917 on the imperative of leadership in seeking to improve the standards of education, J. Edward Mayman argued, "In the first place the high minded teacher demands that the preparation for teaching shall be longer and much more thorough than it now is. Thus, there should be better teaching materials to begin with. Secondly, the teacher demands the professional right to judge and be judged by his peers. This implies a responsible power and a democratic control which would not only purge the system of inefficient teachers and leaders of the educational system, but would also build up strong professional leadership which would not tolerate low standards."[3]

Mayman postulated that the only way this crucial initial step could be taken to restore quality leadership in education was "to have the board of education elected at large and be subject to recall."[4] According to Mayman, this action would also enhance the positive responsiveness of teachers to the needs of students. The ultimate effect of the role of leadership would be that students who were properly educated would offer invaluable service to their community and country. In this regard, students would play proper leadership roles in society. The knowledge of this reality would require a comprehensive understanding at all levels of education that educational leadership must be in place at the administrative level and then extended to all levels of the educational hierarchy to include teachers, students, and members of the community.

Mayman further suggested that educational leadership must never be left to the members of the school board because they are heavily influenced by considerations of personal political benefits at the expense of the education of students. The formulation of any educational principles that failed to take this into account would have no efficacy in the educational system. The failure of the country to develop an alternative method of choosing members of the school board so that they are responsible to the community, rather than to themselves, was primarily the failure of individuals to provide such an option. The whole question of the absence of educational leadership was directly related to the lack of educational innovation. In this regard, the country faced a challenge of immense proportions.

Writing also in 1917 about the role of teachers in developing principles of educational leadership, Abraham Lefkowitz, a teacher at De Witt Clinton High School in New York State, addressed the philosophical question relative to dialogical interaction between teachers and the administration, saying, "How can teachers teach democracy when they are not permitted to live it? Educational leadership requires a special aspect of its efficiency in promoting democracy in the kind of relationship that must develop between teachers and the school board. Democracy must be the substitute for autocracy. This is evident in the manner in which educational system is conducted. Without democracy the quality of education is threatened and society pays the ultimate price. Teachers must not

---

3. J. Edward Mayman, "Business and Education," *The American Teacher* 6, no. 6 (June 1917): p. 85.
4. Ibid., p. 86.

become mere cogs in the educational machine. They must play a real role in educational leadership to enable the system to sustain quality in education."[5]

Lefkowitz argued that the only way to find solutions to the problems of educational leadership was to take teachers as equal partners in formulating principles for its development and implementation; otherwise, he concluded, "the battle for professional rights for teachers to play their proper leadership role in education will continue"[6] with adverse effects on the conduct of the school. The longer the struggle for teachers' rights continued, the more likely education was to suffer, whether the administration recognized it or not. In suggesting that the quality of educational leadership depends on the role that teachers play, Lefkowitz was calling on the AFT to play the role that he argued it must to ensure the educational leadership needed to have quality education. He recognized that the task of bringing this about was not an easy one because the administration often felt threatened by innovative ideas. He concluded his article by urging the AFT to make sure that it seeks out and maintains strong leadership.

THE FORMATIVE YEARS: FROM CHARLES STILLMAN TO MARY BARKER

From the moment that Charles Stillman was elected president of the AFT in 1916, he fully understood the coercive and stressful situation in which teachers in the union found themselves. They faced a relentless campaign by the board of education enveloped in the so-called the Loeb law. Until his death in 1924, Jacob Loeb waged an obsessive campaign against teachers who were members of any organization outside his control. In a landmark decision that strengthened the board's position, the Illinois Supreme Court ruled against teacher organizations in 1917 saying, "The board has the absolute right to decide to employ or to refuse to reemploy any applicant for any reason whatsoever or for no reason at all. The board is not bound to give any reason for its action. It is free to contract with whomever it chooses."[7]

Recognizing the very real peril that teachers in the AFT faced if Illinois boards of education had the right to immediately dismiss any teacher they wanted, Stillman and Freeland G. Stecker realized the urgent need to exercise strong leadership in protecting them. They decided to keep the AFT membership lists away from the office out of concern that it could be raided by the police. They also took this action "to protect teachers against intimidation and discrimination on account of their affiliation with organized labor."[8] This action

---

5. Abraham Lefkowitz, "The Teachers' Union: Past, Present, and Future," *The American Teacher*, no. 6 (June 1917): p. 91.

6. Ibid., p. 92.

7. Chicago Teachers Federation and the Board of Education," *School and Society* 5 (May 5, 1917): 526-27.

8. "Report of the Committee on Adjustment," *Report of the Proceedings of the Fourth Annual Convention of the American Federation of Labor* (Washington, D.C.: The Law Reporter Printing Company, 1920), p. 42.

was a hint of what Stillman would do to provide effective leadership in facing the challenges that the AFT would encounter as a result of the obstacles put in place by court decisions. He mobilized public sentiment and sought the support of the teachers to wage a moral struggle against what he believed was an oppressive system.

When the Illinois Supreme Court issued its landmark decision in 1917 denying teachers any employment rights, the state became the target of AFT activity.[9] Politicians, public officials, parents, and members of the public became the focus of a strategy designed to arouse political consciousness that heralded the need to protect the rights of teachers in order to safeguard the rights of all workers. In addition, the CIO and other labor organizations adopted this justification so as to emphasize the importance of respecting the rights of all workers. For example, as president of the United Auto Workers from 1946 to 1970, Walter Philip Reuther (1907-1970), operated under this principle.[10] It was, therefore, obvious that regardless of the court ruling, the workers pursued their objective without violating the letter of the law.[11]

Stillman skillfully succeeded in convincing the public that in spite of the Illinois Supreme Court ruling against teachers, there was a need to protect the right of teachers to form unions. It was not a question of legal process, but one of a basic political right of all people. He urged the public to realize that when workers are dissatisfied with their working conditions, the level of productivity declines sharply. In this repressive state of affairs the interests of the country as a whole suffer. He called on all those who felt the way he did to come forward and unite to work towards the development of a system that recognized the rights of all people as a prerequisite for establishing positive conditions that enhanced the development of the nation.

Stillman was careful to urge the public not to take action against the ruling of the courts, but to continue their campaign based on the historical democratic precedent that the people have a moral responsibility to change unjust laws. The success of this campaign placed the Illinois Supreme Court in an uncomfortable position as it began to realize that it was arbitrating political issues, rather than defining the law.

As Stillman felt confident that he was gaining the support of the public in his crusade, he shifted his attention to lobbying for the passage of legislation that would protect the rights of workers. He utilized the growing awareness across the country that to deny them those rights would place the country in a state of reduced productivity. As a matter of strategy, he avoided talking directly about the rights of teachers, opting to emphasize workers in general. Using the publicity and acknowledgment he was receiving that he was doing something for the good of the country, Stillman persuaded members of the legislature to make moot the ruling of the Illinois Supreme Court. This is why in 1917 the Illinois

---

9. Stillman was from Wilmette, Illinois.

10. This was made clear in the documentary "UAW and the Rise of Walter Reuther," aired by PBS on September 5, 1993, the eve of the Labor Day holiday.

11. This could not be said about the current struggle between the pro-choice and the pro-life groups on the issue of abortion. This suggests the conclusion that the protagonists in this tragic drama need to learn the lessons from the past.

legislature enacted a law that for the first time provided a system of tenure that stopped the arbitrary and capricious dismissal of teachers by boards of education.

The legislature, now highly sensitive to public opinion, mandated the restructuring of the existing boards of education to enable them to function under the provisions of recent legislation. This was intended to reverse the decision of the Illinois Supreme Court in such a way that strengthened AFT principles and objectives. Stillman's leadership was instrumental in this paradigm shift. Encouraged by this unprecedented success, Stillman shifted his attention to the development of a foundation upon which future educational leadership would be built. After holding discussions with Henry R. Linville, the editor-in-chief of *The American Teacher*, a decision was reached to run an editorial encouraging the AFT to initiate a plan of action to consolidate the gains that had been made. Stressing the importance of the teachers' role in educational decision-making, the editorial presented an impressive argument, stating:

> A teacher's personality may be humanly gauged by the depth and the power of vivid self-expression created in the pupils under his sincerely affectionate guidance. A principal's personality may be measured by his ability to lead and wisely exploit the funds of vital energy, intellectual and spiritual, often copiously welling up in the minds of teachers and students. A principal whose very presence is repressive and inhibitory, conducive to nothing more creative than sullen silence, suspicion and cold detachment, is not fit to continue in his high office. Fit or unfit this species of assassin is not checked in his meanly uneventful career. The triumphant brute reigns unperturbed. How long must the teacher remain on the fringes of educational leadership?[12]

One can see that the editorial was extremely forceful in promoting the leadership role of teachers, premising its argument on the legislation passed by the Illinois legislature. It also based its argument on the support the AFT was receiving from the public and on Stillman's own popularity. As Stillman gained more experience, the influence that Gompers had exercised on the AFT was waning. Stillman had established himself as a leader in his own right. With increasing confidence in himself, he was now providing the leadership the AFT needed to build itself. The editorial that Linville wrote took this development into account in stressing the essence of personality that he said manifested teachers' behavior.

> We, the incorrigibly credulous, have been half-persuaded into believing that personality is the precious quintessence of educational leadership and efficiency. If personality means anything vital, it means the fine talent, ceaselessly evolving, for creating in the hearts and minds of surrounding personalities an intensified desire to express for the fullest whatever compelling inspirations lie latent in their souls."[13]

---

12. "Through the Fluoroscope," (editorial), *The American Teacher* 6, no. 6 (June 1917): p. 88.
13. Ibid.

In rapid succession teachers in cities across the country were voting for an affiliation with the AFT. In 1917 alone, teachers in Schenectady, New York; Gary, Indiana; Jacksonville, Florida; and Washington, D.C., voted for membership in the AFT. In 1918 a total of thirteen new school districts joined the AFT. In 1919 Stillman claimed that the AFT did not need to resort to strikes to resolve conflict between its members and the board of education because members of the public fully understood that the organization was trying to promote quality education for all students by providing job security for teachers.[14]

Stillman was the man of the hour, a rising star in the struggle of wills between the mighty political establishment and a fledgling and fragile labor organization. Although there was considerable ideological difference between Stillman and Linville, the two men approached their responsibility with a sense of earnest importance in making efforts to build a strong foundation on which to structure the future leadership of an organization that meant so much to teachers across the United States.

Once he felt that the AFT had received the recognition that it deserved, Stillman shifted his focus to developing his philosophy of education, especially the curriculum. In 1920 he and Stecker advanced their position on school curriculum. They believed that vocational education must form an acceptable alternative to academic education and that teachers of it form the backbone and future strength of the AFT. Stillman and Stecker shared a belief that if vocational education succeeded in imparting to students the values of vocation, it was critical to have teachers of it become members of the AFT. The two men also argued that the enactment of the Smith Vocational Education Act in 1917 fully recognized the contribution of vocational education teachers to the teaching profession and that they must now be accorded the proper recognition they deserved.[15]

Beginning in 1920 Stillman's leadership skills and style were tested in an unanticipated way. Women teachers were increasingly expressing resentment at the influence the conservative Gompers was still exerting on Stillman at a time when most thought the AFT should be able to stand on its own. Although that influence was less visible and direct, it was, nonetheless, a cause of concern among some teachers. The ratification of the Nineteenth Amendment[16] on August 26, 1920, galvanized and unified women to demand recognition of their right to participate in all matters of national importance.

Women demanded equality in representation, leadership position, improvement in conditions of employment, salary, and so on. They were no longer willing to be treated as second-class citizens; the days of Susan B. Anthony were over as women began to look to the future with great expectations. For the next two years Stillman was overwhelmed by the rapid

---

14. Charles B. Stillman, "Four Months of Progress," *The American Teacher* (January 1919): p. 12.

15. Ibid., p. 13.

16. The amendment, which was proposed on June 4, 1919, stated, "The right of citizens of the United States to vote shall not be denied or abridged by the United States or by any state on account of sex."

pace of events. The criticism from women members of the AFT that Gompers was having undue influence on him proved to be more a tactical method of asserting their rights in the wake of the passage of the Nineteenth Amendment than a genuine expression of concern. It is for this reason that Stillman did nothing to respond.

However, this line of thinking among women resurfaced at the AFT annual convention in 1923. With a debt of $3,500, a considerable amount in those days, Stillman knew that his days of leadership were numbered. For seven years he had been the champion of teachers' rights, a workhorse in the emerging field of social engineering that gave birth to a new social order and a new realism for members of the teaching profession. Now he was becoming tired and overworked at a critical time in the brief history of the union. He was unable to meet the challenges that had to be met to assure the future of the organization that held so much potential for its members.

While women teachers were paid less than male teachers, a practice that has continued to this day, they paid the same amount of dues as male members of the AFT. They criticized Stillman for failing to move the AFT along the lines defined by the Nineteenth Amendment. They criticized him for allowing Gompers to continue exerting influence of him because Gompers was not known for his positive views of women.

Instead of fighting to keep his position, Stillman decided to resign. He felt that a struggle within the AFT would paralyze its ability to pursue the objectives for which it was founded. In 1924, recognizing increasing opposition and in declining health, Stillman, the seemingly steel man of the AFT, was replaced by Florence Rood. She was an influential and powerful teacher with the union's women's movement from St. Paul, Minnesota. Rood was Margaret Haley reincarnated, a consummate visionary of the women's movement and a true believing liberal who had castigated Stillman for his relationship with Gompers. She was the quintessential manifestation of the Nineteenth Amendment, bustling with new ideas for the transformation of both the AFT and American society.

Florence Rood held the view that before teachers ever stepped into the classroom, they must be accorded the respect and the employment protection that they deserved. She believed that female teachers must be treated in the same manner as male teachers. She also believed that the country must implement an affirmative action program to compensate them for the humiliation they had endured in the past. She perceived her election as part of that agenda and felt that the country was poised to enter a new era of unprecedented social transformation unmatched by that of any other prior period. The passage of the Nineteenth Amendment had made this possible. It was therefore in the best interest of all concerned to operate under the new spirit of equality.

In putting together her own plan of action Florence Rood did two things that Stillman did not attempt. The first was to formulate a set of policies that made the AFT different from the NEA in two areas, teacher representation in contract negotiations and curriculum development. Whereas Stillman had expressed philosophical views about the curriculum, Rood actually ordered the revision of it to make education relevant to the needs of students. She shared the view that the strength of the AFT lay in a working balance between these two interrelated components. Second, she sought to strengthen the feminist quality of the original women's movement.[17] This had not been emphasized during Stillman's term of office. Now that a woman was president of a national organization, it was natural to expect that she would place the development and interests of women high on her list of priorities.

The beginning of Rood's term of office coincided with important world and national events. In 1920, the year the Nineteenth Amendment to the Constitution was ratified, Warren G. Harding (1865-1923) was elected president of the United States on the wave of excitement from the adjournment of the Versailles Peace Conference and the promise of new prosperity. In 1922 the Lincoln Memorial was dedicated to symbolize the quest for freedom of all people, including women. In the same year Egypt gained political independence from Britain, Benito Mussolini became the dictator of Italy, the Soviet Union was formed, and international conference was held in Washington, D.C., to limit naval armadas. Harding's national agenda did not include aggressive efforts to improve the status of women in light of the ratification of the Nineteenth Amendment. This came as a great disappointment to Rood and other women. What his death on August 2, 1923, did was reveal the scandal that he kept two mistresses. This may explain his attitude toward women and his reluctance to embrace the views of Margaret Haley and Florence Rood.

The succession of Calvin Coolidge (1872-1933) to the presidency following Harding's death did not mean the introduction of a policy to improve the status of women. The agenda of a liberal leader who symbolized so much hope for the improvement of female teachers and women in general was being overshadowed by more pressing events that were unfolding nationally and internationally. A civil war broke out in China in 1924. The Locarno Conference of 1925 was raising new hopes of peace in Europe over the neutrality of the Rhineland. The first diesel locomotive to run a regular passenger service to New York beginning in 1925 captured the headlines and placed Rood and the AFT on the back pages of major newspapers.

For the next two years, from 1924 to 1926, the fortunes of the AFT steadily declined under Rood's leadership. This was not because she was inefficient, but became events combined to place her at a disadvantage. As a result, the progress that the AFT had witnessed during Stillman's term of office was being reversed. While the agenda that she had set still represented the thrust for the new and struggling union to move forward to meet new challenges, the means of implementing it were not in place. In her enthusiasm to promote the feminist movement Rood alienated an important and powerful segment of the constituency she needed to make her leadership effective-- men.

Cast in a national milieu, the program that Rood was trying to accomplish got lost in the shuffle of competing national issues. The economy, already in a weak state, needed strengthening in order to generate enough revenue to carry out social programs and rejuvenate national confidence about the future. President

---

17. Marjorie Murphy, *Blackboard Unions: The AFT and the NEA, 1900-1980* (Ithaca, N.Y: Cornell University Press, 1990), p. 90.

Coolidge was not aware that continuing Harding's economic policies would eventually lead to the collapse of the entire economic system in only seven months after his leaving office. Rood's options were few. She was caught between idealism and reality, between what was possible and what was not possible. The male members of the AFT were equally caught between giving her enthusiastic support within the spirit of the Nineteenth Amendment and struggling against a prevailing negative attitude toward women's leadership in national affairs. They, too, had few options.

Unable to generate a new enthusiasm among members of the public and the AFT, Rood was desperate. She remembered the circumstance that led to the demise of Charles Stillman in 1924 and how Freeland G. Stecker had reacted to the collapse of his mentor's leadership by saying, "When the committee on nomination and elections met the carefully guarded secret was out. There was not to be a graceful and honorable retirement, not even a vice-president."[18] By 1926 the fiery Florence Rood, who envisaged the complete overhaul of the AFT and the teaching profession, was overwhelmed by a sense of failure to accomplish the objectives that she had established for her term of office.

Feeling abandoned by her close associates and distanced by the members of the organization, Rood resigned, deeply disappointed in both herself and her friends in their failure to make significant gains. Rood's leadership of the AFT was over. Although she was haunted by her inability to accomplish, Florence Rood must not be regarded as a failure. In just two years she demonstrated that a woman could be trusted with the responsibility of leading a national organization. She also proved that when given the opportunity, women were just as capable as men. Indeed, Florence Rood had played her role well in evincing effective leadership during the formative years of the AFT.

When Mary C. Barker of Georgia succeeded Rood in 1926, there was a feeling among the AFT members that her agenda would be realized. Barker's tenure was noted for its focus on making women a new factor in the national politics of education.[19] Barker succeeded in arousing a new awareness about the political ability of women. A graduate of Agnes Scott College for women, founded in 1899 in Decatur, Georgia, Barker learned early in life to identify herself with women's issues. She assumed the responsibility of supporting her widowed mother and two sisters on the salary of an elementary school teacher. At her alma mater Barker distinguished herself as a serious student. Later she was appointed principal of an elementary school in Atlanta, where she distinguished herself as an effective administrator who showed great care for her students and teachers.

Barker administered the school as if it were a family, regarding each teacher and student as a special human being with great potential to contribute to the good of society. She allowed either the students or the teachers to fail in their respective responsibilities. Students were expected to succeed and teachers to

---

18. Freeland G. Stecker to Florine E. Francis, president of the Gary Teachers Federation, December 11, 1924, AFT Files, Washington, D.C.

19. Marjorie Murphy, *Blackboard Unions: The AFT and the NEA, 1900-1980*, p. 118.

inspire. The success of the school attracted the attention and the admiration of both the public and the administration. This was a rare occasion during a time conflict and crisis were the order of things due to the struggle for power and influence.

Barker was as enthusiastic as Margaret Haley, Nancy Cott, Janie McKeon, and Ella Flagg Young in seeking to promote the status of women in the teaching profession. As a teacher, she played an assertive role in supporting local teachers' organizations to go national. She shared the views expressed by Florence Rood and Margaret Haley that teachers, collectively and individually, must be involved in politics because politics reflects every aspect of American society. This is why she regarded the ratification of the Nineteenth Amendment as a monumental milestone in women's struggle for advancement.

Although she was raised in an environment that reminded women of their place in society, Barker became highly sensitive to issues of gender and race. For this reason she became an uncompromising advocate of equal rights for all people, including those of minority groups. Her philosophy was that it was not possible to successfully promote the status of women without trying to promote that of minority groups.[20] Combined with the agenda that Florence Rood tried to carry out, this approach helped to enhance Barker's image among the members of the public that she was a genuinely dedicated national leader. Her own position that "unless we ourselves consider our services valuable and show what we can do, no one else will so recognize us"[21] earned her the respect of the members of the public and those of the organization that she led.

Barker also believed that autonomy and the independence of teachers in making academic decisions, such as the curriculum content, was a manifestation of the professionalism that they all must exercise. She firmly believed that decisions must not be dictated by boards of education. She argued that because traditions of the past inhibited the ability of society to accord them this right, teachers must organize to demand it. This is why she tried to have the superintendent of her school system authorize teachers to exercise decision-making in determining certain aspects of educational policy.

Although by comparison Barker was more indirect than Rood, she exhibited patterns of leadership and cognition that were similar to those of her predecessor. Florence Hanson, the influential president of the Chicago Federation of Women Teachers and Barker's close friend and associate, was a loyal official who played an effective role in promoting the AFT agenda under Barker's leadership.

Another woman who fully supported Barker was Selma Borchardt, who had been a teacher in the Washington school system where she learned the art of hard ball politics relative to the teachers' role in educational policy. Following the ratification of the Nineteenth Amendment, Borchardt readily joined the AFT with a single mission in mind to enable it to realize the goals that teachers were trying to achieve. Among these goals was initiating collective bargaining and

20. Albert Shanker adopted this strategy beginning in 1955, the year the civil rights movement is believed to have started in the United States.

21. Marjorie Murphy, *Blackboard Unions: The AFT and the NEA, 1900-1980*, p. 119.

according teachers improved conditions of service. Borchardt then studied law and devoted her career to protecting children under child labor laws.

Borchardt also aggressively lobbied for legislation that would recognize the rights of children, women, and minority groups. Within a short period of time she became a trusted aide and counsel to Barker. In that position Borchardt proved to be an efficient, loyal, and principal advisor to Barker. Her sole motivation was the promotion of the AFT's agenda to the best of her ability. Borchardt's dedication to the AFT's cause, her ability to bring salient points of view together, and her power of persuasion, created a political and social climate that compelled the public to support both the AFT and Barker's leadership of it.

Barker's qualities of leadership, like those of her predecessors, were put to the test. For Barker it came from a conflict that emerged and settled in between Borchardt and Charles Williams, an official of the NEA. Williams was trying to promote the NEA's legislative educational packages and was seeking a cabinet position in the Coolidge Administration. Fearing that Borchardt's rising star threatened his own fortunes because she decided to work as an AFT national lobbyist, Williams refused to even recognize the AFT as a national organization. But what actually threatened Williams was Borchardt's ability to bring common sense to the discussion of critical issues.[22]

When Williams appeared to solicit the support of Matthew Woll, an official of the AFL, in his campaign against Borchardt and the AFT, Barker could no longer contain her patience. Charging that Woll and Williams were individuals motivated by their disrespect of successful women, Barker fired back, saying, "I do not believe that our program is the root cause of the trouble. Mr. Woll revealed some of his own personal feelings against us. Now Mr. Williams has found a faithful ally to damage the work we are trying to accomplish"[23] and reduce the role that women were playing in the educational and social reconstruction of the country. Recognizing that they had made an error in assessing the situation, Woll and Williams swallowed their pride and let both Borchardt and Barker enjoy the popularity that positive publicity brings.

Another issue that brought forth the best of Mary C. Barker's leadership qualities was the criticism that came from male members of the AFT that she was using the organization to promote the Joint Women's Congressional Union, a national organization that was created after the ratification of the Nineteenth Amendment. Its chief function was to advocate the political advancement of women. William Green, an official of the AFT who was critical of Barker, went even further to argue that she was using male members of the AFT to support her political agenda and cited socialist A. J. Muste as an example.

Barker was infuriated as she responded, "The affinity between the AFL and the NEA has finally dawned on me. As much as two peas in a pod. Autocratic, complaisant, monopolistic, anti-social, fear-ridden, illiberal inherently afraid of

22. Joseph Whitworth Neuwman, "A History of the Atlanta Public School Teachers' Association: Local 89 of the American Federation of Teachers, 1919-1956" (diss., Georgia State University, 1978), p. 95.

23. Mary C. Barker, in a letter dated January 17, 1929, addressed to Florence Hanson, the AFT Collection, Walter Reuther Archives of Labor and Urban Affairs, Wayne State University, Detroit.

progress, Mr. Green is like a fish out of water. I have completely lost confidence in the Woll-Williams ridden machine. I fear I am not a good barometer of Mr. Green's mind."[24] Barker saw Green's attempt to smear Muste as a personal attack on her character. She returned the slander by attacking Green, the AFL, and the NEA.

Indeed, the strength of her personality sustained her leadership of the AFT at a time of great crisis. On June 26, 1928, at the twelfth annual convention, Barker discussed the frustration she had experienced and the hope she envisaged as the motivating factor for her organization, saying, "A year ago the American Federation of Teachers was looking out upon an encouraging prospect for growth and expansion. Up to May 1st our actual increase in membership during the year had been over 13 percent. However, we have encountered some of the social ills that our program is designed to help eradicate."[25]

Barker suggested three possible solutions. The first was to launch a new publicity program to emphasize the goals and accomplishments of the AFT. The second called for the establishment of a reserve fund to assist those teachers who were experiencing economic difficulties. The third involved raising funds to ensure the AFT had sufficient legal representation if the need should arise. That the convention delegates accepted the proposals attests to how effective a leader Barker was.

By the time the AFT held its thirteenth annual convention, also in Chicago in July 1929, Mary C. Barker knew that she was positioned on the top of the popularity ladder. She used this to call attention to issues that had not been addressed in the past. She called for improved living conditions for teachers, including housing. During her presidential address she received a standing ovation when she said, "We are insisting upon housing conditions for teachers that are physically safe and that may be expected to produce socially sound practices. Help yourself to attain the conditions necessary for you to function as human beings and as worthy members of your profession. Endeavor to overcome the obstacles to your aspirations by cooperating with your fellow teachers to get the necessary political power to bring about desirable improvement in all the conditions that affect your work."[26]

Addressing the question of the rights and freedom that she said teachers must have to discharge their responsibility, Barker argued, "The American Federation of Teachers is demanding necessary freedom for teachers and pupils to develop those qualities of citizenship that are most desirable in a democracy. We oppose the practice of overcrowded classes, overworked teachers, and over-exercise of power by the administration. We insist upon just compensation for

---

24. Mary C. Barker to Florence Hanson, June 23, 1929, AFT Collection, Walter Reuther Archives of Labor, Wayne State University, Detroit.

25. Mary C. Barker, "Presidential Address at the AFT Annual Convention, Chicago," June 26, 1928, AFT Files, Walter Reuther Archives of Labor and Urban Affairs, Wayne State University, Detroit.

26. Mary C. Barker, "Presidential Address, at the AFT convention in Chicago, July 2, 1929, AFT Files, Walter Reuther Archives of Labor and Urban Affairs, Wayne State University, Detroit.

teachers and upon every child to receive adequate educational opportunity. We place emphasis upon the teaching of social values."[27]

In 1930, endorsing the program initiated by the Memphis Power and Light Company, Barker argued, "As we see it teaching people how to think is a fundamental purpose of education. It is essential to teach pupils how to understand issues so they can react to them with responsibility. Understanding is a critical element that builds partnership. We would like to be known as partners with people and organizations interested in every worthy enterprise. The Memphis Power and Light Company is attempting a worthy enterprise. It therefore deserves our support."[28] Indeed, Barker was at the top of her game: her star was rising very fast and in a manner that she herself could not comprehend. For the AFT the days of Edwin G. Cooley were over as its members looked to the future with high hopes and anticipation. Barker had become the E. F. Hutton of the new era of ideas: when she spoke, everyone listened.

Amidst this glory and power, disaster struck in a cruel and devastating way. The economic crisis that began with the fall of the stock market in October 1929 had a deleterious effect on the AFT. Not only did President Herbert Hoover (1874-1964) inadvertently mislead the country into believing that there would be no economic collapse, but also he underestimated its impact when it actually occurred. For the AFT this was almost a death sentence as its efforts to raise funds in accordance with the purposes Barker had outlined in her presidential address to the annual convention the previous year were seriously impaired. Although Barker was able to stay the course that she had outlined at the beginning of her term of office, she had neither the means nor the ability to overcome the effects of the economic collapse. She tried under difficult conditions to sustain the program, which had yielded tangible results to the AFT.

Beginning in 1930, one year before she retired as president of the AFT, Barker instituted a new plan to attract new and young members to the organization. In doing so she was thinking about its future. Although the number of dues-paying locals affiliated with the AFT had increased from thirty-four in 1928 to thirty-nine in 1929,[29] she knew that the increase was not significant enough to sustain and strengthen the organization during a period of great economic crisis. Although her spirits were dashed, she managed to provide the kind of leadership that was needed at a crucial period in the development of the organization.

In 1931, tired by the endless struggle, weakened by the complexity of the issues that had to be resolved, and devastated by the collapse of the economy, Mary C. Barker retired from the presidency of the AFT. This was at a time when confidence in the AFT, not only in the quality of its leadership, but also in its ability to plan for the future, was increasing. Her refusal to let the

---

27. Ibid.

28. Marcy C. Barker, "Presidential Address at the AFT Convention," June 30, 1930, AFT Files, Walter Reuther Archives of Labor and Urban Affairs, Wayne State University, Detroit.

29. Florence C. Hanson to Mary C. Barker, June 19, 1929. AFT Files, Walter Reuther Archives of Labor and Urban Affairs, Wayne State University, Detroit.

organization that meant so much to the lives of teachers perish is testimony to the courage of a gallant leader.

Now it was time for a new leader to come forward and take the helm to steer the AFT toward new horizons. Her term of office had been a candlelight flickering in the darkness of the great uncertainty that engulfed the nation. Although she was the last leader of the formative years, Barker had reawaken ed the hearts and minds of the members of the AFT. She provided the steady hand that gave the union the time it needed to allow the cement that she and her predecessors had "poured" to dry so that it formed the solid foundation the AFT required to vigorously move forward into the future.

THE PERIOD OF CONSOLIDATION

At the last annual convention that she presided over, Mary C. Barker tried to leave a lasting imprint of the quality of her leadership when she argued that members of the AFT must become more conscious of the implications of social class because it determined the structure of social institutions. Margaret Haley concurred when she said, "Class consciousness is what we missed in our organizing work."[30] Barker's argument was that if class consciousness became a factor in the AFT operations, it would inhibit the ability of its members to conduct a dialogue between teachers and the administration on educational programs and to resolve disputes involving pedagogical philosophy. She had operated under these considerations during her term of office when the AFT was experiencing serious problems.

By the time Henry R. Linville was elected president of the AFT in 1931 to replace the retiring Barker, he had gained considerable experience in articulating the leadership qualities needed to strengthen the AFT and to lead it into the future. As editor-in-chief of *The American Teacher*, Linville wrote in 1917:

> Education in the new sense in which John Dewey employs the concept can never flourish under autocratic domination. The autocrat lacks inspiration and contemptuously spurns the new forms of educational leadership. The autocrat is an intellectual stand patter. The reasons which to us are all sufficient for the damnation of the autocratic board of education are startling evidence of the need for new forms of educational leadership. Collective power and vision are the means to educational and individual realization, the only true basis of education. For the autocrat freedom of thought and frankness of speech are alien to his bull dogmatic, Medievalist creed. Among us the autocrat is a living nightmare, an even walking ghost, a sinister influence. He radiates, not good but evil.[31]

There can be no question that Linville shared the view of other AFT leaders and members that the effectiveness of the organization rested on the set of

---

30. Margaret Haley to Florence Hanson, May 23, 1934, AFT Files, Walter Reuther Archives of Labor and Urban Affairs, Wayne State University, Detroit.

31. The AFT, "Through the Fluoroscope," p. 88.

fundamental leadership principles that they identified as a cornerstone of its strength. Therefore, the three years that Linville served as president of the AFT ushered in a period of consolidation of the leadership standards that they needed to shape the future development of their organization.

A solid team player and an ethical man, Linville was uncomfortable with the influence that Samuel Gompers had exerted on Charles Stillman's stewardship of the AFT. Stillman and Linville disagreed on a fundamental tenet of the AFT's operations. Stillman felt that he needed the assistance that Gompers gave him to solidly establish the AFT. Linville felt that the AFT must establish its own identity different and apart from the AFL agenda. Although Linville and Stillman were unable to resolve their differences of opinion, they both remained loyal to other key principles that they saw as essential to the strength of the AFT.

It is not surprising, then, that as soon as Linville assumed the presidency of the AFT, he tried to give it an identity different from the one that labor leaders had in mind. The need for the AFT to assume a position relative to its efforts to protect teachers that was different from labor's efforts to protect workers had long been debated among the leadership and the membership. But now prejudice among school officials against Jewish teachers had become a serious problem. Later it was a problem that Shanker faced as well. Linville noticed a pattern of prejudice against Jewish teachers and felt that something had to be done to stop it. He went on to observe, "If a teacher happens to be a Jew and socialist, personally disliked by an official, the technique of indirection takes care of it all through the euphemism of conduct unbecoming a teacher."[32] Linville concluded in a prophetic way that if the harassment of Jewish teachers was not stopped, then it would be a matter of time before the harassment of teachers in general would start.

Indeed, in 1919 the New York state legislature appointed a committee under the chairmanship of Senator Clayton R. Lusk to investigate any influence the Bolshevik Revolution in Russia might have on American schools. The purpose of the investigation was to discover any evidence of unpatriotic sentiments among teachers as result of the influence of the revolution. The Lusk Committee subpoenaed every teacher who was suspected of being unpatriotic. The investigation was a follow-up to the demand of the boards of education in the state of New York in 1917 that teachers sign a loyalty oath before they received their paychecks.[33]

After its investigation the Lusk Committee concluded, "While this Committee has never made an investigation of the public schools or of school teachers in the State of New York, it has found evidence that several teachers in the public schools, duly licensed and having all the prescribed educational attainments, were members of revolutionary organizations dedicated to the

---

32. Henry R. Linville, January 28, 1918, Linville Collection, AFT Files, Walter Reuther Archives of Labor and Urban Affairs, Wayne State University, Detroit.

33. State of New York, *Report and Recommendations of the Joint Legislative Committee Investigating Seditious Activities*, Legislative Document no. 52 (Clayton R. Lusk, chairman) (Albany: Government Printer, 1920), p. 3.

principles of the overthrow of this State and of the United States."[34] The committee then made three recommendations. The first was that all teachers then employed or to be employed in the future in the public schools must obtain a certificate of qualification, which would state that the teacher holding it is a person of good moral character and has shown satisfactorily that he or she would support the constitutions of the state of New York and of the United States.

The second recommendation was that a certificate of qualification must be issued at the direction of the commissioner of education with the state of New York and that the person holding it must conform with the rules adopted by the Board of Regents of the University of New York. The certificate must not be issued until the applicant had been fully examined in accordance with the rules and regulations. That no teacher would be employed in public schools after January 1, 1921, unless he or she showed that he or she did not belong to unions was the third recommendation.

The Lusk Committee then advocated "the passage and immediate adoption of an act putting into effect these recommendations with suitable appropriation to carry the purposes of the act. This committee feels that the education of the citizens and residents is of vital importance to the state, and that all educational enterprises other than those carried out by well-recognized religious denominations or sects should be under the control and supervision of the state."[35] In order to accomplish this objective, the Lusk Committee also recommended that the state commissioner of education be authorized to provide for maintaining and conducting a course of study and for training teachers in normal schools and colleges to ensure compliance with the requirements.

When hundreds of teachers, most of them members of the AFT, protested the conclusions of the Lusk Committee because they felt that their civil rights were violated, a number of them were singled out for further investigation. These and three teachers who proved to be pacifists became the focus of the loyalty investigation. These teachers were then dismissed and were subjected to further attack as a strategy to force them to name other teachers who were considered to be unpatriotic and thus receptive to Bolshevik influences. This sad episode provided a precedence for the notorious McCarthy era that began after the end of the Second World War.

Although these unfortunate developments took place during the leadership of Charles Stillman, Linville defended the dismissed teachers. He argued that they were victims of vindictiveness initiated by the boards of education because the board members felt threatened by the collective intellect of the members of the AFT. In this regard Linville was playing an appropriate leadership role at a critical juncture in the development of the AFT.

As president of Local 5 in New York, Linville and his longtime friend Abraham Lefkowitz had supported the principles they thought were essential to the AFT's cohesion. Among these was their belief that academic freedom for teachers was an absolute must in order to have school boards recognize teaching as a profession. Linville promoted this line of thinking as president of the AFT.

---

34. Ibid., p. 5.
35. Ibid., p. 6.

Although he regarded resorting to strikes as a behavior incompatible with the professional code, Linville felt that teachers should reserve the right to strike in order to convince those in positions of authority that teachers could use strikes to assert their rights. To assure this right Linville argued with city and state officials that only properly qualified teachers must be employed.

In April 1934, just before he left office, Linville placed an added layer of cement upon the foundation of leadership of the AFT. In a letter to the members of the executive council he outlined his views of what that body should be, saying, "We have a function to perform in developing a professional and social spirit of cooperation among teachers, and in furnishing leadership in the battles against the economic drive, and in education. No other group is prepared to undertake these tasks. We could justify our existence on these bases alone. I think, also, that there is a deep rambling in the general social set-up that will bring teachers in the AFT together to fight the injustice imposed on them."[36] This indicates that from its inception to 1934 the leadership of the AFT was gaining strength because it was continuously engaged in consolidating itself.

Recognizing the influence that the AFT was exerting on the character of education, Linville expressed his view that the AFT must operate with a much broader perspective than that of the Chicago local. In the same letter to his executive council Linville advised, "I have about come to the conclusion that the national organization has been so closely identified with the Chicago school situation that we tend to think of our locals there and the national headquarters as being merged into one. Tragic as the Chicago school situation has been, the national organization must now have other priorities and obligations."[37] Linville suggested moving the headquarters of the AFT to a city more centrally located in order to readily reach all its branches.

Indeed, the quality of leadership that Linville had tendered in three years became the foundation that his successor, Jerome Davis (1891-1979), used to build in a new direction for the next three years, from 1936 to 1939. Davis wanted the AFT to function under principles of justice and fairness both in seeking solutions to the problems that teachers were facing and in continuing its endless struggle against the policies adopted by school officials. Davis never lost sight of the need to accomplish this objective. This is his legacy to the future-oriented leadership that the AFT required for its development. For the first time in the history of the AFT Davis moved aggressively to bring about a full integration of the AFT's structure and programs.

By the time his term of office came to an end Davis felt that white members had played a crucial role in the AFT's development and it was now time to welcome black members as equal partners in building an organization that was inclusive in its character and embracing in its content.[38] He also argued that the

---

36. Henry R. Linville to the members of the AFT executive council, April 25, 1934, AFT Files, Walter Reuther Archives of Labor and Urban Affairs, Wayne State University, Detroit.

37. Ibid.

38. The AFT, "The Need of the AFT to Be Inclusive," *The American Teacher*, 23 (March 1939): 5-7.

AFT needed to intensify its recruiting campaign to increase its membership as a true basis for strength and influence.

In 1936, soon after his election, Davis initiated a strategy to have teachers participate more effectively in convention activity. This made it possible for him to bring into the executive council a new caliber of thinkers whose leadership skills he needed to consolidate the foundations that had been built in the past. This not only strengthened the AFT, but also enhanced Davis's leadership position. But in doing so Davis allowed more liberal elements of the AFT to define its operational principles in a way that alienated conservative elements in the organization who had developed a rapport with the union's administrative structure. Although Davis had manifested liberal views as a professor of theology at Yale University, he now came face to face with the difficult realities of the practical application of liberal ideas in the world of teachers.

In 1937, when the staunchly conservative president of the AFL, William Green, launched a campaign to eliminate socialist elements from the AFT, Davis's leadership surfaced to help him play the authoritative role that he believed was essential to strengthen the gains that the AFT had made. Without responding directly to Green's call, Davis convinced the members of the AFT that diversity of ideas strengthened the organization by making it possible to examine all sides of an issue before a solution or decision could be reached. When Matthew Woll argued in 1939 that Davis was allowing Communists to influence the direction that the AFT was taking, there was a united response within the AFT to keep the union strong. Davis, refusing to abandon the diverse composition of the AFT executive council, created an environment that allowed difference of opinion on issues to be a positive attribute of the AFT's character.[39]

At different times during his term of office Davis experienced challenges that tested his skills. In 1936 Mary Foley Grossman, whose loyalty was clearly with the NEA, decided to offer herself as a candidate for the presidency of the AFT. Grossman, a self-proclaimed moderate, showed the conservative side of her philosophy when she argued that Davis was a radical whose continued presidency would alienate many teachers who had supported the AFT. But in doing so, Grossman raised more doubts about her own leadership abilities than about Davis's. In 1937 Davis began a move that would define the legacy of his leadership. He successfully persuaded high school and elementary school teachers to join forces in order to present a united front in their efforts to confront the issues they faced.

Davis's liberal views, however, became a reason for those who opposed him to nominate Lillian Hernstein for the presidency of the AFT. Hernstein was a conservative and a bright strategist from the days of the Chicago Women's Federation. She was also a disciple of Margaret Haley. She had the credentials of the old union struggle reminiscent of the days of Charles Stillman. To the Chicago local Hernstein was a loyal and dedicated member whose ideas were compatible with those of Samuel Gompers.

---

39. Marjorie Murphy, *Blackboard Unions: The AFT and the NEA, 1900-1990,* p. 162.

But when her views were compared with those of the conservative and less popular William Green, Hernstein was found to be no better candidate inadequate than Davis. To members of the AFT outside Chicago, Lillian Hernstein represented the past, a phase of history that only those like William Green represented. It soon became clear to Hernstein and her supporters that her campaign to replace Davis was falling apart, so she quietly withdrew herself from consideration.[40] Not only did Davis emerge the winner, but also his leadership of the AFT was enhanced, giving him the opportunity that he needed to consolidate its foundation and move forward with his mandate.

In 1939, the last year of his presidency, Davis wanted to leave his imprint on the AFT by taking action on an issue that the federation had not addressed in the past, racial segregation in education and society. Meeting in Buffalo, New York, in August, the delegates had spent four days listening to speeches. One of the main speakers was George Googe, who represented William Green. Aware that his appearance in person might trigger a negative response, Green asked Googe to deliver an address that was reconciliatory in tone. As a result, Googe received a warm reception helping Green and the AFL to improve relations with the AFT.

While this was transpiring, Davis worked diligently behind the scenes to help the resolutions committee draft a resolution that called for an end to racial segregation in both education and society. Amelia Yeager, the AFT vice-president, read the resolution to the convention delegates:

> Resolved: That the American Federation of Teachers, in convention assembled, strongly condemn any system of racial segregation which results in the denial, either complete or partial, of equality of educational opportunity to any students on account of race, creed, or color, that all facilities provided under any particular school system shall be made available to white and Negro children alike, that it lend all its support to the program to abolish differences in teachers' salaries based solely on race or color,[41] that it endorse the principle announced by the Supreme Court of the United States in the case of *Gaines v. The University of Missouri*[42] to the effect that it is the duty of the state to furnish like educational opportunities for all of its citizens regardless of race, creed, or color, and that the American Federation of Teachers pledge its unswerving aid to the various state teacher associations and other cooperating organizations

---

40. The AFT, "Annual Convention Proceedings, Buffalo, 1939, AFT Files, Washington, D. C.

41. In her study *The Troubled Crusade: American Education, 1945-1980* (New York: Basic Books, 1983), Diane Ravitch compares the salary of a white woman teacher in Nebraska with a black woman teacher in Mississippi as of 1945 and concludes that the former was paid three times more than the latter.

42. In that 1938 case the U.S. Supreme Court ruled that the state of Missouri must provide Gaines "fact and citings for legal education substantially equal to those which the state has afforded for persons of the white race." (Robert E. Potter, *The Stream of American Education* (New York: Van Nostrand Reinehold Company, 1967), p. 479.

which are working together to remove the blemish of unequal educational opportunity from the face of our democracy.[43]

That the resolution, after being seconded and duly debated, passed overwhelmingly suggests how the AFT was conditioning itself to confront critical educational and social issues that were profoundly impacting American society. In three years Davis made an unusual contribution to the enhancement of leadership standards needed for the future. Now he could pass on that leadership to another person. Fifteen years later, in 1954, when the U.S. Supreme Court ruled in *Brown v. Board of Education of Topeka* that racial segregation in schools was unconstitutional the leadership of the AFT was further strengthened, respected, and consolidated.

This cohesiveness made it possible for the union to address persistent issues that intimately affected the position of teachers. In 1935 it worked closely with the Baltimore chapter to protect the interests of its teachers. In August of that year, the Baltimore chapter issued two resolutions addressing the need to ensure job security for teachers. The first resolution read:

> Whereas in the present period of the Great Depression the tenure rights of teachers have been seriously threatened by the passage of the Ives Law in New York and laws of other similar nature now pending in other states, therefore be it resolved that the American Federation of Teachers initiate a campaign to meet this attack on teacher tenure rights where they have been threatened or destroyed, and be it further resolved that the support of the AFT and other socially minded groups be enlisted for the permanent elimination of legislation of this nature.[44]

The second resolution read:

> Whereas the practice of arbitrarily disciplining teachers and students for their political beliefs and economic activities such as opposing salary cuts and retrenchment in school systems has become a definite tendency, and whereas an increasing number of students and teachers have been disciplined by dismissals and demotional transfers because of their opposition to war and fascism, therefore be it resolved that the American Federation of Teachers and its officiated locals carry out a campaign on a national level to enlist the support and sympathy of organizations on the issue of freedom of thought and action by all people.[45]

---

43. The AFT, "Report of the Resolutions Committee of the Twenty-Third Annual Convention," August 1939, AFT Files, Washington, D. C.

44. Baltimore Teachers Union, "Resolution on Tenure Rights for Teachers," August 10, 1935, AFT Files, Walter Reuther Archives of Labor and Urban Affairs, Wayne State University, Detroit.

45. Baltimore Teachers Union, "Resolution on Denial of Academic and Political Freedom for Teachers," August 10, 1935, AFT Files, Walter Reuther Archives of Labor and Urban Affairs, Wayne State University, Detroit.

These two resolutions show that by 1935 the AFT felt confident enough in itself to launch a new campaign to resolve issues that threatened teachers. Leadership played a key role in these developments.

The period of the consolidation of the AFT leadership showcased itself during the presidency of George Counts (1889-1974) from 1939 to 1942. The circumstances that brought Counts to the office of president had less to do with conditions teachers were serving under and more with dramatic events that were taking place in Europe. On the eve of the AFT annual convention in August 1939 the world came to know about the signing of the treaty of friendship between Adolf Hitler and Joseph Stalin and the stipulation that the Soviet Union would not question Hitler's annexation of Poland and Czechoslovakia. Davis's liberal views had become excess baggage and a liability for the AFT. When he failed to take a position against the Hitler-Stalin pact because he feared it would cause a split within the union and lose the support of socialists, those who opposed him felt that a change in leadership was warranted.

Counts seemed a natural to succeed Davis. Like Davis he was a professor. He had credentials that no one else possessed. From the time he received his Ph.D. degree from the University of Chicago in 1916 to the time he retired in 1971, George Counts distinguished himself as a scholar and teacher. His tenure as professor of education at Yale University, the University of Chicago, Columbia University, and Southern Illinois University, lasting from 1927 to 1971, marked the career of a scholar who was fully qualified to do what he was educated to do. By 1939, the year he was elected president of the AFT, Counts was already an accomplished professional who had demonstrated that he was an authority on education in the Soviet Union.

A prolific writer, Counts authored twenty-nine books, including *The Education of Free Men* (1941) and *The Challenge of Soviet Education* (1957). In these, and other books, Counts examined how the social systems of the twentieth century were inadequate to promote and sustain democracy. He concluded that although both the First World War and the Second World War had an impact on social order, human action created problems that only education could help solve. He believed that education must be designed so as to help the individual develop principles that would promote his or her potential. For this reason Counts suggested that any education not available to all students on equal basis is inappropriate to meet the needs of society and is thus void of any real purpose.[46]

Counts did not fully support John Dewey's progressive education movement . He argued that it was not based on a theory that could be validated. He concluded that "progressive education must face squarely and courageously every social issue. It must come to grips with life in all of its stark reality. It must develop a realistic and comprehensive theory of welfare. It must fashion a compelling and challenging vision of human destiny. Progressive education cannot build a program out of the interests of children alone. It cannot place its

---

46. William van Til, *Education: A Beginning* (Boston: Houghton Mifflin Company, 1974), p. 423.

total trust in a child-centered school. It must reflect the interests of society."[47] It is easy to understand why Counts was criticized not only by those who believed in progressive education, but also by those members of the public who were looking for viable forms of education to meet the challenges of a new age. He appeared unable to discern that by developing education to meet the needs of the individual student, the school was in effect trying to meet the needs of society.

As a professional educator Counts operated under a credo that placed the importance on education structured around a global situation. This is evident in what he said in 1932: "I believe that a critical factor must play an important role in any adequate educational program, at least any program fashioned for the modern world. An education that does not strive to promote the fullest and most thorough understanding of the world is not worthy of the name. I am prepared to defend the thesis that all education contains a large element of imposition that in the very nature of the case this is inevitable, that the existence and evaluation of society depends upon it, that it is consequently desirable, and that the frank acceptance of this fact by the educator is a major professional obligation."[48]

The international reputation that he held placed him in a position to comprehend the complexities of the modern world. It also made it possible for him to understand the problems of leadership within the AFT. These factors were becoming increasingly critical to the future of both the union and its membership. His frequent travels to the Soviet Union, combined with his publications, enabled him to acquire basic knowledge of the issues that teachers faced. For Counts this was a period of immense challenges. The world of 1939 was permanently transformed by a series of events that demanded strong leadership in all major social institutions, including education. No one was able to predict with any degree of certainty what was likely to happen in the wake of the outbreak of the war. Human values, thought process political action, and educational endeavors were all imperiled by a human-made catastrophe that only human intelligence could resolve. Was Counts able meet these challenges?

The test of Counts's leadership ability came soon after his election. Recognizing that "members of the Communist Party are enrolled in the American Federation of Teachers, and that organized units of the party have operated in certain locals and in the national organization,"[49] Counts realized that the effectiveness of the AFT in pursuing its objectives depended upon the support if its members, including socialists whom he did not want to alienate. He did nothing to cause dissension in the ranks of the AFT. Instead, he sought to minimize the role of socialists, saying, "By outwardly abandoning many of their doctrines and deliberately advocating policies which they knew liberal-minded teachers would be inclined to support, the Communists, after dividing themselves into opposing camps in playing their role in leadership, are merely

47. George Counts, "Dare Progressive Education Be Progressive," in *Progressive Education* (April 1932), p. 258.

48. George Counts, *Dare Build a New Social Order* (New York: John Day Company, 1932), p. 11.

49. George Counts, "Is Our Union Controlled by Communists?" *The American Teacher*, 24 (December 1939): 5.

marching with the crowd."[50] He did not think that Communists posed any real threat to both the AFT and American society because, he concluded, "the greatest threat to American democracy comes, not from doctrines imported from beyond the seas, but from our own failure."[51]

Counts argued that instead of trying to get rid of Communists from within its ranks, the AFT must direct its energies toward securing rights for teachers in order to eliminate the threat that some people feared Communism was posing. His narrow victory over Jerome Davis suggested to him the need to follow a moderate stance on issues, especially the threat of Communism in Europe. This gave his opponents a reason to criticize him for placing his sympathy with Communists and later provided an operational base for Senator Joseph McCarthy to launch a campaign against universities and other educational institutions, which McCarthy said were breeding grounds for Communism.

In October 1939, soon after Adolf Hitler's forces invaded Poland and triggered the outbreak of the Second World War, Counts recognized the need to exert an assertive leadership role in an effort to create stable working conditions so teachers could do their work properly. He observed, "As our federation begins its 24th year, we live in fear of a second world war. Our first responsibility is to defend and improve public education. Regardless of wars and rumors of wars, children come into the world and grow to maturity. They will need good education to prepare themselves for the future."[52]

During the next two years the war created problems for Counts which he was not quite able to resolve. At the annual convention in 1941 a resolution was introduced to expel four locals that were under the influence of Communists. When the resolution carried by the vote of 1,600 to 1,100, Counts felt that he had lost the confidence of the AFT membership and that he had served his purpose. He recommended a successor. In a farewell address in October 1942, Counts said, "We welcome the opportunity to live in an age of great decisions and to help shape the future, not only of our own America, but also of all mankind throughout the world. The challenges are great, so is the human spirit to meet them."[53]

The question posed is, What contribution did Counts make to the efforts that the AFT was undertaking in consolidating its leadership? On November 10, 1974, the day that Counts died, Albert Shanker, newly elected president of the AFT, and Robert Porter, the AFT secretary treasurer, issued a joint statement about Counts, "The AFT mourns the death of its former president who served the interest of public education and teacher unions with diligence and dedication. He established that one can defend and expand democracy and liberty in education and the larger society by a combination of sound scholarship with militant teacher advocacy.

---

50. George Counts, "Communists in the AFT," *New York Times*, (December 15, 1939): 6.

51. Ibid.

52. William van Til, *Education: The Beginning*, p. 424.

53. Ibid., p. 425.

Counts made an unusual contribution to the quality of leadership of the AFT at a very critical period. We join others in mourning the loss of a great leader."[54] One must conclude that this tribute is a testimony to the leadership qualities of a dedicated man whose vision helped the organization he led toward future greatness. Counts operated by these qualities and so left a legacy that future leaders would use to build an organization destined to play an unusual role in the struggle teachers would be engaged in to give them a new sense of the future. Counts's term of office put the finishing touch on the consolidation of leadership of the AFT.

THE ERA OF NEW DIRECTIONS

By the time that Carl Megel was elected president of the AFT in 1952, the leadership of the federation was strong enough to take new risks in seeking out new directions of development. Marjorie Murphy concludes, "Megel's election was seen as a call for more aggressive leadership on economic issues."[55] He immediately recognized that "the average salary for teachers in the United States during the past year was approximately $400 less than the income for the average factory worker."[56] His term of office, from 1952 to 1965, was directed toward seeking improvement in the conditions of service for teachers under the new principle known as collective bargaining.

Megel was the first leader of the AFT to operate under the belief that in the new postwar social era the AFT must seek solid improvement in teachers' salaries and that collective bargaining was the means to ensure this goal. Although in the past the AFT had occasionally thought about this strategy of interacting with school administrations in seeking solutions to the problems of education, Megel's term of office was the first time that the AFT formulated the principle of collective bargaining as a fundamental tenet in its operations.

Megel outlined the benefits that he believed collective bargaining would bring to teachers. It would compel boards of education to recognize that conditions of service for teachers could no longer be dictated. The AFT would be recognized as an official representative of the teachers. For this to happen, Megel exercised appropriate leadership to influence developments needed to bring this about. After President John Kennedy issued an executive order in 1962 requiring agents of the federal government to observe collective bargaining, Megel worked hard to persuade states to repeal the no-strike legislation that had placed so many hardships on teachers. By 1965, at the end of Megel's term of office, the AFT had won the legal right to resort to strikes in order to end the economic injustice that teachers had faced.

---

54. Albert Shanker and Robert Porter, "Tribute to George Counts," November 10, 1974, AFT Files, Washington, D. C.

55. Marjorie Murphy, *Blackboard Unions: The AFT and the NEA, 1900-1980*, p. 210.

56. Carl Megel, "Economic Conditions for Teachers," *The American Teacher*, (October 1952), p. 16.

Another critical issue that brought Megel's leadership qualities to the surface was the question of racial segregation in education. This was an issue that the AFT, under the leadership of Jerome Davis, had tried to address in 1939. Megel realized that since that time there had been no significant progress made in this area. Following the *Brown* decision in 1954, Megel decided to ask locals to voluntarily integrate. Matters came to a crisis in 1961 when the Virginia Education Association suspended the Arlington Education Association for voting to integrate its membership in accordance with guidelines outlined by the AFT. Megel denounced the Virginia Education Association and accused it of practicing racial segregation at a time when the country was trying to end it. Embarrassed by its action and Megel's reaction, the Virginia Education Association reversed itself and designed a new policy to ensure the desegregation of all aspects of education.

In a profile published on Megel in *The American Teacher* in February 1977, an article that Megel himself said should not be published because "people will think that I'm on my way out,"[57] Albert Shanker and Robert Healy, president of the Chicago Teachers' Union and the AFT vice-president, representing paid tribute to his leadership. Shanker said, "Carl has seen us through hard times. I have had the greatest respect and admiration for him. He is fair. He is deeply committed to the ideas of teacher organizations. He is an effective leader for a new era in directions."[58] Healy added, "Many people in Illinois fondly remember Carl Megel as the founder and leader of the locals. We worked together closely and he always gave me good advice. As far as we are concerned, Carl Megel really Mr. AFT."[59] What this indicates is that Carl Megel had charted a new course of assertive leadership in the AFT, which enabled it to address new critical issues arising out of a rapidly changing society.

The beginning of Charles Cogen's term of office as president of the AFT in 1965 was marked by new efforts to make collective bargaining a standard operating procedure in negotiations between the AFT and a school administration. Cogen initiated this thrust in response to a series of developments that began to unfold in January 1962 when President Kennedy issued Executive Order 10988. This allowed federal employees to exercise the right to engage in collective bargaining. By 1964 at least seven states had recognized the principle of collective bargaining as a legitimate practice in negotiating working conditions, making it possible for teachers to reject unreasonable demands through the threat of a strike. Many feared that this could lead to an abuse of power on the part of teachers' unions.

This fear is what Kennedy's secretary of labor, Arthur Goldberg, had in mind when he insisted that teachers must not go on strike just because they and the board of education failed to reach agreement, but must continue their dialogue until an agreement could be reached. By the time that David Selden succeeded

---

57. *The American Teacher* (February 1977), p. 12.
58. Albert Shanker, "Tribute to Carl Megel," *The American Teacher*, (February 1977) p. 15.
59. Robert Healy, "Tribute to Carl Megel," *The American Teacher* (February 1977), p. 17.

Megel in 1965, the principle of collective bargaining was being applied in most states. But it was during David Selden's term of office from that year to 1974 that teachers across the country recognized that the leadership of the AFT had shaped new and positive directions for teachers. How these directions factored into the leadership of Albert Shanker is the subject of the remainder of this study. To put these developments into a proper perspective, Chapter 3 focuses on the United States during Shanker's lifetime.

SUMMARY AND CONCLUSION

In discussing the development of the leadership of the AFT, one needs to remember that there were three phases crucial in the formation of its character. The formative years, from the leadership of Charles Stillman beginning in 1916 to the end of that of Mary C. Barker in 1931, was characterized by efforts to design an organization that tried to generate a new level of consciousness about the importance of protecting the interests of teachers. The second phase, from the leadership of Henry R. Linville beginning in 1931 to the to end of that of George Counts in 1942, was a period of consolidation of the core principles that the AFT had formulated during its formative years.

The third phase, from the leadership of Carl Megel in 1952 to the end of David Selden's guidance in 1974, was a period of searching for new directions in the development of the union. The principle of collective bargaining began to take on meaning and force during the third phase. Collective bargaining, as a product of the kind of leadership exercised by these individuals, is a development that Albert Shanker has utilized to lead the AFT into new areas of endeavor. Without vision and tenacious determination, the problems that American teachers have encountered would not have been resolved. Because Shanker has been the leader of the AFT longer than any of his predecessors, it is necessary to examine his accomplishments within the context of the legacy left to him.

3

The United States of Shanker's Times

Racial discrimination in the opportunity for school facilities is as spectacular as it is well known.

Gunnar Myrdal, 1944

The defense of this nation depends upon the mastery of modern techniques developed from complex scientific principles.

The National Defense Education Act, 1958

THE POLITICAL ENVIRONMENT OF 1928

Dramatic and unprecedented events began to take place in the United States with Herbert Hoover's announcement in February 1928 that he was a Republican candidate for president of the United States. Hoover seemed a natural successor to President Calvin Coolidge, who was elected in 1924. Coolidge had announced six months earlier, on August 2, 1927,[1] that he would not seek a second term. That Coolidge succeeded to the presidency when President Warren G. Harding died in 1923 added an irony to events that were already rapidly unfolding during that period. In 1921 President Harding had named Hoover secretary of commerce, an office he continued to hold under President Coolidge. At the 1928 Republican convention held in Kansas City, Hoover was nominated on the first ballot. The purpose of this chapter is to present historical events like these that have influenced the life of Albert Shanker and the role he has played as president of the AFT.

In that year Amelia Earhart (1897-1937) embodied the national spirit when she became the first female pilot to fly solo from Newfoundland to Burry Port in

---

1. President Harding died on August 2, 1923. It is not clear why Coolidge chose this date to make his announcement. This author thinks that he chose the anniversary of Harding's death to show his respect for the memory of a man he admired and to give his successor publicity in launching a successful election campaign. Indeed, his successor, Herbert Hoover, won the election in 1928.

Wales. On May 20, 1932, when her spirit of adventure led her to fly across the Atlantic, she rekindled a new determination to overcome the devastation caused to national morale by the Depression. In doing so she put into proper perspective the fear that President Franklin Roosevelt said was the only thing Americans had to fear. In this way she galvanized the national determination needed to meet the challenges posed by the Depression.

If the Depression had created the impression in the minds of Americans that all was lost, Earhart's determination and spirit of adventure proved that human spirit can prevail over adversity of immense proportions. If the years from 1928 to 1932 represented the worst of times for the country, the period after proved that the best of times was yet to come. In her disappearance on July 2, 1937, the nation lost a true pioneer at a critical time during a period of great crisis.

The year 1924 also saw J. Edgar Hoover (1895-1972) appointed director of the FBI, a position he held from that year until his death in 1972. During the formative years of his career, Hoover became famous for his relentless campaigns against persons considered public enemies and those who belonged to organized crime. As soon as he took office, Hoover replaced untrained men with lawyers and accountants. This enabled him to develop the FBI into one of the most efficient law-enforcement agencies in the world. But over the years the abuse of power became a hallmark of Hoover's reign.

In 1917, after graduating from high school, Hoover worked as a messenger in the Library of Congress. As director of the FBI also coordinated investigations of suspected subversive persons and groups in the United States. His books *Masters of Deceit* (1958) and *A Study of Communism* (1962) discuss the dangers of Communism and methods for combating it. By the time of Herbert Hoover's nomination for president of the United States, J. Edgar Hoover was well on his way to becoming an American institution.

In their state of euphoria the Republicans celebrated Herbert Hoover's nomination as if it were the election itself. They wanted the entire country to know that the best of times were here at last, totally unaware that the worst of times was about to begin under their leadership. Hoover's Democratic opponent, Alfred E. Smith (1873-1944), held impressive credentials. He was first elected to the New York state legislature in 1903. From that time to 1919, when he was elected governor of New York, Smith distinguished himself as a powerful politician. His understanding of critical national issues was comprehensive. He used his failure to win the Democratic nomination in 1924 to build a national image for himself as the Democrat who displayed qualities of leadership far better than anyone else within the party.

But with all the political skills he possessed and in spite of the fact that both Harding and Coolidge manifested weaknesses in national leadership[2] at a critical point in the development of the country, American voters decided to

---

2. As vice-president in the Harding Administration Coolidge could not escape the Teapot Dome and other such scandals. Although in 1924 he forced the resignation of Attorney General Harry M. Dougherty and replaced him with Harlan F. Stone, Coolidge remained tarnished by the scandals. The fact that as President he pursued Harding's policies added doubt to the problems of confidence he was having with the public. This is partly the reason he decided against running for a second term in 1928.

place their trust in Hoover by electing him president. He garnered 21.4 million votes to Smith's 15.0 million. Hoover was not a particularly exciting politician, nor was Coolidge. In the election of 1924, Coolidge managed to win over his Democratic opponent John W. Davis (1873-1955), a former ambassador to Britain from 1913 to 1918, but who was hardly known outside the inner circle of the Democratic party. Davis, a constitutional lawyer, represented a wide range of clients and argued hundred and forty cases before the U.S. Supreme Court, but lost his last and most famous case when he defended the board of education in the *Brown* case in 1954.

The fact that James M. Cox, the Democratic nominee who ran against Harding in 1920, won only 9.1 million votes against Harding's 16.1 millions appeared to indicate by the election of 1928 that Democrats were unable to present strong candidates for president. This perception clearly worked against Smith. But the Republicans and the country did not know that Hoover would be the last Republican president until Dwight D. Eisenhower was elected in 1952.

When Shanker was born on September 14, 1928, the election campaign was getting under way. Hoover campaigned on his plan to improve the economy and end poverty. Smith warned against overconfidence, suggesting that the economy showed signs of weakness and serious decline within a short time. The voters seemed to believe Hoover, who predicted that American families would have two chickens in the pot and a car in every garage, more than they did Smith, who was seen as not being positive enough to plan the future development of the country. This took away the excitement of the campaign as Smith was unable to generate enthusiasm in his candidacy and in himself as a viable alternative to Hoover. Brilliant lawyer that he was, Smith failed to develop both a strategy for his campaign and a plan to revive the economy. Although some people doubted Hoover's ability to deliver what he was promising, they thought the future of the country would be better under his presidency than under that of Smith.

Among those who believed that Hoover was promising more than he could deliver was John Dewey, the well-known educator whose philosophy of progressive education had attracted the attention of leading thinkers throughout the world. As voters were about to go to the polls, Dewey, then sixty-nine years old, not only supported Smith's candidacy, but also criticized Hoover for failing to develop and fully explain his plan to revive the economy. He also faulted Hoover for not presenting other domestic and international policies that would ensure the development of the country and the security of the world. Dewey went on to add, "If he has any human insight, dedicated by consciousness of social needs, into the policies called for by the day-to-day life of his fellow human beings, either in domestic or international affairs, I have never seen the signs of it."[3]

Dewey's concern was based on his argument that "lying just below the optimism, prosperity and gaiety that is our abiding image of the roaring twenties, there seems to be flowing a strong undercurrent of dissatisfaction ready to surface. The whole creed of complaisant capitalistic individualism and the

---

3. Herbert Kliebard, *The Struggle for the American Curriculum, 1893-1958* (New York: Routledge and Kegan Paul, 1987), p. 180.

right and duty of economic success commits him to the continuation of that hypocritical religion of prosperity."[4] Dewey then predicted that Hoover's economic policies would lead, not to two chickens in the pot and a car in every garage of every family, but to an unprecedented economic disaster. However, the Republicans believed that Hoover had what it takes to lead the country into the era of great economic prosperity and so refused to consider the ominous signs of impending doom.

ECONOMIC DISASTER AND THE CHALLENGE OF RECOVERY

With Hoover's election, events began to unfold in dramatic fashion. The country had been on a course towards a major economic collapse. Farmers had not shared in the relatively reasonable prosperity that followed the end of the First World War. In the coal mining and textile industries working conditions had not improved since President Theodore Roosevelt had intervened in 1902.[5] By 1929 the economy was also weakened by widespread buying on credit. Thousands of Americans had borrowed money to pay for stocks, giving Hoover and his administration an erroneous impression that the country was enjoying a new era of socioeconomic prosperity as stock prices soared to new heights. Then in October 1929 the stock market collapsed, and the Great Depression was under way.

Unable to comprehend the magnitude and the seriousness of the problem, Hoover tried to assure Americans that the economic problems amounted to nothing more than a temporary setback. But when, by the end of 1929, the collapse had caused losses estimated at $40 billion, everyone knew that the country was in a very serious economic situation. The value of stock listed on the New York Stock Exchange had dropped by 40 percent. Individuals lost their personal savings and employment opportunities. Within a few months the two chickens and a car for every American family that Hoover had promised became a delusion that existed only their minds. Although the Republicans nominated Hoover for a second term as president in 1932, he knew that he had little chance of being reelected.

By the end of the year Franklin D. Roosevelt (1882-1945), then governor of New York, was a force to be reckoned with in the Democratic party. His speech nominating Alfred Smith in 1928 had helped raise his own political fortunes, generating hope within the party that he could become a viable candidate in the future. Many people within the Democratic party were hardly aware that the future was only four years away. It was only natural for the Democratic party to turn to him as its candidate for president to salvage the party and save the country.

In a nation wide radio address, Roosevelt outlined a program to meet the economic problems the nation was facing. He was nominated on the fourth

---

4. Ibid., p. 181.
5. This has been discussed in Chapter 1 of this study.

ballot and went on to defeat Hoover by a vote of 20.8 to 15.7 million. Roosevelt's victory was largely the result of James A. Farley (1888-1976), chairman of the Democratic party in New York and his campaign manager. There was a new sense of hope for new directions not only within the Democratic party, but also within the country in general. Americans began to blame Hoover for the Depression because he failed to acknowledge the extent of the problems and so was unable to design a program to combat them.

In 1932, as the country was entering a period of political transformation, tragedy struck an all-American family in a way that devastated the nation. Charles A. Lindbergh, Jr., infant son of an American hero, Charles A. Lindbergh (1902-1974), who had flown non-stop from Roosevelt Field near New York City on May 20, 1927, to Paris, France, in 33.5 hours,[6] was kidnapped and murdered. The enthusiasm for the future exhibited by the citizens of St. Louis who sponsored Lindbergh's plane, christened the *Spirit of St. Louis*, quickly gave way to the reality that the Great Depression was having other devastating effects on people's behavior that were hard to measure, let alone accept.

That kidnapping became a very common crime in the United States during the Depression suggests the negative side of human experience and thinking while under stress. Although the Congress responded by enacting the Lindbergh law, which made kidnapping a federal crime if the victim was carried out of state, it did little to curb this crime. The arrest, trial, conviction, and death sentence of Bruno Richard Houptmann, a German immigrant, for the crime added a sad twist to a national tragedy. It reminded Americans that the country was vulnerable to a combination of forces that were working against it.

By the time Roosevelt took office on March 4 1933,[7] the Depression had grown steadily worse. Thousands of unemployed workers were standing in bread lines to receive food for their families. Many farmers and workers were rapidly losing their homes, and many more were about to lose them because they could not pay the mortgages. Roosevelt applied a wide range of programs that he had used successfully in New York at the beginning of the Depression to restore the confidence of the people in the future.

The New Deal was the beginning of major reform in the structure of national institutions and the introduction of programs that were designed to enable Americans to have a fresh new vision of the future.[8] But in initiating these programs Roosevelt was under no illusion. He knew that the task was great and the challenge was compelling. He also knew that it was a challenge that had to be accepted and a task that had to be undertaken because the survival of the nation was at stake.

---

6. The record shows that Lindbergh took off at 5:21 p.m. from Roosevelt Field near New York on May 20 and landed at Le Bouget Field near Paris at 10:21 p.m. Paris time on May 21, covering a distance of 3,600 miles.

7. The inauguration was the last to be held in March. Under the Twentieth Amendment of 20 to the Constitution proposed March 3, 1932, and ratified February 3, 1933, all future inaugurations would be held in January.

8. Robert E. Potter, *The Stream of American Education* (New York: The American Book Company, 1974), p. 371.

As part of the New Deal Roosevelt initiated relief programs for farmers in an effort to control the devastation of that segment of the economy, which was so vital to the survival of the state. On March 6, 1933, Roosevelt declared a "bank holiday" to allow his administration to formulate a new monetary policy. Three days later, on March 9, Roosevelt called a special session of Congress to begin dealing with urgent economic matters. This special session of Congress lasted ninety-nine days, but it is known as the "Hundred Days Session of Congress."[9] On March 12 Roosevelt began the first of his famous fireside chats in which he addressed the many measures that his administration was proposing to fight the effects of the Depression.

While the main purpose of the New Deal was to combat the effects of the Depression, it was also designed to initiate long-term solutions to other problems. It included programs designed to bring visible benefits to education as a preparation for the future. One of these programs was the introduction of the school lunch. When it was initiated in 1935 to provide an expanding market for the farmers, it was believed that it would be a temporary measure. But by 1946 it had been so successful that it was made a permanent part of educational programs. The national lunch program is still in operation today.[10] The legislation creating this program also authorized the secretary of agriculture to purchase and distribute agricultural surplus among individuals devastated by the Depression. The school lunch program became the second largest single program of aid to education, totaling nearly $400 million by 1964.[11]

In spite of these efforts to sustain education as an investment for the future, the Depression had a devastating effect on education. By 1932 teachers' salaries had been reduced to poverty levels all across the country. In Chicago, the birthplace of the AFT, teachers had gone without pay for months bringing untold misery and financial ruin. To add insult to injury, the leadership of the National Association of Manufacturers attributed the economic disaster to the laziness of the workers and the failure of schools to educate students well.[12] This is why in his study *Dare the School Build a New Social Order*, published in 1932, George Counts argued that the failure of society to support education created a national disgrace that led to the crisis in which it now found itself. Counts suggested the expansion of the curriculum to assure that students were adequately prepared to play their role in society.[13]

This reaction to conditions of education as one of the chief effects of the Depression suggests the conclusion that just as the New Deal initiative was intended to plant a new hope in the minds of the people about the general conditions of the economy, George Counts's initiative in education was generating a new level of confidence in educators as they were collectively trying to restructure the elements of leadership that was needed for the future. By the

9. The special session of Congress lasted from March 9 to June 16, 1933, a total of one hundred days.

10. Robert E. Potter, *The Stream of American Education*, p. 391.

11. Ibid., p. 340.

12. Herbert Kliebard, *The Struggle for the American Curriculum, 1893-1958*, p. 187.

13. Ibid., p. 195.

time he assumed the presidency of the AFT in 1939, Counts had become a major national figure in the efforts that were being made to restore the country to its feet. By 1934, seeing Roosevelt's persistence, Americans were steadily gaining confidence that they could recreate social and economic conditions that would eventually make the country better in the future than it was the past.

When a new journal, *Social Frontier*, appeared in 1934, it provided a forum for debate on national critical issues, especially the position of teachers and the direction that education was taking.[14] What this indicates is that Roosevelt had planted in the minds of the people that distinct combative determination to rise to the occasion and meet the challenges posed by the Depression, to fight to regain their sense of vision and purpose, and to struggle against the odds to overcome the problems it had created.

THE UNITED STATES AND THE WORLD SITUATION

In 1931 the situation in the world created problems that placed the United States in a dilemma. Should it become involved in the effort to create stable conditions beneficial to the international community at the expense of possibly failing to pay adequate attention to problems at home, or could it remain isolated and create conditions that could have an adverse effect on recovery programs at home? It was a crisis with no easy solutions. In that year Japanese military forces invaded Manchuria to reestablish its influence after Chinese revolutionary forces invaded it in 1911 and ousted the Manchu dynasty.

Since that time Japan had opposed Chinese action and waited until 1931 when it thought conditions were appropriate to reassert its dominance. The League of Nations, weakened by the United States Senate's refusal to ratify its creation under President Wilson's plan as outlined in his Fourteen Points presented at the Versailles Peace Conference in 1919, called for the imposition of economic sanctions. The sanctions, however, proved to be ineffective, which served as a green light for Japan and other nations with similar ambitions to expand their boundaries through territorial gains. In 1937, Japan, feeling no ill effects from the League of Nations sanctions, invaded China itself. This set the stage for the progression of events that culminated in the outbreak of war in 1939. When the war ended in 1945, the character of international relationships was altered forever.

In 1935, encouraged by the failure of the League to do anything to stop the Japanese occupation of Manchuria, Benito Mussolini ordered his forces to invade Ethiopia. Its leader, Emperor Haile Selassie, fled and appealed to the international community to do something to force Italy to remove its forces from his land. But, as in the case of the Japanese invasion of Manchuria, the League of Nations was unable to do anything to stop this aggression. In both situations Roosevelt was equally unable to do anything that might have helped find solutions to the escalating international problems. The following year, 1936, the time for presidential elections in the United States, Francisco Franco

---

14. Ibid., p. 196.

(1892-1975) led a revolution that established him as dictator of Spain, a position of absolute power he maintained for nearly fifty years. For much of Franco's dictatorial rule the standard of living for the Spanish populace remained one of the lowest in Europe.

During this time the declining economic position of teachers united many locals of the AFT in order to do something to resolve it. They formulated various strategies for seeking improvement. This is why the Baltimore Teachers Union passed a resolution in August 1935 stating, "Whereas the teachers in the United States have suffered repeated pay cuts in the past five years of the depression, and whereas the rising cost of living has still further depressed teachers' salaries. Therefore, be it resolved that the American Federation of Teachers begin a national campaign of meetings, public petitions, media speeches, etc. in order to arouse public opinion in favor of restitution of teachers to restore salaries to their previous level and to ensure a further increase to meet the rising cost of living. Be it further resolved that all teachers' unions in the AFT and other organizations sympathetic to labor be enlisted in this campaign."[15] Although there were no immediate changes in the position of teachers as a result of this resolution, the country could not remain ignorant of the plight of teachers any longer.

Members of the AFT were seriously concerned about the critical nature of the world situation and how it could have a profound impact on conditions at home. The Baltimore Teachers Union recognized this fact and passed a resolution in 1935 condemning the preparation for war that was under way in Europe. The resolution stated,

> Whereas the danger of an impending war threatens more and more ominously aggravated by a suicidal race in preparing arms and other war materials, and whereas such organizations as the ROTC, CMTC, CCC, etc., are indoctrinating our youth in the military and nationalist spirit, therefore be it resolved that teachers counteract such preparation by the doctrine of peace and internationalism for the settlement of national disputes and international conflict. Be it further be resolved that armament expenditures be diverted to educational channels for the benefit of children and undereducated adults. Be it further resolved that this convention urge the AFT to reorganize a nation-wide opposition to imperialist war bringing together all organizations opposed to war.[16]

It is not surprising that those who saw the peril of Nazi and Fascist imperialism regarded the resolution as supporting Hitler and Mussolini. However, the failure of the Munich conference between Hitler and Neville Chamberlain (1869-1940),

---

15. Baltimore Teachers Union, "Resolution on the Position of Teachers," August 10, 1935, AFT Files, Walter Reuther Archives of Labor and Urban Affairs, Wayne State University, Detroit.

16. Baltimore Teachers Union, "Resolution on the Danger of War," August 10, 1935, AFT Files, Walter Reuther Archives of Labor and Urban Affairs, Wayne State University, Detroit.

the British leader, can be attributed not to the beliefs of this nature, but to Chamberlain's appeasement of Hitler.

To make sure that the Baltimore Teachers Union was not misunderstood, it passed another resolution the same day stating,

> Whereas fascism is a reactionary force in society interested in the destruction of all liberal and progressive thinking about trade unions, fraternal organizations, and political parties, and whereas fascism incites the population against minority races and groups, and whereas fascism is spreading an international network of reaction and race hatred awakening in this country, be it resolved therefore that this convention reiterate its unalterable opposition to fascism. Be it further resolved that the teachers, as directors of the union, use their influence in combating fascist thought and activity. Be it further resolved that the extension of credits or loans to the Nazi government by the United States be condemned and that the AFT request the U. S. government to prevent such credits or loans.[17]

It is clear that the Baltimore Teachers Union saw events in Europe in the context of events that were rapidly unfolding in the United States, especially the deterioration of the economic position of teachers. On that same day the Baltimore Teachers Union passed two more resolutions, one addressing the need to recognize human rights for teachers, and the other calling for a system of tenure.

The outbreak of war in September 1939, when Albert Shanker was eleven years old, transformed the way people thought about themselves and their world. The Japanese attack on Pearl Harbor on December 7, 1941, forced the United States to end its neutrality. In January the President underscored the importance of four freedoms he believed must be preserved for all people, saying, "In the future day, which we seek to make secure, we look forward to a world founded upon four essential human freedoms. The first is freedom of speech and expression everywhere in the world. The second is freedom of every person to worship God in his own way. The third is freedom from want. The fourth is freedom from fear."[18]

When France surrendered on June 22, 1940, Germany launched its blitz against Britain, believing that it would not be able to withstand the power and destruction that its air force and missile attack unleashed. For several months Winston Churchill (1874-1965) pleaded with Roosevelt to come to Britain's aid, arguing that united German and Italian forces would force Britain to surrender, which posed serious implications for the United States. After meeting secretly the two leaders issued what became known as the Atlantic Charter on August 11, 1941, consisting of eight principles. The third principle stated, "We respect the right of all peoples to choose the form of government under which they will

---

17. Ibid.
18. Franklin D. Roosevelt, *The State of the Union Message*, January 6, 1941 (Washington, D.C.: U.S. Government Printing Office, 1941).

live, and wish to see sovereign rights and self-government restored to those who have been forcibly deprived of them."[19]

This statement shows two things. The first is that the United States was now willing to consider its involvement in world events that held implications for its own future. The second is that it implied that colonial systems in Africa had forcibly deprived the Africans of their right to self-determination. Both implications would have serious consequences for the future as both Africans and African-Americans began to demand better treatment soon after the war. In the United States it meant the beginning of the civil rights movement. In Africa it meant the rise of African nationalism. Both movements had a profound impact on social conditions in both continents.

The passage of the Lanham Act in 1941 made it possible for the federal government to provide funds for school districts to build and operate schools where federal war-related activity created problems that local governments could not resolve. Three years later, in 1944, two events occurred that would have a profound impact on the country. The first was the passage of the Servicemen Readjustment Act, better known as the GI Bill. This legislation provided education and training for returning war veterans. Later the benefits it provided were expanded to include veterans of the Korean and Vietnam wars. The ability of the country to initiate educational plans for the future in an environment of war suggests a critical feature of the human struggle for existence. The GI Bill made it possible for Americans returning from the war to receive the education that they needed to prepare themselves for the future.

The second event took place in 1944, was the publication of a report entitled *An American Dilemma: The Negro Problem and Modern Democracy* by Gunnar Myrdal (1898-1987), a Swedish sociologist and researcher. In his well-documented study Myrdal predicted that unless racial discrimination soon ended, the United States was likely to encounter serious racial and social problems in the not so distant future. Myrdal suggested the causes of this social conflict, saying, "The crowdedness in the Negro ghettos, the poverty and the economic insecurity, the lack of wholesome recreation are factors which all work in the direction of fostering anti-social tendencies leading to conflict. Racial discrimination in the opportunity for school facilities is as spectacular as it is well known. The current expenditure per pupil in daily attendance per year in elementary and secondary schools in ten southern states in 1935 and 1936 was $17.04 for Negroes and $49.50 for white children."[20] This difference meant that black Americans were receiving less educational opportunity than white Americans, a fact that contributed to both the *Brown* decision in 1954 and the beginning of the civil rights movement in 1955.

The violent deaths of Adolf Hitler and Benito Mussolini in 1945 meant that only Japan remained determined to continue the war against the Allied forces.

---

19. President Franklin Roosevelt and Prime Minister Winston Churchill, *The Atlantic Charter*, August 11, 1941 (Washington, D.C.: U.S. Government Printing Office, 1941).

20. Gunnar Myrdal, *An American Dilemma: The Negro Problem and Modern Democracy* (London: Harper and Brothers, 1944), p. 332.

After nearly six years of fighting, the world was getting tired of it. On July 16, 1945, the United States tested an atomic bomb in New Mexico. On August 6 the United States dropped one such bomb over Hiroshima, killing more than 70,000 persons. Three days later a second atomic bomb was dropped on Nagasaki, killing nearly 40,000 persons.

This brought the war to an end, but the use of the bomb created conditions of increasing global insecurity and danger. The atomic bomb had ushered in the era of nuclear weapons which posed the possibility of destroying the world. In spite of the end of the Second World War the wars in Korea and Vietnam brought the United States into the arena of international relationships more intimately than it had done in the past.[21] Since that time the world has not been the same. The United States has since been involved in seeking solutions to a plethora of global problems.

DEVELOPMENTS IN THE UNITED STATES

One year following the end of the war in 1945 dramatic events began to rapidly take place in succession in the United States. In 1946 a 38-year-old conservative Republican politician from Wisconsin, Joseph McCarthy (1908-1957), was elected to the U.S. Senate. Four years later, in 1950, McCarthy attracted public attention by accusing of some members of the U.S. State Department of harboring Communists. McCarthy capitalized this publicity by writing two books, *America's Retreat from Victory* (1951) and *McCarthyism: The Fight for America* (1952). Although both books were less than successful, McCarthy used them to stage a massive investigation of individuals he suspected of Communist activity. In the process of carrying out his self-assigned inquisition, McCarthy initiated a witch hunt that violated the basic constitutional principles that he claimed he was trying to protect.

When Dwight Eisenhower (1890-1969) was elected president of the United States in 1952, McCarthy was already at the height of his investigations. He singled out teachers and college professors because of their activities during the Depression. During what has become known as the McCarthy Era, careers were destroyed. Eisenhower, fearing to divide the Republican party, tried to ignore McCarthy and his activities. But, by 1953, Eisenhower and his administration soon realized that McCarthy was an embarrassment to both the Republican party and the country.[22]

The president tried an approach of quiet diplomacy to have McCarthy cease his activities. In 1954 McCarthy was censured by the U.S. Senate, bringing his infamous activities to a halt. Education scholar Diane Ravitch concluded, "With

---

21. For example, since the United States recognized the formation of the government of Israel in 1948, it has tried to mediate between Israel and its Arab neighbors. Its efforts remained unsuccessful until September 14, 1993, when the government of Israel and representatives of the Palestinian Liberation Organization (PLO) met in Washington, D.C., to sign an agreement that they had reached.

22. Diane Ravitch, *The Troubled Crusade: American Education, 1945-1980* (New York: Basic Books, 1983), p. 110.

Eisenhower as President, McCarthy could no longer call upon and sustain an atmosphere of suspicion. The efforts to oust teachers suspected of being communists continued for a time in some school districts."[23]

Among the dramatic events that had a profound impact on the United States during this time was the Supreme Court decision in *Brown v. Board of Education of Topeka.* Since the end of Reconstruction and the passage of Jim Crow laws, there had developed a thinking that differences in skin color represented differences in intellectual potential and that the black race was inferior to the white race. A conclusion was then reached that because of this difference, separate facilities must be established for whites and blacks. This thinking was seen as receiving official approval by the U.S. Supreme Court in its 1896 *Plessy v. Ferguson* decision. From this decision, the doctrine of separate but equal became the modus operandi until the *Brown* decision of 1954.

From 1952 to 1953 the Supreme Court heard arguments against this policy and the specific application of separate but equal relative to segregation in education. These arguments were directed at schools in South Carolina, Virginia, Delaware, the District of Columbia, and Kansas, which were the objects of similar lawsuits, combined into the *Brown v. Board of Education of Topeka* case that put John W. Davis on the national spotlight for the last time. He, arguing in favor of maintaining segregation, cited the *Plessy* decision to conclude that the issue of race had been settled once and for all and that the constitutionality of racial segregation had been substantiated by that decision. He further argued that nothing must be done to change it.

The lawyers in favor of integration, led by Thurgood Marshall (1908-1993), the chief counsel for the plaintiff, and later the first African-American to serve on the U.S. Supreme court, argued that segregation did great damage to black students because separate was not equal. Robert L. Carter, arguing for the plaintiffs, advanced a compelling argument, saying, "No state has any authority under the equal protection clause of the Fourteenth Amendment to use race as a factor in affording educational opportunity among its citizens."[24] Marshall, who had attended the Howard Law School directed by Charles H. Houston (1895-1950), added, "that there were no recognizable differences from a racial standpoint between children."[25]

On May 17, 1954, after hearing the arguments, the Supreme Court reached a unanimous decision that the doctrine of separate but equal as enunciated by the *Plessy* decision was no longer applicable to conditions of the day. Chief Justice Earl Warren (1891-1974)[26] wrote the decision saying, "Does separation of children in public schools on the basis of race, even though the physical facilities and other tangible factors may be equal, deprive the children of the

---

23. Ibid. p. 111.
24. Leon Friedman (ed.), *Argument: The Oral Argument Before the Supreme Court in Brown vs. Board of Education of Topeka, 1952-1955* (New York: Chelsea House, 1969), p. 14.
25. Ibid., p. 15.
26. Warren had been named chief justice by President Dwight D. Eisenhower in 1953 to replace Frederick Vinson (1890-1953), who died suddenly.

minority groups of equal educational opportunity? We believe that it does. Such segregation is a denial of equal protection of the law."[27]

The reaction to the historic decision can be understood in the context of the events that began to immediately unfold. The formation of the infamous White Citizens Council in close cooperation with the Ku Klux Klan to coordinate efforts to disobey the ruling was the beginning of a decade of unprecedented social turmoil. Some U.S. senators from the South, especially South Carolina and Mississippi, were actively involved in efforts to disregard the decision and to maintain racial segregation. James Eastland and John Stannis, U.S. Senators from Mississippi, both took the center stage in their resistance to the *Brown* decision.

When Albert Einstein (1879-1955) died on April 18, 1955, the theory of relativity that he first enunciated in 1915 had become a touchstone that physicists tried to apply to a variety of situations in order to find solutions to problems of human existence. In that year Shanker, already a successful mathematics teacher, saw the applicability of the theory of relativity to conditions of education by recognizing its central tenet that all laws of physics have the same mathematical form regardless of the system of reference to which they are applied. This is why he tried to adopt "a strong stand and not allow the school district to renege on its contract in order to satisfy an experiment in education and allow a superintendent to use the community against the union."[28] In this approach Shanker was now trying to apply the logic of scientific and mathematical methods to find solutions to problems of society.

On August 20, 1955, Emmett Till, a black youth of fourteen, almost missed his train from Chicago to the Mississippi Delta, where he was going to spend part of the summer with his relatives. Till caught his train but never made it back to Chicago. He was murdered and those responsible for his death were acquitted of the crime. A decade after the end of the Second World War southern states, especially Mississippi, felt that the *Brown* decision had plunged the United States into "another war to protect its way of life."[29] Those responsible for Till's death did not know that they were helping arouse a new level of consciousness among black Americans about the need to initiate a protest movement to gain their civil rights.

In the same year that Till was murdered, a crisis was rapidly developing in Alabama. Racial segregation on the Montgomery bus lines had been entrenched by tradition. When black passengers boarded the bus, they paid the fares at the front, and then they were expected to leave the bus to reboard at the rear door because the front seats were reserved for white passengers. Black passengers were also expected to give up their seats to allow white passengers to have them if more white passengers got on. On December 1, 1955, Rosa Parks, secretary to the Montgomery branch of the National Association for the Advancement of the

---

27. *Brown vs. Board of Education of Topeka*, 347 U.S.483 (May 17, 1954).

28. Marjorie Murphy, *Blackboard Unions: The AFT and the NEA, 1900-1980* (Ithaca, N. Y.: Cornell University Press, 1990), p. 246.

29. Henry Hampton and Steve Fayer, *Voices of Freedom: An Oral History of the Civil Rights Movement from the 1950s Through the 1980s* (New York: Bantam Books, 1990), p. 2.

Colored People (NAACP) and a tailor's assistant at the Montgomery Fair department store, was on her way home after a long and tiring day. There was one vacant seat on the Cleveland Avenue bus that she took to go home. She took the seat in front across the aisle from one white man and two black women.

By the time the bus got to the third stop all the seats in the front were taken, and a white man stood next to Parks. The driver, in accordance with the practice, asked Parks and the other two black women to give up their seats to the white passengers. The two black women gave up their seats, but Parks refused to give up hers. The driver called the police, and Parks was immediately arrested. E. D. Nixon, chairman of the local NAACP, posted bail and got her out of jail.

The next morning Nixon called a number of people, including Martin Luther King, Jr. (1929-1968), a young minister at the Dexter Street Baptist Church, to discuss a strategy for action. Coretta Scott King, Martin's wife, explained what they planned to do: "They decided that they wanted to call together the ministerial group and some leaders. They had the meeting at Dexter Street Baptist Church to formulate a plan of action. The plan called for a one-day boycott of the buses for one day in December. They sent out leaflets all over town."[30] When the boycott extended beyond the one day the committee had recommended, Montgomery city authorities were compelled to change the policy in 1956 because the boycott had caused severe economic strains. Thus, the civil rights movement was under way, and the United States would never be the same.

On September 4, 1957, the world awoke to a major crisis that was emerging in Little Rock, Arkansas. There, national guardsmen, with fixed bayonets, stopped a fifteen-year-old black girl from entering Central High School as a mob of white protesters threatened to lynch her. In a scene reminiscent of the Reconstruction Period, a major crisis was rapidly developing between the governor of Arkansas, Orval Faubus (born in 1910), and President Eisenhower. To enforce the *Brown* decision the president federalized the Arkansas national guard, depriving Faubus of the means to resist integration.

But the anger and outrage with which the white community responded in being forced to give up its exclusive power and position of privilege were manifested in violence against black Americans. While the Court required the end of discrimination, it did not order integration, and "the Constitution does not require integration as a result of voluntary action, it merely forbids the use of governmental power to enforce segregation."[31] Regardless of this action the United States was forging ahead with plans for the future. There was no going back to conditions of the past. This was the course of action the AFT had advocated since 1937.

The crisis in Little Rock occupied the back pages of national newspapers when the Soviet Union launched the first satellite Sputnik (Voyager) on October 4, 1957. The satellite circled the earth once every ninety-five minutes at a speed of 18,000 miles her hour until it returned to the earth on January 4, 1958. The entire world was caught by surprise. Few people believed that the Soviet Union,

---

30. Ibid., p. 22.
31. Diane Ravitch, *The Troubled Crusade: American Education, 1945-1980*, p. 165.

coming out of the Second World War weakened to the point where its recovery would take years, was capable of rising above its third-rate development to the status of a major nuclear power in the way that it did.[32] By 1959 the Soviet leader, Nikita Khrushchev (1894-1972), exploited the Sputnik's success for his own political advantage and threatened to bury the West in the intense ideological competition that was rapidly developing as part of the Cold War.

The impact of Sputnik was felt more profoundly by the United States than by any other country in the world. The United States saw the success of Sputnik as a challenge and decided to respond in two specific ways. The first had to do with a change of attitude about the involvement of the federal government in education. Out of this new thinking emerged a national call for the federal government to think of new ways of encouraging development in key areas of research and technology. This in turn required funding for certain academic areas, especially mathematics and the hard sciences. President Eisenhower had vigorously opposed any federal role other than that of offering encouragement in education.

Eisenhower's reason for this position was that federal involvement would lead to federal control of education, a situation the Constitution of the United States avoided by delegating education to the states. However, knowing that the era of the baby boom was placing considerable financial strains and demands on those who were formulating strategies for action, President Eisenhower was compelled to seek congressional action in initiating construction projects to improve education.[33] But many Americans saw the country's response to an educational need in terms of a number of political factors that included religion, gender, and race. That the southern states saw this effort as a way of seeking to impose the *Brown* decision accentuated the controversy surrounding the federal involvement in education that Eisenhower was now seeking in order to ensure its development as a response to Sputnik.

The second specific way in which the United States reacted to Sputnik was that as soon as it returned to earth, President Eisenhower pushed through the Congress the National Defense Education Bill. Due to congressional procedures the bill did not become law until September 1, 1958, still a relatively short period in the history of legislative action in the U.S. Congress. The first paragraph of the act stated clearly what its purpose was: "The Congress hereby finds and declares that the security of the nation requiring the fullest development of the mental resources and technical skills of its men and women. The present emergency demands that additional and more adequate educational opportunities be made available. The defense of this nation depends upon the mastery of modern techniques developed from complex scientific principles."[34]

Among the major provisions of this legislation designed to respond to Sputnik was the need to include in the curriculum at all levels more comprehensive studies in science, mathematics, foreign languages, and research.

---

32. Ibid., p. 228.
33. Ibid., p. 229.
34. U.S. Public Law 85-864, National Defense Education Act, 85th Congress, September 2, 1958.

University professors saw in these provisions opportunities to initiate research in various areas related to the U. S. efforts to sustain its interests during the Cold War. It was the beginning of new graduation requirements in both high school and college.[35]

In 1959, while attempting to gain technological ground lost to Sputnik, Eisenhower invited Khrushchev to visit the United States. In June of that year, Soviet First Deputy Premier F. R. Kozlov, visited the United States to prepare for Khrushchev's visit. Khrushchev seemed to understand the impact that Sputnik was having on the thinking of people in the United States. On his return to the Soviet Union Kozlov carried an official letter of invitation from Eisenhower to Khrushchev. Khrushchev reacted, "Our relations had been extremely strained. Yet here was Eisenhower, President of the United States, inviting us to head a government delegation on a friendly visit. America had been boycotting us completely, even to the point of issuing a special ban on the purchase of crab meat from the Soviet Union. They said our goods were manufactured by slave labor. They also refused to buy our caviar and vodka. How does one explain this sudden invitation? What did it mean? It was hard to believe."[36]

Conscious of the impact of the invitation, Khrushchev submitted the letter of invitation to the Soviet Presidium for discussion and decision. It was decided to accept the invitation in principle, but to urge the United States to do more to reduce the tension that was building up between the two countries. M. A. Menshikov, the Soviet ambassador in Washington from 1958 to 1961, was instructed to relay the acceptance of the invitation to Eisenhower and to make appropriate arrangements for the visit.

The trip lasted thirteen days in September 1959, shortly after the first anniversary of the passage of the National Defense Education Act. Khrushchev and his entourage would visit seven cities and the United Nations. His wife, his son Sergei, his two daughters Yalia Gentor and Rada Adzhubei, and his son-in-law, A. J. Adzhubei, the editor of *Izvestia*, were among the party. This raised the question in Moscow about the wisdom of taking the entire family to the United States in one plane during the height of tensions between the two countries.

Khrushchev's tour of the United States would have been completed without incident were it not for the remarks made by Norris Poulson, the mayor of Los Angeles, during a reception hosted by the World Affairs Council. Poulson chided Khrushchev for his "We will bury you" remark. Khrushchev recalled his reaction in an interview with his biographer, Strobe Talbott, "Everything was going fine until the mayor got up to make a speech. His remarks were brief but very offensive to us. He stuck all kinds of pins in the Soviet Union and our system, most in the form of comparisons with the United States. I was furious. I could not pretend that I did not know what he was really saying. So I decided to deal a

---

35. This author recalls that when he arrived in the United States to attend college in 1961, the liberal studies requirements were already in place, and he took courses under provisions of the legislation.

36. Edward Crankshaw and Jerrold Schecter, *Khrushchev Remembers: The Last Testament* (Boston: Brown and Company, 1974), p. 369.

counter blow as I said, 'Mr. Mayor, I am here as a guest of the President of the United States. I did not come to your city to be insulted or to listen to you denigrate our great country and our great people. If my presence is unwelcome, then my plane is always ready to take me straight back to the Soviet Union.' In my indignation I might have been a bit rude."[37]

Instead of returning to the Soviet Union with a favorable impression of the United States, Khrushchev returned with a strong suspicion that the United States was about to increase its anti-Soviet activity, including espionage. Indeed, Khrushchev did not have to wait too long to substantiate his suspicion. Early on May 1, 1960, Marshall Malinovsky, head of the national security system, called Khrushchev to report that an American U-2 reconnaissance airplane had crossed the border of Afghanistan into Soviet airspace and was flying toward Sverdlovsk, a strategic defense center. Khrushchev ordered the Soviet defense forces to shoot the plane down and not to allow it to get away as had happened in April when another U-2 plane had flown into Soviet airspace.

As soon as the plane was hit, the pilot, Francis Gary Powers (1929-1977), a lieutenant in the U.S. Air Force who was also in the service of the CIA, parachuted and was immediately placed under arrest. When Eisenhower refused to acknowledge the espionage purpose of the flight, Khrushchev angrily denounced the United States and canceled the summit conference that was scheduled for mid-May among himself, Charles de Gaulle (1890-1970), and Eisenhower to discuss postwar German issues and disarmament in general. This incident represented the lowest point in Eisenhower's presidency. He even purportedly considered resigning because he felt that he had let his country down. After this incident the Cold War took a dramatic turn for the worse. Neither leader could trust the intentions of the other. Khrushchev's recent visit to the United States was no more than a minor episode in the relationships between the two countries.

These developments had placed the United States in what a film documentary called the dangerous years.[38] By the time that the Cuban missile crisis occurred in 1962, the United States was increasingly coming to the realization that the diplomacy that it was initiating in order to improve relationships and reduce tension between it and the Soviet Union must take a back seat to the need to strengthen its military forces. The arms race represented a bold approach that included space exploration to counteract the prediction that Khrushchev had made during his tour of the United States. In Khrushchev's opinion, the United States must abandon its capitalist policies in favor of a socialist agenda; otherwise, the country would fall farther and farther behind the Soviet Union. On February 20, 1962, John Glenn became the first American astronaut to orbit the earth. The arms race soon acquired expanding and perilous dimensions.

The AFT's members, like the rest of the world, became helpless participants in the doctrine known as MAD (mutually assured destruction) that these two

---

37. Ibid., p. 388. Twice in 1993 the author requested a copy of Poulson's remarks from the office of the mayor in Los Angeles, but he received no response.

38. Arts and Entertainment, *Eisenhower: The Dangerous Years*, (documentary film), July 1988.

superpowers obsessively embraced. Schoolchildren all around the world soon took part in two kinds of emergency classroom drills: fire and atom bomb.

KENNEDY AND THE NEW FRONTIER

The tragic death of President John F. Kennedy on November 22, 1963, did not slow down the intensity of the arms race and the Cold War in general. Kennedy's successor, President Lyndon B. Johnson (1908-1973) continued the programs Kennedy had started. The installment of the Kennedy administration gave Americans an opportunity to reevaluate the relationship that their country had with other countries. This could only be realistically done in the context of posing fundamental questions about the United States' own national character and domestic programs. This is why, on taking office on January 20, 1961, Kennedy recognized the need to develop a national program that would reach out for improved relationships with other nations.

Kennedy's concept of the New Frontier was born out of this endeavor. It was significant because it acknowledged a basic tenet in human relationships: the freedom of all people is essential to stability and peace among all nations. For Kennedy the exploration of space was only meaningful within the context of seeking to recognize the exploration of the aspirations of all people, both in fulfilling their personal ambitions and in meeting new challenges leading to national enrichment. This is why in 1961 Kennedy enunciated new policies regarding the rise of African nationalism. The appointment of Dean Rusk as U.S. Secretary of State brought a fresh new approach that saw a departure from past policies pursued by the State Department under John Foster Dulles. Up until the Kennedy years prior administrations believed that the consequences of the rise of African nationalism were the sole responsibility of the colonial governments.[39]

Kennedy also fully recognized the momentum that the civil rights movement was gathering in the United States. In it he saw a struggle that gave the country an emerging national character that was necessary to enable the country to recognize its proper role in critical issues of international relationships. His basic conviction was that unless the United States found solutions to problems at home, it would not be able to play an effective role in international developments. The New Frontier demanded the administration take all pertinent factors into account in designing a domestic policy and agenda that were closely related to events abroad. This is the reason why Kennedy submitted to the Congress the most comprehensive bill on civil rights, which became law in 1964.

The creation of the Peace Corps in 1961, under the direction of Sargent Shriver, Kennedy's brother-in-law, brought to the country to the ultimate New Frontier. The Peace Corps because a cultural bridge that helped build international relationships by providing the U.S. government and its people with

---

39. Dickson A. Mungazi, *The Struggle for Social Change in Southern Africa: Visions of Liberty* (New York: Taylor and Francis, 1989), p. 100.

an opportunity to understand the nature of other cultures and the problems that other countries faced in their struggle for advancement.

Americans from all walks of life were called upon to join the Peace Corps and then participate in a national program intended to give Kennedy's transformation vision a practical application to human understanding and cooperation. They were asked to live and work with people in foreign countries, studying and advising them on various aspects of national development. They would immerse themselves in foreign cultures and avoid trying to persuade the people in those lands to adopt the American culture. They symbolized mankind's ability to appreciate cultural diversity as a means toward global enrichment. Kennedy envisioned this as constituting an understanding that was a prerequisite in creating an atmosphere of peace and cooperation. Nurses, teachers, agricultural specialists, engineers, and industrial workers all came forward in the spirit of Kennedy's call to offer their service in a national program designed to improve understanding between the United States and other countries.

In this rare new venture Americans came to understand themselves within the context of a global community. It also enabled their country to rediscover itself in an effort to redefine its proper role in international relationships. In this context Peace Corps volunteers were found all over the world. The quest for human understanding came alive when agricultural specialists worked alongside people in Chile to raise food, when educators went to the Philippines to be both students and teachers, when health workers helped establish health care facilities in Tunisia, and when geologists went to Tanzania to assist in extracting minerals that were needed to reap the benefits of natural resources without doing damage to the ecosystem. There was no age limit to be a Peace Corps volunteer, indicating awareness that all Americans had the potential for accepting an assignment in a foreign country in the service of their nation. The AFT fully supported the Peace Corps mission. It allowed Peace Corps teachers to return to American classrooms with a wealth of experience and knowledge to share.

This approach to national policy created an environment that helped define a new paradigm, which held new meaning for the United States. This New Frontier manifested itself in variety of program initiatives at home. The Higher Education Act of 1963 authorized $935 million in matching funds and $360 million in loans extended over a period of five years to institutions of higher education, both public and private, for constructing new educational establishments that included athletic and recreational facilities and buildings for all purposes, even sectarian.[40] At the same time the Vocational Education Act, also passed in 1963, "extended and expanded all previous vocational programs including the Smith-Hughes Act of 1917."[41]

In 1965, having won the 1964 presidential election on his own merit against his Republican opponent, Barry Goldwater (born in 1909) of Arizona, Lyndon B. Johnson set out to define in his own way the New Frontier. On April 11, 1965, President Johnson initiated what he regarded as a new definition of the New Frontier by signing the Elementary and Secondary Education Act. This

---

40. Robert E. Potter, *The Stream of American Education*, p. 406.
41. Ibid., p. 402.

legislation represented the most comprehensive provisions for education since
the National Defense Education Act of 1958.

The law provided for annual appropriations for education that enabled
students from low-income families to avail themselves of educational
opportunities. The implementation of the law began with $100 million for the
1965 academic year. It allowed for the purchase of textbooks, library resources,
and other published materials needed in the promotion of education among the
children of economically deprived families. States were required to assure that
fiscal control of the funds ensured fair and equitable distribution of resources.

On November 8 President Johnson expanded the concept of the New
Frontier in the area of higher education by signing the Higher Education Act.
Coming one year after the passage of the Civil Rights Act of 1964, this
legislation prompted Johnson to acknowledge its importance by saying, "This is
only one of more than two dozen educational measures enacted by the first
session of the 89th Congress. History will forever record that this session did
more for the cause of education in America than all the previous 176 regular
sessions of Congress did put together."[42]

While this was happening, African-Americans were trying to define the New
Frontier in their own way. Since the *Brown* decision, they were increasingly
demanding their fair share of the educational pie. The constitutional conclusion
of the Supreme Court in that decision that separation of children on the basis of
color gave them the stamp of inferiority became the basis of a fresh approach to
their quest for educational opportunities. Those who continued to argue that the
black race was intellectually inferior, such as Arthur R. Jensen,[43] saw the earlier
Plessey decision as supporting their line of thinking.

Those who argued that race was not a factor in human intelligence also used
the *Plessy* decision to support their view. This brought the question of research
into play. The *Brown* decision, however, validated a new line of thinking that
environment plays a major and crucial role in academic achievement. This belief
led African-Americans to argue that society has a duty to provide an environment
that is conducive to their learning. The reality of this aspect of the New Frontier
is that success or failure in both education and society in general must be
measured by the guarantee of equality in all aspects of national life.

This line of thinking was the reason why from provisions of the Civil
Rights Act and of the Economic Opportunity Act of 1964 efforts were made to
assist students from economically disadvantaged family backgrounds. They
received special attention to help them overcome the effects of the denial of equal
opportunity.   Known as the anti-poverty initiative, the Economic Opportunity Act
was intended to help students recognize their potential and to encourage them to
use it in their educational efforts.

---

42. U.S. Senate, Committee on Labor and Public Welfare, *Enactments by the 89th
Congress Concerning Education and Training* (Washington, D.C: U.S Government
Printing Office, 1966), p. 18.

43. William van Til, *Education: A Beginning* (Boston: Houghton Mifflin
Company, 1974), p. 346.

In this connection Johnson's understanding of the New Frontier was evident in his desire to initiate Head Start, a program for preschool children. The rationale behind Head Start was that a culturally disadvantaged background made it more difficult for a student to learn. This was due to the lack of racially integrated social interaction. This situation also deprived them of access to quality teachers and appropriate educational resources. As they did with the Peace Corps venture, the AFT and Albert Shanker lauded the implementation of Head Start.

This paradigm change in education held meaning and renewed hope for those responsible for education. They understood that educational materials and adequate environment were critical variables for educational success. Shanker has persistently addressed the critical nature of the relationships that exist between these educational building blocks. The U.S. Office of Economic Opportunity has also argued that this disadvantage can be corrected by appropriate remedial strategies designed early in the life of students.[44] This is precisely the position that African-Americans took in their understanding of Kennedy's original concept of the New Frontier. With the passage of this legislation they felt that the concept was within their grasp. With this recognition they felt that they and the country stood on the verge of a new era, an era of social cooperation and acceptance.

RICHARD NIXON, POLITICAL CORRUPTION AND BEYOND

That Johnson translated the spirit of the New Frontier into a vision of the Great Society suggests the critical nature of the national programs he began, especially in education. This gave Americans a clearer sense of what it meant to live in a world of conflict. From preschool through post secondary education, from rural to urban settings, he regarded education as the chief instrument necessary to allow in giving Americans to fulfill their aspirations. In relying on education to accomplish this objective, individuals would also become involved in proactive ways in seeking an end to conflict in the world .

Johnson might have gone down in history as one of the great presidents were it not for the war in Vietnam. Realizing that his domestic priorities were misunderstood because of the conflict in Vietnam, Johnson announced in 1967 that he would not seek the nomination of the Democratic party for a second term as president. The tragic deaths of Martin Luther King, Jr., in April 1968 and of Robert Kennedy (1925-1968) in June of the same year appear to have closed the era of the New Frontier. But was the country ready to enter the period of Richard M. Nixon?

The presidential election of 1968 was marked by violent demonstrations throughout the nation. Protesters clashed with police at the Democratic National Convention, held in Chicago. Mayor Richard Daley (1902-1976) wielded a heavy hand in dealing with the demonstrators. Although Hubert Humphrey (1911-

---

44. U.S. Public Law 88-482, Economic Opportunity Act (1964).

1978), Johnson's vice-president and heir-in-waiting, received the Democratic nomination, he lost the election to Richard Milhous Nixon (1913-1994), the Republican candidate who had lost to Kennedy eight years prior. Nixon exploited the violence in Chicago by portraying Humphrey and the Democratic party as being unable to provide effective national leadership at a critical point in the history of the country. The deterioration of the war in Vietnam, where American soldiers were being killed every day, was being seen on television with deleterious results for the administration and the Democratic party.

President Nixon recognized that the war in Vietnam must soon come to an end if the United States was to search for a newly defined role as the world's greatest superpower. Nixon dispatched his secretary of state, Henry Kissinger, on what would be referred to as shuttle diplomacy. This led to a premature announcement in 1973 that peace was at hand. The Supreme Court's decision in *Roe v. Wade* in the same year had further far-reaching social and educational implications for the United States. The case addressed the question of reproductive choice--a concept associated with democracy and freedom.

This decision is represents a period of time when the Supreme Court stepped boldly forward to address certain social issues that could not be addressed in any other way, knowing full well that it was the final arbiter in the land.[45] Indeed, the *Roe* decision placed the country in a situation that has compelled it to reexamine its value system. This re-evaluation still continues to plague and disunite large segments in the United States. Whereas protesters in the 1960s and 1970s addressed the moral issue of war in faraway lands, the 1980s and 1990s have witnessed protests about the right to terminate human life while it is still gestating in the womb.

The decision in *Roe* was not merely about the right of women to terminate unwanted pregnancies, but also about the exercise of their rights in a variety of settings. It has extended to following question: Should school districts retain an unmarried pregnant teacher? Could the school district employ a couple living together outside marriage? If so, what kind of influence would they have on students and society? These were just some issues the United States had not yet encountered. During these troubled times the AFT began to formulate its own position on the controversies that these issues raised in order to remain effective in discharging its proper responsibility to both education and society.

In 1972 Nixon accentuated the drama of moral decline ascribed to the so-called era of the hippie movements by putting together a highly controversial reelection committee, consisting of individuals of questionable integrity. Nixon then authorized the burglary of the national headquarters of the Democratic party, located in the Watergate Hotel, to search for materials he thought might embarrass the Democratic party and his opponent, George McGovern. Nixon hoped to use the information against both McGovern and the Democrats to win

---

45. In 1975, during an official visit to Washington arranged by the U.S. State Department, this author had an occasion to visit with Justice Potter Stewart, who said to him and to other guests, "We are final not because we are infallible, but we are infallible only because we are final."

the election.   Although Nixon won reelection, the action caused his political demise.

Two years later, when the full extent of his involvement in this unprecedented scandal was made known, Nixon had no choice but to resign from the presidency on August 9, 1974. In doing so he became the only president in the history of the United States to resign. Gerald Ford, who had become vice-president some months earlier when Spiro T. Agnew resigned because of his questionable financial dealings, assumed the office of President at a period of turbulence in the history of the United States. This author holds the opinion that interest in the Nixon years will increase with the passage of time because the complete story of the Nixon presidency has not yet been told.[46] But at this point it is clear that his political behavior represented a low point in the development of a nation struggling to find an effective place in the world.

Although Nixon helped to bring about formal relations with China, through what has become known as ping-pong diplomacy, his legacy is rooted in the Watergate scandal. The moment Nixon's name is mentioned, one immediately associates him with political corruption. The introduction of court-ordered busing to achieve racial balance in schools reached a crisis during the Nixon presidency. Both white parents and black parents began to reject court-ordered busing as a means to achieve equality of educational opportunity. While Nixon expressed his opposition to forced busing, he did not offer any viable alternative plan to achieve the objectives the federal courts had outlined. In this regard Nixon failed to exercise proper national leadership when the country needed it.

In 1969 the war in Vietnam brought the U.S. Supreme Court into the controversy in a way Nixon never anticipated. In the famous *Tinker v. Des Moines Independent School District* case, the Supreme Court ruled that students had a constitutional right to protest the war. The Court stated, "A student may express his opinion, even on controversial subjects like the conflict in Vietnam. Under the Constitution, free speech is not a right that is given only to be so circumscribed that it exists in principle but not in fact."[47]

In May of 1993 Shanker reflected upon the impact that, by 1974, these developments were having on the United States. He told the author,

> As you know the country was going through a national crisis caused by the Watergate scandal. Although the scandal affected the political process more than it affected education, it had a tremendous impact on national morale. Inflation was rising rapidly, giving teachers less buying capacity. The war in Vietnam was reaching a critical stage. The curriculum in general was not developing as much as it should have developed. Teachers were in a state of confusion. Students were in doubt about the future. The traditional American family was experiencing unprecedented problems. Social and moral values were in a state of decline. These were among the conditions that prevailed in

---

46. On August 7, 1994, PBS aired a program entitled "The Nixon Years: Rise and Eclipse," but offered no new information that was not previously known.

47. *Tinker v. Des Moines Independent School District*, 393 U.S. 503 (1969).

the country. We felt we had to reflect upon them in the activities of the AFT."[48]

When Ford assumed the presidency, he was preoccupied with minimizing the impact of his pardon of Nixon. Because of his presidential pardon Ford immediately alienated himself from the American people, causing serious political problems for himself.[49] During the primary election campaign beginning in 1975, Ford faced a considerable challenge from former California Governor Ronald Reagan, an actor turned politician.

Although Ford won the Republican nomination in 1976, he lost the election to Jimmy Carter, a one-term governor from Georgia. In 1993 Shanker looked back upon the Ford presidency, saying, "President Ford was so preoccupied with the damage control of his pardon of President Nixon that he was unable to do anything else. He also vetoed education legislation to the extent that he was known as the veto president. His term of office from 1974 to 1976 was not distinguished in terms of defining an education needed for the future."[50]

When Jimmy Carter assumed office in January 1977, he was keenly aware of the promise he had made to the country during an address to the NEA in 1976. He proclaimed that if elected he would create a separate department of education, replete with cabinet ranking, to make it more effective in responding to the increasing educational needs of the populace.

As a result Carter received enthusiastic endorsements from both the NEA and the AFT. One of his major accomplishments as president was the creation of the U.S. Department of Education, a move Shanker opposed because, as he told the author, "I felt that education should not be isolated from other national issues."[51] But Carter believed he had to fulfill his promise to those who had helped elect him. For this reason Shanker changed his position because he saw Carter's commitment to education as a distinct feature of his administration, one that was genuine.

During the election campaign in 1980, the Republicans formed an educational alliance with special interest groups such as the Moral Majority led by Jerry Falwell and Eagle Forum led by Phyllis Schlafly, which attempted to draw votes away from Carter. These groups formed a coalition that functioned under an umbrella organization known as the Committee for the Survival of Free Congress. The organization chose Ronald Reagan as its candidate for President, as did the Republican party. Throughout his term of office Reagan responded to the dictates of the organization, raising serious questions in some people's minds about the purpose of government in a democracy. Should it dictate a national education policy?

---

48. Albert Shanker, interview with author, Washington, D.C., May 17, 1993.

49. During a graduate course in political science at the University of Nebraska the author conducted a survey that asked 500 people what they thought about the pardon. Eighty percent had a negative response to it.

50. Albert Shanker, interview with author, Washington, D.C., May 17, 1993.

51. Ibid.

Although Carter was supported by the AFT and other organizations in his bid for reelection, the financial contributions and publicity generated by the special interest groups supporting Reagan proved too much for him, and Carter lost the election. During his two terms of office, from 1981 to 1989, Reagan tried to dismantle the U.S. Department of Education, which Carter had created. He appointed Terrel H. Bell to preside over its dissolution and William Bennett when Bell could not.

Critics of the Reagan administration argue that he failed to accomplish any significant progress in any national education programs because he was operating under the influence of special interest groups and was preoccupied with defending himself in the Iran-Contra scandal. Reagan also defended action of the principal player in the scandal, Oliver North, an ambitious former marine who hoped to make capital political gains by playing a major role that he believed to be patriotic. In spite of his admission that he had misled the Congress, North became a Republican candidate for the U.S. senator from Virginia in 1994.

An embarrassing moment for the Reagan presidency came in 1983 with the publication of *A Nation at Risk*. On April 26, 1981 Bell had named the National Commission on Excellence in Education to examine the quality of education in the country and to submit a report making recommendations on how it could be improved. In 1983, after traveling across the country to gather the evidence it needed to reach its conclusions and ancillary recommendations, the commission submitted a report that was disturbing in its indictment of education in general and specifically the Reagan administration:

> If an unfriendly foreign power had attempted to impose on America the mediocre educational performance that exists today, we might well have viewed it as an act of war. As it stands, we have allowed this to happen to ourselves. We have even squandered the gains in student achievement made in the wake of the Sputnik challenge. Moreover, we have dismantled essential support systems which helped make those gains possible. We have, in effect, been committing an act of unthinking, unilateral educational disarmament.[52]

Bell had no choice but to resign. His successor, William Bennett, the conservative Republican who did not appear to have an adequate understanding of critical issues in education, did little to confront the educational problems that plagued the administration he served. It appeared to many that the Reagan administration lacked any real understanding of the need to fully stress the ongoing and proactive development of education as the principal component in national development.

When George Bush, Reagan's vice-president, was elected president in 1988, he seemed to recognize the serious nature of the problems that country faced. He lost the support of the people, however, when he announced that he wanted to be known as the education president, but then added:

---

52. National Commission on Excellence in Education, *A Nation at Risk* (Washington, D.C.: U.S. Department of Education, 1983), p. 5.

People who want Washington to solve our educational problems are missing the point. We can lend appropriate help through such programs as Head Start. But what happens here in Washington will not matter half as much as what may happen in schools. Each local community and, yes, in each home. Still the federal government will serve as a catalyst for change in several important ways.[53]

This suggests that under Bush the federal government had chosen a small role for itself to play in the enhancement of education. Bush also seems to have ignored the perilous concerns that he National Commission on Excellence in Education had raised in 1983. How could he possibly initiate a new policy before solutions to these entrenched problems were found? Bush was not in touch with reality as far as education was concerned. By 1991 the war with Iraq and the declining economy combined to create serious political problems, which he could not overcome. These are some of the reasons behind his loss of the presidential election to Bill Clinton, the governor of Arkansas.

During the presidential election campaign in 1992 Clinton outlined his proposals for the recovery of the American economy through education in a clear and articulate manner, saying, "Education today is more than the key to climbing the ladder of opportunity. In today's global economy, it is an imperative for our nation. Our economic life is on the line. Washington shows little concern[54] as people pay more and get less for what matters most to them: educating their children."[55]

As he took office in January 1993, Clinton faced many national problems that were not solved during the Reagan-Bush and the Bush-Quayle administrations. But the improvement of the economy at the beginning of 1994 gave Clinton and the American people a period of great expectations, a fact he took into account in his State of the Union address delivered to a joint session of Congress on January 25. In 1994, one of the major national issues that Americans were asked to consider was the health reform proposals that President Clinton and his wife, Hillary, had initiated.[56]

In 1992 Clinton outlined the problems he saw in the existing national medical care, saying, "Washington has ignored the needs of middle class families and let health care costs soar out of control. American drug companies have raised their prices three times faster than the rate of inflation, forcing American consumers to pay up to six time more than Canadians or Europeans for the same drugs. Insurance companies routinely deny coverage to consumers with "pre-existing conditions" and waste billions on bureaucracy and administration.

---

53. George Bush, *America 2000: An Education Strategy* (Washington, D.C: U.S. Department of Education, 1991), p. 5.

54. This was a clear reference to the lack of interest by by both the Reagan and the Bush administrations.

55. Bill Clinton, *Putting People First: A National Economic Strategy for America* (Little Rock, Ark.: Bill Clinton for President Committee, 1992), p. 6.

56. The author received a letter dated July 13, 1994, from the Democratic National Committee (Washington, D.C.), saying. "President Bill Clinton would greatly appreciate your opinion concerning his administration and agenda."

Twelve years ago Americans spent $240 billion on health care. This year we will spend more than $800 billion."[57] In the face of mounting medical cost in 1994, it was a call the American people could not afford to ignore. This national issue, the baseball strike, and the arrest and trial of O.J. Simpson, who was accused of murdering his former wife Nicole, were among the major events that took place in the United States during the second half of 1994.

In August 1994 a major crisis was developing within the ranks of the NAACP. In June Mary Stansel, former administrative assistant to NAACP president, Benjamin Chavis, sued the organization for sexual harassment and discrimination. Chavis decided to pay her $332,400 without the knowledge and approval of the board of directors.[58] The board then voted to ask Chavis to submit his resignation. This action divided the black community and the NAACP itself into two opposing camps paralyzing its operations. Since its founding in 1909 the NAACP had not experienced a crisis of this magnitude. It was imperative to find a solution to it quickly if the organization hoped to carry out its responsibility of promoting the development of African-Americans.

SUMMARY AND CONCLUSION

The discussion in this chapter touched upon events that began to take place in 1928, the year that Albert Shanker was born. These were presented in order to build an understanding of the backdrop from which he emerged. The politics of the nation and its influence on education cannot help but have had an impact on his leadership of the AFT. The two go hand in hand.

One arrives at two conclusions from the discussion. The first is that from the beginning of the Depression and Herbert Hoover to the era of economic and educational reconstruction under Bill Clinton, the United States has faced serious socioeconomic problems that leaders have strived to resolve. The national spirit has always surged higher to assert itself in a struggle to sustain a national character consistent with the demands of the time. In this endeavor the AFT has played a major role in convincing the people of the importance of making education a high priority and of investing in students as an investment in the future. Throughout its history the AFT has never lost sight of that objective. In playing this role the AFT has helped reconstruct a national agenda for the future.

The second conclusion is that the era of civil rights that began in December 1955 with Rosa Parks and Martin Luther King, Jr., quickly led to a national campaign to recognize the need to extend civil rights to all people. The *Brown* decision in 1954, the passage of the Civil Rights Act in 1964, the *Tinker* decision in 1969, and the *Roe* decision in 1973 all testify to the degree to which the United States was struggling to put the civil rights movement into proper perspective and to further create conditions that were conducive to the improvement of the lives of all people. Kennedy's concept of the New Frontier

---

57. Bill Clinton, *Putting People First: A National Economic Strategy for America*, p. 17.

58. *Time* (August 29, 1994), p. 40.

held wider significance and implications far beyond the extent of his thinking and vision.

The crisis that the NAACP faced in 1994 over Benjamin Chavis inflicted considerable damage to the struggle of African-Americans for development. It had to be resolved quickly and fully. In the same way, reform of medical care had to be successfully carried out if all Americans hoped to have access to adequate medical care. When the U.S. Senate joined the House of Representatives in voting to pass the crime bill on August 25, 1994, President Clinton expressed hope that the Congress would then move on to grapple with the issue of medical care reform. The unfortunate thing about this initiative is that members of the Congress saw it in political terms.

On September 19, 1994 an invasion of Haiti by the United States was narrowly averted when a U.S. delegation led by former U.S. president Jimmy Carter and included former Chairman of the Joint Chiefs of Staffs Colin Powell and Senate Armed Services chairman, Sam Nunn succeeded in persuading the military government headed by General Raoul Cedras to resign in favor of restoring Jean-Bertrand Aristide, who had been duly elected in 1990 but whom the military removed from office in a coup staged in 1991. Aristide fled to the United States where, in 1993, he succeeded in persuading President Bill Clinton to take action toward restoring him to office. Clinton then regarded the military coup as a threat to democracy and decided that the military government must go.

When the economic embargo failed to force the military government to resign, Clinton decided to use U.S. military force to restore Aristide to office. When everything seemed ready to launch the invasion, Clinton sent the Carter delegation to Haiti to give the military government the last opportunity to resign by October 15. When Cedras agreed to do so the invasion was then averted. For Clinton the crisis in Haiti was a test of the American will. For the United States it was a test of national purpose. The results of the mid-term elections held on November 8 constituted that test. For the first time in forty years the Republicans gained control of both the U.S. Senate and the House of Representatives putting Clinton programs in serious doubt. Chapter 4 discusses Shanker, the man and his mission.

4

Albert Shanker:
The Man and His Mission

What we tried to do in the past by economic means can now be done by education. We want to create more effective and more humane schools.

Albert Shanker, 1989

As I grew older and gained new experiences, I realized that I had an obligation to play my role in society.

Albert Shanker, 1993

SHANKER'S ROOTS

To appreciate Albert Shanker and understand his mission of service one needs to be aware of the social conditions that shaped his life. The political environment discussed in Chapter 3 not only molded his personality, but also influenced his outlook on and participation in the American Federation of Teachers. As a child growing up in the Great Depression, Shanker's character was further developed by the socioeconomic and political conditions that his family endured.

Both his parents had immigrated from Russia during the reign of Czar Nicholas II (1868-1918), whose oppressive rule came to an end with the Bolshevik Revolution in 1917. The war of 1904 between Japan and Russia had resulted in a humiliating defeat for Nicholas and the Russian people. When the peace terms forced Russia to make major concessions to Japan, the Russian people concluded that a change of national leadership was needed and that extreme measures might have to be used to bring it about.

By 1905, facing widespread dissatisfaction among both the serfs, who were struggling for economic survival, and the general population, who were dissatisfied over losing the war with Japan, Nicholas became even more oppressive. His creation of a parliament-like body, the Duma, was an attempt to pacify the masses. Even this effort, however, yielded only marginal results. As Nicholas's fortunes continued to decline, the Russian people endured the weight of an increasingly repressive political and economic system. By the time Russia entered the First World War on the side of Britain and France, it had been so weakened that its people took advantage of the situation to stage a successful revolution that brought Nicholas's rule to an end in 1917.

While this was happening, many Russians began to leave the country. Shanker's parents were among those who left. Upon their arrival in the United States, Morris and Mamie Shanker fully understood what it meant to live in a country that was considered the land of opportunity. But to realize the dream they sought, they knew that hard work was an indispensable condition for success. They also soon realized that hard work alone was insufficient to enable their family to attain the improved economic conditions they strived for.

Morris and Mamie Shanker had experienced poverty and they wanted something better. Therefore, because of unacceptable economic conditions, Mamie was forced to take a job as a sewing machine operator. Soon she was recognized by both management and her co-workers as being efficient and thorough. She demonstrated a clear understanding and acceptance of responsibility. The company management and her fellow workers admired her integrity and honesty. Mamie Shanker was the kind of person that anyone would like to associate with.

Soon Sidney Hillman (1887-1946), a union organizer, recognized Mamie Shanker's unusual talent and invited her to join his Amalgamated Clothing Workers of America (ACWA).[1] Hillman had founded it in 1914 to improve and protect the economic conditions of the workers. Under his leadership the union pioneered the development of collaborative processes that led to improved working relationships between management and workers. Hillman also brought about health and welfare programs for workers, and he initiated, in cooperation with management, an unemployment insurance plan. Hillman was also a founding member of the Congress for Industrial Organizations, established in 1938.

Hillman had immigrated from Zagare, Lithuania, when he was twenty years old. In this regard he and Morris and Mamie Shanker shared something in common in their backgrounds. Hillman was born during the height of the Industrial Revolution, which placed an emphasis on the ability of individuals to use technology to advance themselves and their societies. Although he was not a Marxist, Hillman saw what Karl Marx saw in 1848: that future social and industrial development would largely depend upon the kind of relationships that existed between management and the workers. He, like Marx, knew that it was up to the workers to make sure that they were not exploited by management in its desire to maximize profit. This has always been the core catalyst from which unions have been formed.

The opportunity to work with Hillman provided Mamie an opportunity to learn about the importance of various strategies that labor utilized in realizing its objectives. Hillman became the godfather and guiding spirit of the labor movement in New York. His leadership of the Amalgamated Clothing Workers

---

1. Timothy Noah, "The Fiery Unionist as Educational Leader: Albert Shanker, Statesman," in *The New Republic*, June 24, 1993, p. 4.

of America was characterized by a vision of workers protected by their ability to resist any policy that attempted to exploit them. As soon as the ACWA was formed, Hillman aggressively sought continued improvement in the working conditions of ACWA members. He also sought better salaries for them. In Mamie Shanker he saw a reliable worker who grasped the importance of what he was trying to accomplish.

Mamie saw in Hillman the kind of leader whose devotion to the organization he founded was shaped by the values that she, too, believed in. The entire Shanker family soon admired Hillman as a person and leader of principle, and Hillman, in turn, admired the Shanker family for their commitment to the ACWA. Hillman's success came partly from the fact that from 1910 to 1913 Mayor William Jay Gaynor (1849-1913) had adopted policies that were sympathetic toward laborers. Gaynor, a liberal Democrat who had been a justice on the New York Supreme Court from 1894 to 1909, helped reform the police department and sought to improve the image of the city. His efforts to improve working conditions attracted the attention of city officials throughout the country.

Gaynor's innovative ideas were based on his belief that city workers can make a viable contribution to the effectiveness of the services they offer if they operate under conditions that made them happy. These were the considerations that Hillman took into account in structuring the ACWA so that it would be what he knew it had to be if it was to be effective. The relationship that developed between Hillman and the Shanker family held a special significance in the development of industrial relations in New York City. When Hillman died in 1946, Albert Shanker was eighteen years old. This shows that when he reached manhood, Albert had already been fully socialized to the inner workings of labor organizations. In May 1993 Albert Shanker told this author that when Hillman died his family felt a profound loss.

From the moment he was able to understand the events that shaped his world, Albert quickly learned that the world was what it was because people behaved in ways that reflected their attitude about it. His parents taught him to understand the importance of politics in human relationships, and in the functions and operations of national institutions.

Edward B. Fiske observes on this aspect of Shanker's background, "Politics was part of the air his parents breathed. Mamie, his mother, was an ardent member of the Amalgamated Clothing Workers of America, but remained haunted by her past."[2] Fiske goes on to quote Shanker himself as saying in 1989 of his mother, "She never got over the injustices of the old [Russian] system. Wherever politics came up around the dinner table, she would go and open the door and look to be sure no one was listening."[3]

When Shanker was fifteen years old, he developed an intense interest in public issues. He used to frequent Columbus Circle to listen to public figures debate issues of the day. He began to admire a number of individuals whose ideas

2. Edward B. Fiske, "Albert Shanker: Where He Stands," (*New York Times*, 1989).

3. Ibid.

he respected, including Bayard Rustin, the civil rights leader; Clarence Darrow, the famous lawyer whose campaign to promote justice endeared him to many; and Sidney Hook, whose philosophy Shanker deeply admired because it addressed the need for social justice.

As an adolescent, Shanker began to seriously read Hook's works. He paid tribute to Hook, saying, "He got involved, sometimes at considerable personal cost, in virtually every major human rights issue of his time. I very much admired the kind of life he lived."[4] This suggests that while he was influenced by his parents, Shanker developed an identity separate from theirs as a social activist early in his life.

Shanker's fascination with social issues and justice as an adult had its roots during his boyhood days. His father delivered newspapers and read extensively every single day. As a boy Albert would walk over the Queensboro Bridge to search for newsstands on 42nd Street, where he read extensively, just like his father. He immersed himself in *The Partisan Reviews* by the time he was fifteen years old and subscribed to *The Commentary* in 1944, when he was sixteen years old. By this time the mayor of New City, Fiorello Henry La Guardia (1882-1947), a liberal Republican who served from 1934 to 1945, had had a profound impact on Shanker because of his dedication to social justice.

What impressed Shanker even more about La Guardia was his role in the enactment of the Norris-La Guardia Federal Anti-Injunction Act of 1932. This protected the rights of striking workers who were struggling for economic survival during the Depression.[5] For Shanker, who was growing up in a family of staunchly partisan Democrats, to admire La Guardia, a Republican, shows he was an independent thinker who was always searching for ideas that he would use to shape his own future.

Party affiliation and labels meant little to him in his search for self. This position allowed Shanker to remain open to all ideas regardless of where they came from. In this way he was on his way to becoming a leader of a new generation of professional people who sought to render service to their country. By 1945, when Shanker was seventeen years old, he began to formulate his own ideas based upon the roots his family had established and the conditions that were present in his society.

EDUCATION AND THE CHALLENGE OF LEADERSHIP

With an enormous curiosity and desire to learn, Shanker was now ready to pursue his formal education aggressively and with enthusiasm. After graduating from Stuyvesant High School, ranking 125 out of 625 students, Shanker failed to gain admission to Harvard University. He was, however, admitted to the University of Illinois at Champaign-Urbana, where he earned a B.A. with honors in philosophy. He had devoted himself to the study of philosophy and

---

4. Ibid.
5. La Guardia served in the U.S. House of Representatives from 1917 to 1921 and from 1923 to 1933.

mathematics. Shanker's exposure to Sidney Hook now began to influence his own course of study. The philosophy of Bertrand Russell also came into play as Shanker engaged in his studies. The thoughts and ideas of these individuals became the core of his educational foundation. For Shanker his studies in philosophy and mathematics supplemented each other in ways that enabled him to see the issues society was facing from their proper and logical perspectives.

After graduating from the University of Illinois Shanker applied for admission to the graduate school at Columbia University, where he studied philosophy. His enthusiasm for learning manifested itself as his emerging scholarship. His love of reading developed into a passion for knowledge, a practice that he still follows. In 1952 he completed his course requirements for the Ph.D. degree. He had hoped to become a professor of philosophy at one of the nation's leading universities.

But, exhausted by a combination of events and the uncertainty of the teaching profession in the university setting, Shanker ran out of both patience and money. He accepted a position as a teacher of mathematics in a junior high school in New York City with the idea of going back to Columbia to complete his dissertation. But the need to earn a living forced him to continue his teaching. From that time to 1959 Shanker exhibited the traits of a master teacher. His knowledge of philosophy and mathematics helped him perceive the world as it was, rather than what it should be, and share his perspective of it with his students.

Shanker's perception of reality indicated a grim picture regarding the socioeconomic status of teachers. He knew firsthand that they worked long hours and were not paid what they were worth. The average annual salary was $3,600 for teachers in 1952 compared to $4,100 for industrial workers.[6] This situation was a graphic reminder of Shanker's boyhood when, as a six foot tall, 110-pound, twelve-year-old Russian Jew, he recalled, "I was a Jew living in an Irish Catholic neighborhood of Queens, so everybody took turns beating up the biggest lad. I'd ask myself: Why are they beating me up?"[7] His earlier physical abuse had been replaced by the economic abuse cast upon teachers.

As a teacher struggling to make ends meet, Shanker applied lessons from his painful experiences as a boy to his efforts in seeking improvement in the conditions under which he and other teachers served. He concluded metaphorically that teachers were the biggest Jewish kids living in an Irish Catholic neighborhood and everybody took turns beating them up. He was determined that this economic pummeling must stop. This is why he became a full-time teachers' union organizer in 1959. This launched a career that has made him an international figure. The teaching profession would no longer be the same. He immediately began to utilize the combative spirit and strategies that he had learned from his parents and combined them with a real knowledge of the problems teachers faced. These were transformed into objectives he felt must be achieved in order to give teachers a respectable position in society.

---

6. Barnard Yabroff and Lily Mary David, "Collective Bargaining and Work Stoppages Involving Teachers," *Monthly Labor Review* 76 (May 1953): 478.

7. Edward B. Fiske, "Albert Shanker: Where He Stands".

For Shanker this conviction was destined to shape his career, based upon his total dedication to teachers' needs and their struggle to obtain them. The American public's perception of classroom teaching was soon to change forever. In this setting Shanker became the Freeland G. Stecker and the school officials the personification of Edwin G. Cooley. Both were ready to engage in a combat of ideas and a deadly collision of conflicting agendas. The position of teachers became the battleground. The realignment of confrontational politics was about to reemerge in a way that would have a profound impact on education in the United States.

From 1959 to 1964 Shanker dedicated himself to the task of securing the rights of teachers that he believed they must exercise. In doing so, he proceeded knowing full well the effect of the low wages, the severely restrictive and humiliating conditions teachers worked under the meager benefits, the long hours, the additional duties they had to carry out, the political impotence, and the lack of academic freedom. He knew from personal experience how teachers were made powerless in areas that were essential to their work.

The curriculum was decided upon by the school board. The salary scale was arbitrarily decided by politicians. Sick leave and other conditions of service were outlined by the administration without consulting them. Maternity leave for female teachers, class size, disciplinary procedures, educational facilities, equipment, supplies, and general school policy were all designed and implemented without teacher involvement. The people on the front lines in the war to improve human thinking and understanding had absolutely no say whatsoever in how it was to be waged.

In order to grasp the extent of the need for basic reform on these critical issues, Shanker posed a fundamental question: How can teachers effectively discharge their responsibilities without playing a role in the development of policy covering these areas? He determined that it was his responsibility to make sure that teachers in New York fully understood the implications of their state of powerlessness and to do something to change it. He was a determined man with a mission to improve the condition of education by improving the lot of teachers.

FORMULATING AND APPLYING THE PRINCIPLE OF COLLECTIVE BARGAINING

In 1964 Shanker generated a new way of thinking among teachers that would make it possible for them to recognize the need to initiate collective action in order to seek improvement in their working conditions. In that year he was elected president of the New York United Federation of Teachers (UFT) due to his leadership skills, dedication, and knowledge of the issues. The spirit of Margaret Haley, Janie McKeon, and Catherine Goggin was resurrected in him. New York City became the new battleground for the struggle of teachers, just as Chicago had once been at the turn of the century. The combatants were the UFT and the New York City school administration. Each side was fully determined to sustain its position on the issues that divided them.

In the forthcoming battle of wills Shanker operated under the assumption that in any democratic society dialogue and consensus[8] must remain an essential operative principle. If the country took pride in its claim of upholding democratic values, then he assumed that the school administration must stop dictating conditions under which teachers worked because this action inhibited their ability to discharge their proper responsibility to their students. These conditions had to be discussed with teachers by their duly elected local representatives. As soon as Shanker assumed the office of UFT president, he introduced the principle of collective bargaining as specified in Executive Order 10988, issued by President John Kennedy in January 1962. He expected the school administration to do the same in its relationships with public school teachers.

Aware that Shanker and the UFT were committed to the operating principle of collective bargaining, the New York City Board of Education agreed to respect Shanker's insistence on it. A key tenet of the principle of collective bargaining was that elections must be held to determine who would represent teachers. In spite of the efforts made by the NEA to discourage such elections, the UFT won the elections. This greatly enhanced Shanker's sphere of influence and solidified his power as president of the UFT.

This was a major victory for him and the organization he led. The final vote count gave the UFT 20,040 compound to 9,770 for the NEA. Just as Sidney Hillman had succeeded with the aid of the policies designed by Mayor William Jay Gaynor, Shanker had utilized the spirit created by Kennedy's executive order to initiate a new and fresh approach to seeking improvements in the conditions under which teachers taught.

Discussions for a new contract under the principle of collective bargaining began immediately. But due to a lack of experience and lingering questions about how the principle would be applied, the negotiations moved at a snail's pace.[9] As early as the spring of 1962 Shanker and his UFT warned that the teachers would go on strike if progress was not forthcoming in the negotiations. With the assistance of an effective executive council that included David Selden, Carl Megel and Charles Cogen,[10] Shanker displayed strong and decisive leadership at a time when conditions were favorable to the agenda the UFT was promoting.

As a matter of strategy the UFT recognized that just as auto workers during the Depression had been successful in uniting to demand improvement in the conditions of their work, teachers had a similar responsibility to show that boards of education must negotiate with them in good faith, or the boards would

---

8. For a detailed discussion of the effect of the lack of dialogue in seeking solutions to national problems, see, for example, Dickson A. Mungazi, *Colonial Policy and Conflict in Zimbabwe: A Study of Cultures in Collision, 1809-1979* (New York: Taylor and Francis, 1992).

9. Marjorie Murphy, *Blackboard Unions: The AFT and the NEA, 1900-1980* (Ithaca, N. Y.: Cornell University Press, 1990), p. 215.

10. Each of these three men served as president of the AFT. See Chapter 2 of this volume for details.

face a united demand that they do so.[11] Once assured that he had the support of the teachers, Shanker called for a strike on April 12, 1962.

Twenty-five thousand teachers went out on strike.[12] Shanker was arrested, the first of two times, for leading what the board of education regarded as an illegal strike. The longer he stayed in jail, the more teachers rallied behind him to stress the fact that the issues in dispute could only be resolved through dialogue guided by the principle of collective bargaining. They stressed that keeping the leaders of the organization in jail would only accentuate the problems between the two sides.

Shanker and the UFT fully comprehended the issues in dispute. These included the need to raise teachers' salaries, extend free lunch periods, improve structural conditions in schools, eliminate non-teaching duties for teachers, increase the role of staff members in the operations of the schools, provide adequate textbook supplies, and end demands made by the administration that teachers prepare and submit detailed lesson plans for inspection.

Last, but not least, Shanker and his UFT were not pleased with the practice adopted by the administration in which "staff conferences often find principals lecturing to teachers dogmatically on organizational details rather than encouraging the kind of academic exchange of views."[13] They firmly believed that part of the preparation of students for involvement in a democracy was the modeling of democratic principles by the schools themselves. Furthermore, Shanker and the UFT were not arguing that the board of education must accept these terms as a condition for ceasing the threat of more strikes; rather, they were arguing that it must negotiate with them in good faith, as required by the principle of collective bargaining.

Recognizing that they had presented to the board of education a long list of issues to be resolved through dialogue, Shanker and the UFT decided to concentrate on seeking improvement in the salaries for teachers. Realizing that it was caught between making efforts to utilize dialogue to resolve the issues between it and the UFT and utilizing traditional authoritarian measures, the board of education showed a willingness to settle the issues by negotiation. But in order to meet the demand made by the UFT, it realized that it had to come up with $13 million, an amount it did not have.[14] The amount was not in dispute. How to raise it was, however, a major problem that the board wanted the UFT to acknowledge. Mayor Robert P. Wagner, Jr. (1910-1991), a Kennedy Democrat who served from 1954 to 1965, was sympathetic to the UFT position. This helped to establish rapport between the two sides and to create an atmosphere in which dialogue could take place in an effort to resolve the issues.

---

11. Marjorie Murphy, *Blackboard Unions: The AFT and the NEA, 1900-1980*, p. 216.

12. During Shanker's leadership of the UFT membership grew from 2,500 in 1959 to 85,00 in 1985.

13. New York Teachers Union, "Statement on Collective Bargaining," April 12, 1962, AFT Files, Washington, D. C.

14. Marjorie Murphy, *Blackboard Unions: The AFT and the NEA, 1900-1980*, p. 217.

Recognizing that public opinion and the momentum it generated were moving in its favor, the UFT decided to stay positive in its efforts to promote collective bargaining and let it become a standard practice in all matters relating to relations between it and the board. David Selden, acting on behalf of the UFT, suggested that Governor Nelson A. Rockefeller (1908-1979) lend the city the amount of $13 million to meet the need to raise the salaries for teachers. The suggestion was not without a historical precedent. During the Depression the state of New York, under the governorship of Franklin D. Roosevelt, had advanced money to meet educational costs.[15]

Because in 1962 the economy was stronger than it was during the Depression, Rockefeller thought the suggestion was a reasonable one. Within days Mayor Wagner, Governor Rockefeller, and the UFT met to finalize the arrangement. The principle of collective bargaining had yielded tangible results for the good of education. Although Shanker and the UFT claimed victory, not for themselves but for democratic principles, the agreement had enhanced their standing within the teaching profession. Shanker was on his way to becoming a giant figure in the educational enterprise of the nation.

It is important to remember that what was happening in New York had a profound impact on teachers throughout the country. The *New York Times* carried news headlines that were read with intense interest across the country. Albert Shanker became a household name. Teachers across the country looked to the activities of the UFT with envy and admiration. A teacher in Flagstaff, Arizona, recalled in September 1993 the meaning of the events that were taking place in New York under Shanker's leadership of the UFT:

> In 1963 the name Albert Shanker fired the imagination of teachers all over the state of Arizona. Wherever you went his name became the chief topic of conversation among teachers. There was nothing more important than the knowledge that the powerful mayor of New York, Robert P. Wagner, Jr. and Governor Nelson A. Rockefeller had come to recognize him as a major figure in the struggle that teachers in New York were engaged in to gain decent salaries and other conditions of service. Today teachers in Arizona must think of utilizing the same methods to regain the loss they have endured recently. The current governor has demonstrated a lack of interest in developing an effective educational policy, especially improving the salaries for teachers.[16] Here we can learn from the success that Shanker achieved on behalf of the members of an organization he led. If we do not do something now we will have only ourselves to blame when the conditions we serve under continue to deteriorate.[17]

---

15. Ibid., p. 219.

16. In Arizona in 1993 Republican Governor Fife Symington was not known for his progressive educational policy.

17. A teacher during a conversation with the author in Flagstaff, Arizona, September 23, 1993. The teacher declined to be identified because, he said, "I realize that Arizona is a Republican state, and I do not wish to give the impression that I am actively involved in state politics."

Many shared Charles Cogen's opinion that "this is the greatest day in the history of education in New York."[18] While this was transpiring, the board of education seemed to have second thoughts about the political implications of operating under the principle of collective bargaining. Although, by 1965, more than fifteen states had bills before their legislatures covering this form of conflict resolution they were worried by their belief that in time teacher organizations would make unreasonable demands under the guise of collective bargaining.

Individuals such as Archibald Cox, the famous independent counsel who investigated wrong-doing in the Nixon administration, became active in providing legal advice to the UFT on issues relative to collective bargaining. By 1968, when some states had laws in place covering collective bargaining, Shanker was fined $250,000 for leading a strike that the board of education and the courts considered illegal.

When Selden warned that leaders of teachers' unions must be willing to go to jail to assert their right to resort to strikes if boards of education derailed collective bargaining, there emerged a new spirit of understanding and willingness to negotiate in good faith. It is not fully known if the board of education was genuinely trying to respect the spirit of collective bargaining or if it was trying to show the courts that it was respecting its guidelines. Perhaps everyone recognized that strikes hurt all concerned, so it was in everyone's best interest to engage in conflict resolution via collective bargaining.

In 1989 Shanker seemed to understand the applicability of the principle of collective bargaining in the context of its benefits to the teachers, students, and society itself, saying:

> In the past when teachers used the word professionalism they meant paying them more and leaving them alone. Now we are talking about assembling a knowledge base, functioning in the interest of students and being accountable for student performance. In the 1930s unions kept people from being exploited. Economic conditions are much better now, largely because of the success of the labor movement. But now you have the new problems of the underclass. What we tried to do in the past by economic means can now be done by education. We want to create more effective and more humane schools and to do that you need a new kind of union and new approaches."[19]

In 1993 Shanker went on to add that without a union, the board of education would always act in an arbitrary manner. Even today, the ability of teachers to organize and establish an agenda for action to fulfill their objectives is what makes collective bargaining possible. He concluded, "As I grew older and gained new experiences, I realized that I had an obligation to play my role in society. What role one plays, one must realize that it goes a long way in building the character of one's community and society."[20] Shanker regarded achieving this

---

18. Marjorie Murphy, *Blackboard Unions: The AFT and the NEA, 1900-1980*, p. 220.

19. Edward B. Fiske, "Albert Shanker: Where He Stands."

20. Albert Shanker, interview with author, Washington, D.C., May 17, 1993.

objective as a commitment that would influence his actions as president of the AFT.

SHANKER'S MISSION

As soon as he was elected president of the AFT in 1974, replacing David Selden, Shanker pursued objectives clearly defined to meet the needs of teachers and students alike. One of these objectives was to increase the membership of the AFT. He believed that strength lay in numbers. He envisaged that this increase in union membership would result in a powerful and politically charged organization. His presidency has witnessed an increase of 600 per cent in AFT membership, from 125,000 in 1974 to 750,000 in 1990. Timothy Noah concludes that throughout his career, both as a teacher and as president of the UFT and the AFT, "over the years Shanker has demonstrated that he is a total believer in the thinking that teachers must have more than adequate academic training to become professional. He has also advocated his position that teachers should be treated like those in other specified professions, such as doctors and lawyers."[21]

For teachers to demand to be treated as professionals, they must demonstrate a clear knowledge of the subjects they teach, and they must receive the professional training that makes them unique in the delivery of the services they provide. Their impact will be seen in what students do after they leave school. Their interest in and ability to motivate students, to teach values that will make them good citizens in the future, constitute essential components of the profession that teachers must acquire in order to be considered professionals.

Shanker has persistently argued that once teachers have reached this level of professional competency, they must demand nothing less than total recognition from their respective school boards. Recognition comes in the form of better conditions of service including salaries and the freedom to make decision relative to their carrying out their responsibilities.

In arguing that teachers must be accorded more professional status than they have thus far enjoyed, Shanker defines a profession as follows: "A profession describes someone who is an expert in his or her field and who thus requires little or no supervision because he/she has a high degree of decision-making power."[22] Shanker is aware that some policies and practices that school authorities have pursued are an infringement on teachers' rights as a professional class of people.

Shanker believes that the application of these policies, influenced heavily by the politics of power, has made it possible for school authorities to treat teachers with less than the respect typically afforded a professional group of people. Shanker argues that this is why superintendents, principals, members of the school board, and politicians all impose conditions that have made teachers

---

21. Timothy Noah, "The Fiery Unionist as Educational Leader: Albert Shanker," *The New Republic*, June 24, 1993, p. 3.
22. Ibid., p. 4.

servants instead of classroom leaders. He has repeatedly argued that as long as this situation exists, communities must not expect teachers to perform their best under such prohibitive conditions.[23]

A study of conditions affecting teachers beginning in 1952, the year that Shanker first became a teacher, would indicate that his zealous insistence that teachers be recognized as members of a profession is fully justified. In that year his weekly salary was less than that of a factory worker who may or may not have finished the eighth grade. Although the image of public schools and their teachers had improved considerably by this time, teaching was still considered a low-income occupation. In the era of civil rights, when many disenfranchised groups demanded their fair share of the educational pie, Jews, Catholics, Hispanics, and African-Americans found themselves involved in the politics and acquisition of education more than in the past.

The so-called white flight to avoid integration meant that inner-city public schools were rapidly becoming predominantly black or Hispanic. Shanker saw this development as totally negative because, as Henry Barnard and Horace Mann had envisaged during the reform movement of the nineteenth century, the purpose of the civil rights movement was to bring about integration of the schools as a means toward social reform and development. Mann saw racial integration as the balance wheel of the new social order that education was expected to bring about. This is exactly how Shanker has seen it. This is why he has directed his mission toward bringing to an end any manner of discrimination.

When Shanker was first hired as a mathematics teacher in a junior high school in East Harlem, he adopted a strategy of teaching the solving of mathematics problems in ways that compelled the attention of his students. His methodology generated an interest in transferring the process of learning mathematics to seeking solutions to the problems of society. He explained, "If it takes four ounces of poison to kill a person, how many ounces would it take to kill your mother, your father, your sister, and your brother?"[24]

Although this approach to mathematics was an unfortunate example, it was real and was relevant to human conditions. Four ounces of poison may be the same as behaving in ways that are inconsistent with human expectations or adopting attitudes that may damage relationships between people or demonstrating ignorance about human issues. In this approach Shanker hoped to accomplish two objectives: to teach students how to solve mathematics problems and to apply those principles to find solutions to the problems of society.

In 1968 Shanker put his ideas of professional status for teachers to the test in the Ocean Hill-Brownsville dispute. When a community board that was fully controlled by black militants dismissed nineteen white school administrators and teachers, Shanker felt that he had an opportunity to confront a major national problem: racial conflict. In a way that was typical of the black political movement, the board gave a number of reasons for its action. When the city board of education reversed the decision of the community board, the students,

23. Albert Shanker, interview with author, Washington, D.C., May 17, 1993.
24. Timothy Noah, "The Fiery Unionist as Educational Leader: Albert Shanker."

most of them black and Hispanic, boycotted classes. A serious crisis was developing that could have serious implications for education in the city as a whole. Shanker, feeling that the black community was accentuating the problem of race, decided to intervene.

While Shanker attempted to mediate this dispute, a militant African-American teacher recited an anti-Semitic poem over the local radio station. Shanker felt that the poem was directed at him personally and tried to bring the two sides together to resolve the dispute through dialogue. Things came to a head when a white pregnant teacher was hit in the stomach, threatening the life of her unborn baby. Shanker refused to give up efforts to mediate between the administration and the African-American communities, arguing that both groups had so much to lose by division.

While he saw no clear possible solution to the crisis, Shanker simply appealed to both sides to apply common sense. He encouraged dialogue, rather than confrontation; understanding, rather than placing demands; cooperation, rather than competition, reason, rather than rancor; persuasion, rather than threats. He advocated what Jesse Jackson later called the Rainbow Coalition, consisting of dispossessed and disenfranchised people who, he said, needed cooperation and unity to bring about meaningful change.

Through his insistence that solutions to the problem lay in the dialogical process, Shanker succeeded in convincing his political antagonists about the real cause of the dispute in the Ocean Hill-Brownsville district. He argued that the situation was not caused by dispute over whether the school board should be controlled by militant African-Americans under the local control principle recommended by McGeorge Bundy, then president of the Ford Foundation.

Rather, the cause of the dispute was that, as members of a profession, teachers must no longer continue to teach in any school or district in which decisions involving their professional functions and operations are made by groups of people who have no knowledge of the educational issues, but are purely influenced by political considerations. He also succeeded in convincing the parties in the dispute that when political considerations heavily influence educational decisions, the result is and has always been that the educational process suffers. This is why he vehemently argues that teachers must be allowed to make decisions relative to education.

Although New York City introduced a broad decentralization plan in 1969 in accordance with the Bundy proposal, Shanker and his UFT ended up exercising substantial influence over the process. Seeing the critical nature of the need to elevate teachers to a higher professional status, Shanker and his UFT endorsed candidates for the school board who demonstrated a clear knowledge and understanding of educational issues. Voters came forward to cast ballots for candidates who expressed views favorable to the need to accord teachers the kind of professional status Shanker and the UFT had sought. He was clearly a man with a mission. This mission was to place him in the national spotlight.

In 1972, when the UFT seemed to experience considerable difficulties caused by increasing criticism that it was becoming too militant, too aggressive, and too political in seeking improvement in the conditions of service for teachers, Shanker sought help and advice from George Meany (1894-1980), president of

AFL-CIO. In 1993 Shanker recalled the reason for this action and what Meany came to mean to his cause. "When I was somewhat young and trying to organize the teachers of New York City, I met with George Meany and asked him for some help, which at first he did not give because he did not think that I would be able to organize the teachers to fulfill the objectives that the UFT had identified. But after he recognized that I was capable of doing so, he readily gave me the advice I needed."[25] When Meany gave Shanker and his UFT the assistance they required, he suggested a closer association between himself and David Selden, then president of the AFT. Selden at first had doubts about the wisdom of a closer relationship with the AFL-CIO because he, like Shanker, opposed the war in Vietnam and Meany supported it.

In a strategy designed to enhance the position of teachers Shanker accepted a nomination for membership into the executive council of the AFL-CIO. When he was elected, he began to work closely with Meany in seeking improvement in the conditions of workers in general. In doing so Shanker invited criticism that in associating himself so closely with Meany he was reducing teachers to the level of mere laborers. From 1972 to 1976 the relationship between Meany and Shanker actually helped Shanker as Selden's popularity began to decline as a result of his failure to articulate clear views on relevant issues. In May 1993, when asked to give reasons for his seeking a closer association between himself and Meany, Shanker replied:

> Meany was a very generous person. He would acknowledge when he was wrong and he always tried to make up for it. He liked and respected me because of my fights, the battles and strikes that I led. The fact that I went to jail, that I was organizing when it was difficult to organize impressed him about me. He nominated me and I was elected to the executive council of the AFL-CIO. I became a personal friend and I was one of the people he had dinner with at almost every council meeting. Meany was a remarkable person with a wonderful mind and a terrific sense of humor. He was trying to do through the AFL-CIO what we were trying to do through the UFT and the AFT. We found that we had a common mission. These are among the reasons for that association.[26]

When Shanker announced his candidacy for president of the AFT in 1974, Selden knew that his term of office was about to come to an end. When the election was held, Shanker won, and he has held the office ever since, having been reelected every two years. Upon being elected Shanker immediately set out an impressive agenda for action to improve the status of education in the country through the activities of the AFT. Part of this strategy was to help teachers and the public understand that public education has been the backbone of the educational system since the time of Horace Mann and Henry Barnard and that it was in serious trouble because of the conflicting views that politicians had expressed. To bring this message to the people Shanker succeeded in persuading

25. Albert Shanker, interview with author, Washington, D.C. , May 17, 1993.
26. Ibid.

the AFT executive council to run a weekly column that addressed critical issues in education in the *New York Times* at a cost of $100,000.[27]

In this series of articles Shanker called attention to issues he believed were critical to education. Among them was his argument that teachers were not being properly trained to teach the subjects they were assigned to teach. He suggested that the requirements stipulated by the state be tightened to improve quality. He also argued that bilingual education, especially for Hispanic students, had the effect of isolating them from the mainstream of the culture in which they were expected to survive. But by November 1974, soon after he assumed the presidency of the AFT, he saw the wisdom in bilingual education and fully endorsed it.[28]

Shanker's opinion that Hispanic students used bilingual education not to make a transition to functional English, but to communicate among themselves was the basis of President Ronald Reagan's opposition to it. But unlike Reagan, Shanker saw value in it as a means of generating confidence among students whose first language was not English. The critical point that Shanker stressed was that in utilizing bilingual education as an educational tool, the school system and society at large must make sure that those students do not remain isolated from the mainstream of the American socioeconomic system. Also, unlike Reagan, Shanker suggested that bilingual educational programs be designed so as to promote ethnic cooperation and understanding, rather than division and strife.

Shanker also argued that because only a small percentage of qualified college graduates were going into teaching, it was in the best interests of the country to design a means to attract more. Part of the reason for this small percentage was that tuition costs were rising rapidly, and national measures were directed toward other priorities, such as the military. He proposed that the federal government pay for the college costs for those students who demonstrated a willingness to spend at least as many years teaching as they received financial assistance,[29] as has been done in the case of medical students.

In making these proposals Shanker did not think them radical. As his voice for change grew louder a large cross section of the American educational community began to listen to his message. Shanker's popularity grew with the publicity generated by his proposal for the country "to establish mandatory national examination for teachers to test the basic skills and knowledge of the subjects they will teach."[30] He suggested that national proficiency examinations should replace state examinations, which, as Shanker described them, were intended to test minimum competency.

---

27. Timothy Noah, "The Fiery Unionist as Educational Leader: Albert Shanker."

28. See Chapter 6 of this volume for Shanker's support of bilingual education.

29. This is a practice adopted in many Third World countries, and Shanker believed that it could be applied to the United States with success. But one must be realistic in saying that for the United States to adopt methods that Third World countries have adopted to solve social and educational problems would constitute an admission of the failure of its conventional wisdom.

30. Timothy Noah, "The Fiery Unionist Educational Leader: Albert Shanker," p. 4.

Minimum competency was no longer sufficient to meet the needs of students facing a complex world. "Minimum competency tests would be a joke in any other profession,"[31] Shanker concluded. Although Mary Futrell, then president of the NEA, argued that Shanker's proposal would be a violation of the basic right of states to determine who is qualified to teach, the press concluded that the proposal showed that Shanker and the AFT were committed to seeking improvement in education, while the NEA was only interested in protecting its members.

Throughout his term of office as president of the AFT, Shanker has insisted that the United States cannot attract good people to become teachers if it cannot promise them security. This is why he has opposed competency tests for teachers who are already employed and who have demonstrated their ability to teach effectively. What has bothered Shanker about teacher competency is that prospective teachers have consistently performed below the average on the SAT scale. He has also argued that stringent teacher certification requirements have had the effect of discouraging those with a potential and interest for good teachers from entering colleges of education. He has, therefore, recommended a system of selection of teachers based on intellect, talent, interest, thorough academic preparation, and good salaries.

Soon after assuming the office of president of the United States on August 9, 1974, Gerald Ford was faced with two serious problems that he never could resolve. The first was the erosion of public confidence in his administration following his pardon of Richard M. Nixon. The second was his inability to control inflation. Speaking at Ohio University in September, Ford suggested that all segments of the American society ought to take steps to increase productivity as a way of fighting inflation. Shanker was asked what the AFT should do to improve productivity.

Recognizing that teachers with a master's degree and eleven years of service earned an average income of $19,100 per year, Shanker responded: "I think that the teachers productivity can be measured very easily by the number of students they educate. One has to look at computer people, lawyers, doctors to see how productive teachers have been. The fact that we have moved so quickly indicates that if teachers had not done their job the level of that productivity would not have been there."[32] Shanker took the opportunity to stress the need to raise the standard of living for teachers. This is why he went on to add, "Teachers and their families are finding it increasingly difficult to pay for clothing, housing, transportation, health care, and other necessities."[33]

Early in his term of office as president of the AFT, Shanker enlisted the assistance of his mentor and friend George Meany in seeking to accomplish his objectives. In September 1974, in response to that request for assistance, Meany delivered a message to labor in a way that showed his support for Shanker, saying:

---

31. Ibid., p. 3.
32. The AFT, "Shanker Meets the Press," *The American Teacher*, (September 1974): 94.
33. Ibid., p. 95.

Along with the whole nation, American labor breathed a sigh of relief when Richard Nixon left the White House and the ordeal of Watergate came to an end. American labor pledged its support to President Gerald Ford. While Watergate is now behind us, inflation is not. Richard Nixon is behind us, but inflation is not. Spiro Agnew is behind us, but the light money policies and record-high interest rates are still with us. Instead of slashing programs that the people need the Congress must raise more than $30 billion to meet the needs of the people."[34]

These were the issues that Shanker had raised, and Meany appeared to aid him in his mission to initiate fundamental change in American education and labor. Meany joined Shanker in calling for change that restructured the way teachers and boards of education interacted. Soon after assuming the office of president of the AFT in 1974, Shanker explained the agenda he held: "In 1960 the AFT was a tiny organization of 50,000 members, a small dedicated group which had great vision. Within this short period of time, we have brought collective bargaining and militancy to American teachers against the opposition of school boards. We have grown to 414,000 members and we will soon cross the half a million mark."[35]

As Shanker looked ahead, he quickly realized that he would have to wield the growing political influence of the AFT to accomplish his objectives. Behind the scenes he began to work toward increasing the membership of the AFT in all fifty states. He hoped to accomplish this by strengthening local union chapters. The numbers were impressive, and the support from labor was at an all-time high. For the first time in its history the AFT was being recognized as a major national power in education, labor, and politics alike. Teachers across the country were made to believe that they would have influence not only in making the AFT what it should be, but also in shaping social policies. Shanker concluded, "Ours is the most powerful voice for better education because it is the voice not only of teachers, but also of the 15 million members of unions who want good education for their children."[36]

Shanker also realized that the success of his mission would be a culmination of a long and arduous struggle in which one of his most difficult problems was to convince teachers themselves of the powerful role that they could play in shaping their own profession. He knew that while they had come a long way, there was still a long way to go. As in the past their future success would depend on the objectives they outlined and the strategies they designed to fulfill them. Shanker knew that to be secure in his position, he needed to establish a national base with widespread political connections.

This is why, in September 1974, he appeared before the U.S. House Education and Labor Committee to advocate enforcement of hiring policies in higher education. Shanker took the opportunity to take his mission to new

---

34. George Meany, "For a People's Congress: Now More than Ever," in *The American Teacher* (September 1974): 24.

35. Albert Shanker, "From the President," *The American Teacher* (September 1974): 94.

36. Ibid., p. 96.

heights in urging the adoption of affirmative action to enhance educational opportunity for all students. He suggested an approach that had not been thought of before, saying, "Our view of what an affirmative action program should be is to start with open admission, free tuition, interest-free loans, and grant money which will not only open the doors of educational opportunity to minority students, but would also encourage their pursuit of professional careers."[37]

In arguing in support of affirmative action, Shanker took the position that any significant increase in minority hiring on faculties must start with a significant increase in the pool of available personnel. He knew that four years earlier, in 1970, approximately 10.6 percent of all undergraduate admissions were African-Americans, Native Americans, and Hispanics combined. These groups collectively constituted 16.8 percent of the U.S. population. He also knew that of the bachelor's degrees awarded in 1970, 5.2 percent were awarded to African-American students, 1.2 percent to Hispanic students, and 1.0 percent to Native American students.

From this information Shanker reached the conclusion that "what the enrollment figures show is that in selecting faculty, one is not drawing candidates from the population at large, but from a significantly smaller pool of qualified candidates. The only way to increase minority educational and employment opportunity in higher education is to increase the number of qualified applicants, and at the same time, increase the available positions."[38]

On October 9, 1974, two months to the day after President Nixon had resigned, President Ford indicated at a press conference that he favored tax credits for parents who sent their children to private and parochial schools[39] and that he was satisfied with the role his administration was playing in supporting education in general. This position gave Shanker an opportunity to advance his mission further as he responded, "At a time when public education is being starved while public funding remains the same as inflation eats away the dollars, it is an outrage that the President of the United States is discussing ways of diverting public dollars to private and religious schools. The AFT will organize a nation-wide campaign against the diversion of funds which should go to the public schools."[40]

Shanker's displeasure with Ford's position was accentuated by the fact that by September 1976, Ford had vetoed fifty-five bills that the Congress had passed to fight inflation and to improve the economy and education.[41] Shanker was

---

37. "Shanker Urges Affirmative Action Through Better Training and More Jobs," *The American Teacher* (October 1974): 22.

38. Ibid., p. 23.

39. Shanker has persistently expressed strong opposition to this thinking. The two Republican presidents who served after Ford, Ronald Reagan and George Bush, took the same position as Ford. But Democratic presidents Jimmy Carter and Bill Clinton took the same position as Shanker: that tax credits and and loans free-interest for education must be directed only toward students in public schools, the backbone of the American educational system.

40. Albert Shanker, "Response to President Gerald Ford's Statement on Education of October 9, 1974," *The American Teacher*, (October 1974): 20.

41. For details, see *The American Teacher* (September 1976): B-3.

particularly disappointed with Ford's veto of H.R. 4222: the School Lunch Bill, passed by the Congress on October 31, 1975. The bill would have provided funding for school breakfast programs for children of poor and low-income families and for children in institutions such as orphanages and homes for the handicapped. He argued that Ford exercised the veto because he lacked the basic understanding of the importance of proper nutrition to educational success. From that point on he decided to campaign against Ford, supporting, instead, Jimmy Carter's candidacy for president. When Carter was elected in 1976, Shanker felt that there was real hope for a new beginning. His steadfastness had yielded tangible results.

In deciding to campaign against Ford and in favor of Carter, Shanker and the AFT concluded that Ford's veto record and his budget had the effect of eliminating $4.7 billion from financing resources that were needed to support various educational programs that the Congress had passed. They also felt that they had a mission to reverse trends that they saw as being initiated by an administration that was handicapped by a major scandal and was totally out of touch with the educational needs of the country. Ford was a politically marked man because "in the eyes of many, like the labor movement and the teaching profession, these crises have continued to kill the national spirit."[42]

In September 1976 Shanker was at his best when he submitted a report proposing that all teachers, not just members of the AFT, should be actively involved in both international and national politics. He began the report by saying, "For the past six years the American Federation of Teachers has been sounding an alarm. We have warned America's teachers that things are about to change for the worse."[43] In the report he identified four issues he believed to be crucial to education. The first was the large-scale teacher unemployment due to the declining birth rate, which was accentuated by the declining economy as a result of high inflation. Shanker's concern was that the country was not aware of the extent of this problem. The second critical issue was the large-scale layoffs of teachers because of local budget cuts caused by a rising trade deficit and skyrocketing interest rates. This placed serious financial constraints that local boards of education would not be able to sustain.

The third was the continuing labor unrest, which reduced the level of productivity. This was mainly caused by the bad fiscal and economic policies of the Nixon and Ford administrations. Shanker concluded that as long as Ford remained in office, public confidence in the future would continue to decline, resulting in serious national problems. The fourth critical issue was the legal setbacks caused by federal court decisions that stemmed from suits filed by members of militant anti-teacher organizations and anti-public employee groups. Shanker concluded, "Unfortunately, our warnings turned out to be accurate. It would be hard to recall a year which was as bad for teachers as this

---

42. "The Big Question for 1976: More Vetoes or a Pro-education President," (editorial) *The American Teacher* (April 1976): 15.

43. Albert Shanker, "Teachers in Politics: The American Heritage, A Report," September 1976, AFT Files, Washington, D.C. See also *The American Teacher* (September 1976): 98.

year. Jail sentences, fines, layoffs, and reduced benefits were common experiences for teachers."[44]

Shanker then directed his report to a discussion of the negative attitudes of the federal courts toward teachers. He cited the *Hortonville* case, upholding the right of the board of education to dismiss striking teachers without giving them an opportunity to negotiate within the spirit of collective bargaining and without observing due process procedures. He also cited the *National League of Cities* case, in which the Supreme Court ruled 5-4 that the minimum wage and maximum hours provisions of the Fair Labor Standards Act would not be applied to teachers and all other non-federal public employees. The effect of these decisions, according to Shanker, was to weaken teacher organizations and strengthen boards of education in the application of the principle of collective bargaining, which he considered central for the improvement of teachers' working conditions.

In spite of these difficulties Shanker was not willing to concede defeat or to abandon his efforts. He considered them part of the trials and tribulations he must endure in order to achieve what he believed was needed. This is why he went on to argue, "We can press the issue by demanding change in programs previously attached to federal legislation and requiring the states to bargain collectively with their employees."[45]

What one sees in all this is that even with the problems Shanker and the AFT were determined to remedy, they would not lose sight of the objectives they were promoting, among them to raise the status of the teaching profession to the level of other professions. Shanker and the AFT decided to work closely with such groups as the American Association of School Administrators, the National Parental-Teacher Association, the American Association of Colleges for Teacher Education, the National Association of State Boards of Education, and the Council of Chief State School Officers seek solutions to the problems that teachers were facing in achieving the agenda that they had set for themselves.

Among the items included on that agenda were strategies that would strengthen the principle of collective bargaining in order to improve conditions under which teachers worked, including salary and benefits. Shanker proposed a logical formula for achieving this goal, saying, "If the federal government assumes the responsibility of welfare costs and health security, billions of dollars will be free at the state and local level for schools and other necessary services."[46]

These were not the ideas of a leader who was about to give up his vision. To accomplish it, Shanker suggested three strategies. The first was to increase membership of the AFT because he argued that its strength lay in numbers. The second was to maintain the AFT's affiliation with the AFL-CIO. The third was to increase political involvement and activity. To do this he initiated a training program to enable teachers to become more knowledgeable about the relationships that existed between education and politics. The enthusiasm with

---

44. Ibid.
45. Ibid.
46. Ibid.

which teachers across the country responded to his leadership provided both the encouragement and the power he needed to continue forth.

Having been convinced that the national morale was in a state of perpetual decline under the Ford administration, Shanker called for members of the AFT to vote for Jimmy Carter and Walter Mondale. In October 1976, at the height of his campaign, candidate Carter was asked to explain what his administration would do to help unemployed teachers. Carter gave an answer that pleased Shanker and the AFT as he said:

> I believe that our long-range goal should be to ensure that no deserving student is denied access to post-secondary education because of financial need. We should try to increase allotment of teachers at the first three levels of school and the number of extra remedial teachers. We should add a thousand new special education teachers each year for children with learning difficulties. We should increase the number of libraries and student counselors. We should reduce the pupil-teacher ratio."[47]

When Carter concluded that these measures would assist teachers who were unemployed, Shanker succeeded in persuading teachers to vote for the Carter-Mondale ticket that November. Carter also indicated that if elected he would give serious consideration to the creation of U.S. Department of Education.

When Carter assumed the office of President of the United States in January 1977, he brought with him a group of impressive individuals very different from those who served in the Nixon and Ford administrations. These included Cyrus R. Vance,[48] secretary of state, who had considerable experience in foreign affairs. Ray Marshall, a professor of economics at the University of Texas, served as secretary of labor. Marshall told the Senate Labor Committee during his confirmation hearing that his priority was to end unemployment. Juanita Morris Kreps, vice-president of Duke University, became secretary of commerce. Patricia Roberts Harris, a successful lawyer in Washington. D.C., became secretary for Housing and Urban Development.

Joseph A. Califano, a successful lawyer in New York, was appointed secretary of health, education, and welfare. Califano, a Kennedy and Johnson Democrat, had served as a top aide to President Johnson from 1965 to 1969. He and Shanker had mutual admiration for one another. Andrew Young, a civil rights activist and civic leader in Atlanta, was named ambassador to the United Nations. Shanker and the AFT were so pleased with Carter's cabinet

---

47. *The AFT,* "Carter on Education,"*The American Teacher* (October 1976): B-1.

48. Vance, an unassuming and knowledgeable man whom the author was privileged to correspond with and to meet with over U.S. policy in southern Africa, had carried out peace missions in various parts of the world on behalf of the U.S. government. In 1993 he and Lord David Owen of Britain successfully laid the basis for the peace dialogue that finally resulted in signing ceremonies in Washington, D.C., between the Palestine Liberation Organization (PLO) and Israel in September 1993.

appointments that they decided to laud them by publishing them in *The American Teacher*.[49]

While the advent of the Carter administration seemed to indicate the return of national pride and optimism, Shanker and the AFT did not allow complacence to water down their agenda. The federal courts were run by individuals who had been appointed during the Nixon and Ford administrations. They were individuals who subscribed to the central tenet of the political philosophy of the Republican party that government is best when it governs least and it should not interfere in most issues, even those that have national significance.

To Shanker and the AFT this philosophy was synonymous with federal abandonment of its responsibility to govern. With a friendly administration now in office Shanker did his best to consolidate the gains he had made. In February 1977, during the Presidential Classroom for Young Americans, a week-long seminar initiated in Washington, D.C. by Carter for 2,000 high school students selected from schools across the country, Shanker had a unique opportunity to explain what his evolving vision was all about.

During the seminar one student, admitting that his exposure to organized labor had been mainly through the press in his home state of Louisiana, which had recently passed a right-to-work law, asked Shanker, "Don't you think that denying a man his right to work unless he joins a union is a violation of his Fourteenth Amendment rights?"[50] From the spontaneous approval of the group, Shanker knew that the issue of labor unions was not fully understood. He took the opportunity to set the minds of the students straight, saying, "I can see that a lot of people have been mis-educated. No one is denied the right to work because he does not belong to a union. Unions make it possible to improve conditions of work and to ensure collective bargaining so that employers do not dictate those conditions to the workers. If a union does not do a good job it can be voted out. Once a contract is negotiated it is taken back to the workers for a vote on whether they wish to accept it or not. When a contract is ratified, it covers everyone including those who do not belong to unions."[51]

To Shanker a question posed about George Meany was as amusing as it was disturbing. One student who thought that Meany lived in the White House wanted to know why it was that Meany was the only one elected permanently to the White House. She concluded that other people in the federal government came and went, but Meany had been there many years.[52] The question was amusing because Shanker felt that the student ought to know that Meany was not elected to the White House. If this was the kind of information high school students had about national events and civics, then the educational system must

49. For details see *The American Teacher* (February 1977): 15.

50. The AFT, "Shanker on Student Seminar,"*The American Teacher* (March 1977): 7.

51. Ibid.

52. Indeed, Meany was elected president of the AFL-CIO in 1955 and remained in office until his death in 1980. But it must be remembered that other labor leaders such as Sidney Hillman and Walter Reuther also stayed in office a long time. It was a practice labor organizations put in place to ensure continuity of leadership when a leader was good.

be made to assume new responsibilities in educating students properly. The question was disturbing in that this faulty information was a common experience among many Americans, not just students.

Nevertheless, Shanker took the opportunity to correct the misunderstanding, saying with considerable intensity, "George Meany is not in the White House. He lives across the park and looks down on it. Meany faces election every two years. Some 250 affiliated unions have the opportunity to vote him out if they think he is not doing a good job representing their interest. Since 1955 Meany has done a good job. That is why he has been reelected many times."[53]

In 1977 Shanker was surprised to receive widespread support for an awareness that he had seeded as president of the UFT and that had stayed with him throughout the years as part of his overall mission. This was the national recognition that drugs, violence, and crime in schools had become three of the most serious problems the country was facing. On February 25 of that year the U.S. Senate Subcommittee on Juvenile Delinquency chaired by Senator Birch Bayh, an Indiana Democrat, reported that there was a disturbing trend of increasing violence and crime in the nation's schools. This threatened to make the primary object of public schools "no longer education but preservation."[54]

Entitled *The Challenge for the Third Century: Education in a Safe Environment*, the report concluded that on a national scale, the country had spent $600 million each of the past several years on repairs caused by vandalism and crime. "This staggering waste of scarce resources needed in education is more money than what was spent on text books in 1972 and is enough to hire 50,000 additional teachers without raising taxes by one penny."[55] Because Shanker and the AFT considered the report critical to their crusade, they decided to feature it in *The American Teacher* to highlight some of its conclusions.

Among these conclusions were the following: "Nearly 70,000 serious physical assaults were committed against teachers in 1975 alone; the number of these assaults had increased by 58 percent from 1970 to 1974; during the same period sex offenses increased by 62 percent; drug-related crimes went up by 81 percent and robberies escalated by 117 percent. Bayh concluded, "It is time to stop pointing accusatory fingers at our education system as being solely responsible for these problems. Our schools are only one facet of a society that has seen juvenile crime increase by 245 percent over thirteen years."[56] Bayh then introduced in the Senate the Juvenile Delinquency in the Schools Bill to combat the problem. Shanker was pleased to see that the nation had at last recognized the problem that he had addressed in 1973.

In 1981, when Shanker thought that the country fully understood the nature and extent of the problems it was facing, a new administration came to Washington, D.C. President Ronald Reagan, a conservative Republican who was once a Democrat, tried to reverse the progressive social engineering that had been

---

53. *The AFT,* "Shanker on Meany,"*The American Teacher* (March 1977): 7.

54. U.S. Senate, *The Challenge in the Third Century: Education in a Safe Environment* (Birch Bayh, chairman) (Washington, D.C. U.S. Government Printing Office, 1977).

55. Ibid.

56. Ibid.

attempted during the Carter years. In his annual report for 1980-81 Shanker decried what he saw as the erosion of the progress that had been made during the past four years. He went on to say, "We now have a president who proposes to cut back one-fourth of the federal education budget and a Congress that appears to go along.[57] We face a resurrected scheme to provide federal tax credits of up to $500 per year for the costs of private school tuition for each child in a family. Looking back over the past year we see almost unprecedented threats to education and other public services."[58]

The election of George Bush as President of the United States in 1988 sent a further signal to Shanker that he needed to redefine the components of his vision and its parameters to suit the demands of new conditions. When Bush published in 1991 his views of and policy on education in *America 2000: An Educational Strategy,* Shanker reacted, "The Bush administration has kept secret its infatuation with giving public funds to private schools as the key to educational reform. What is surprising is just how far the administration is willing to go to undermine America's common school tradition in the name of private school choice. This choice would dilute the effectiveness of Chapter 1 and even destroy it."[59]

The election of Bill Clinton in 1992 was an event of hope for Shanker. In 1993 he explained the reason for his hope, saying, "President Bill Clinton and his wife Hillary[60] know more about education than anybody who has arrived at the White House. They have read more books, they have brought people more knowledgeable about education than most administrations. They brought more education to the state of Arkansas."[61] However, on July 9, 1993, Shanker expressed disappointment with the results of a study conducted by the AFT, showing how much more pay the following countries paid their teachers than the United States:

---

57. In what has become known as the Reagan revolution, many Democrats, mostly from the South, became disillusioned with the Carter program and voted with Reagan on almost all issues. However, this author thinks that in spite of his apparent popularity, Reagan did not accomplish much that the nation can point to as a legacy of the future. His preoccupation with control of the Iran-Contra scandal limited the effectiveness of his administration and programs.

58. Albert Shanker, "Annual Report of the AFT: The State of the Union," 1981, AFT Files, Washington, D.C.

59. Albert Shanker, "Bush's 2000 Plan: A Feast for Private Schools," *The American Teacher* (November 1991): 9.

60. See a tribute to Hillary Clinton entitled "Ascent of a Woman: Hillary Rodham Clinton," *Time* , May 10, 1993. On September 22, 1993, Mrs. Clinton received a standing ovation during a speech delivered by her husband on health reform proposals, which she had worked so hard to formulate over the previous several months.

61. Albert Shanker, interview with author, Washington, D. C., May 17, 1993.

Primary Teachers		Pay for High School Teachers	
Country	**Pay More than the U.S.**	**Country**	**Pay**
Japan	$5,000	Germany	$43,000
Canada	$10,000	Japan	$45,000
Switzerland	$18,000	Canada	$47,000
		United States	$38,000

Source: The AFT, "Study of Teachers' Pay: The United States Compared with Other Countries," July 9, 1993. AFT Files, Washington, D.C.

From these figures Shanker concluded that "American education often does not measure up when compared with our international competitors."[62]

SUMMARY AND CONCLUSION

The discussion in this chapter leads to two conclusions. The first is that from the moment he was able to comprehend his world to the time that he assumed the leadership of the AFT, Albert Shanker, the man, could not be separated from Albert Shanker, the professional. The very nature of the conditions that produced him invariably led to the conditions that would later thrust him into a position of national prominence.

It is clear that Shanker transformed the hardships of the Great Depression into the elements of his union endeavor. He also felt compelled to make the national conscience aware of the fate of people belonging to a profession that he loved and led. The result was the emergence of a national leader whose knowledge of the past helped to define the direction the future was to take.

The second deduction is that in assuming the leadership of the AFT in 1974, Shanker never compromised the principles he identified in 1959 when he became a full-time official of the teachers' union in New York City. He strived to elevate the status of teachers to one of respectability. He has worked hard to extend the principle of collective bargaining. He sought the improvement of working conditions for teachers. He has labored to have teachers participate in politics in more meaningful ways than they had in the past. These activities constituted the core of his vision and defined the focus of his energies. With the preceding historical context as a backdrop, Chapter 5 presents the philosophies of Albert Shanker, father, husband, teacher, and union leader.

---

62. The AFT, "Study of Teachers' Pay: The United States Compared with Other Countries," July 9, 1993, AFT Files, Washington, D.C.

Portrait of Albert Shanker, 1968. "As I grew older I realized that I had an obligation to play my role in society." Courtesy of the Archives of Labor and Urban Affairs, Wayne State University.

Albert Shanker, president of the UFT, at a press conference in 1968. "Professional describes someone who is an expert in his or her field." Courtesy of the Archives of Labor and Urban Affairs, Wayne State University.

Robert Kennedy (left) and Albert Shanker, 1968. "We are looking for a contract, not a strike. Government must act like government." Courtesy of the Archives of Labor and Urban Affairs, Wayne State University.

The AFT president Carl Megel (center) flanked by supporters during a trip to Arizona, March 17, 1957. "Many people remembered Carl Megel as the founder and leader of their locals." Courtesy of the Archives of Labor and Urban Affairs, Wayne State University.

Albert Shanker (center) seated with two other delegates to the New York State AFL-CIO convention, 1969. "I was elected to AFL-CIO council executive before I was elected president of the AFT." Courtesy of the Archives of Labor and Urban Affairs, Wayne State University.

Albert Shanker and Senator Jacob Javitz, 1975. From left to right: Senator Jacob Javitz (R-N.Y.), Charles Cogen, Albert Shanker. "Politics was part of the air Shanker's parents breathed." Courtesy of the Archives of Labor and Urban Affairs, Wayne State University.

Albert Shanker (center) at the AFL-CIO convention, September 1970. From left to right: Jack Rubenstein, Albert Shanker, David Siegel. "Ours is the voice not only of teachers but also of 15 million members of unions who want good education for their children." Courtesy of the Archives of Labor and Urban Affairs, Wayne State University.

David Selden, president of the AFT, with Carole Graves, president of the AFT Local 48, Newark, New Jersey, after his release from jail, February 1970. "Jail sentences, fines, lay-offs, and reduced benefits were common." Courtesy of the Archives of Labor and Urban Affairs, Wayne State University.

Albert Shanker speaking to delegates to the UFT conference, 1968. "Our long-range goal should be to insure that no deserving student is denied access to education because of financial need." Courtesy of the Archives of Labor and Urban Affairs, Wayne State University.

Hubert Horatio Humphrey (center) meeting with members of the Central Labor Council, 1968. Albert Shanker is far right. "Without federal guidance any educational efforts remain fragmented." Courtesy of the Archives of Labor and Urban Affairs, Wayne State University.

Albert Shanker speaking with participants at a meeting of the UFT, June, 1968. "Our aim is to create for effective and more humane schools." Courtesy of the Archives of Labor and Urban Affairs, Wayne State University.

Albert Shanker with UFT officials leaving the New York State Courthouse in Manhattan, October 1975. From left to right: Jeannette DiLorenzo, George Altomare, Albert Shanker, Morris Shapiro, Sidney Harris. "Unless national effort is perceived as federal responsibility, there is little likelihood that a comprehensive approach can be developed to solve problems." Courtesy of the Archives of Labor and Urban Affairs, Wayne State University.

Albert Shanker (right) being interviewed during a demonstration in support of striking teachers in Newark, New Jersey, December 1971. "The problems are great, but we are stronger than we have ever been." Courtesy of the Archives of Labor and Urban Affairs, Wayne State University.

Albert Shanker addressing a meeting, 1968. "Child development programs, free from detractors, should be available to all children." Courtesy of the Archives of Labor and Urban
Affairs, Wayne State University.

Albert Shanker with participants in a strategy meeting, 1972. "The task of bringing about freedom of any dimension of education is a national responsibility." Courtesy of the Archives of Labor and Urban Affairs, Wayne State University.

Mrs. Eve Sacks, Secretary to the AFT since 1967. "Mr. Shanker has had a profound impact on American education and society in ways few people have done."
Photo by the author, May 1993.

Albert Shanker and Greg Humphreies, executive associate secretary-treasurer of the AFT, studying problems of the AFT in Washington, D.C. 1993. "Seeking solutions to problems of society determines national character." Photo by the author.

Albert Shanker and the author, 1993. "We believe that putting the responsibility in the schools is the best way to create a program that works." Photo by the author.

Shanker's Philosophy:
The Nature of Freedom

We believe that putting the responsibility in the schools as an act of recognizing academic freedom is the best way to create an educational program that can grow.

Albert Shanker, 1975

The balance between unity and diversity is the central principle of freedom of all people because it is the strength of the American society.

Albert Shanker, 1993

THE BASIS OF SHANKER'S PHILOSOPHY

Albert Shanker's involvement in major national labor organizations has enabled him to perceive the character of society in a way that has made him a unique national leader. Since 1959 Shanker has consistently demonstrated a keen mind; his cognitive prowess has effectively shown how achievement spawned by new ideas can bring needed change to institutions of public instruction. Politicians, civic leaders, and religious leaders have all come to recognize Shanker as a prominent and shrewd national leader who "helps shape national, state, and local educational policy through his work, ideas and philosophy."[1] Shanker's philosophy is the subject of this chapter. In discussing this dimension of Shanker the chapter presents elements of his philosophy of education and society to suggest how both have helped shape the U.S. educational system and its influence on American society.

Shanker's role in guiding the character of national teachers' labor unions of which he is a member has placed him in a pivotal position of influence. An

---

1. The AFT, "Albert Shanker, President of the American Federation of Teachers," October 1990, AFT Files, Washington, D.C.

AFT memorandum indicated in October 1990, that "Shanker's influence goes beyond New York. He has taken the lead in the educational reform movement by recognizing trends, pinpointing shortcomings, and proposing bold solutions to the complex issues facing American public schools and society. Shanker's speeches are crystal balls which accurately predict and diagnose the trend for specific educational reform initiatives."[2]

The fact that the AFT membership grew from 375,000 in 1974 to 750,000 in 1990, the fact that he sits on the National Board for Professional Teaching Standards, the fact that he first proposed such a board during a speech delivered to the National Press Club in 1985, and the fact that he is one of the seventy-five members of the National Academy of Education all would seem to indicate that Shanker's ability to contribute to the development of the country has been well recognized on a national scale.

Shanker's influence in national developments is not the only level at which he has been recognized. He is equally a major figure in international events. That he is a member of a number of international organizations serves to underscore his involvement as the president of the International Federation of Free Teachers Union, which has over seven million members in democratic countries spread all over the world. He has also been actively involved in organizations dedicated to the promotion of human understanding and civil rights, including the Committee for the Defense of Soviet Political Prisoners.[3] This interaction and exposure have enabled Shanker to formulate his system of beliefs and values. Because Shanker is an educator, his philosophy addresses the relationships that he believes must exist between education and the society it serves.

SHANKER'S PHILOSOPHY OF EDUCATION

From his early days as a junior high school mathematics teacher up to the present, Shanker has held certain fundamental philosophical tenets about both education and society. One of these positions is that the school must be a place to promote the human mind through the process of inquiry, not a place to practice ideological indoctrination. Once the school succeeds in operating by this philosophy, it provides both the teachers and their students an opportunity to be their very best. Shanker believes that because the human being is a product of his or her milieu, society has a responsibility to provide a healthy and secure environment so that learning can take place. This is why Shanker argues, "You cannot think of kids as products who are taken from one station to another on the assembly line."[4]

Shanker also argues that because students are fully human, society must ensure their basic needs such as comfort, love, support, and safety. Whatever society does with respect to the comfort of students is bound to have an impact on them. Shanker seems to share the view expressed by Abraham Maslow

---

2. Ibid.
3. Ibid.
4. Ibid.

(1908-1970) that before the school attempts to educate a student, society must first provide for his or her biological needs and safety needs.

Once this objective is accomplished, then the student's social growth needs, both personal and intellectual, can and must be met in order for formal education to effectively occur. In his study *Motivation and Personality*, Maslow suggests that society must recognize the variation and intensity of growth needs among students so as to properly meet them.[5] Like Maslow, Shanker believes that a fundamental law in the behavioral sciences, one on which educational programs and the learning process must be based, is the concept of individuality.

Shanker further believes that individuality is fundamental to the growth of society because it is essential for the growth of the individual. It provides a climate of rejuvenation, which promotes creativity; it procreates new ideas. Shanker believes that for the student to develop these basic human qualities, society has an absolute responsibility to provide the conditions necessary for their development. These conditions are essential for a society to allow students to see themselves in relationship to the needs of that social network.

But only when students are taught problem-solving skills can they learn to seek solutions to problems endemic to their place and time on this planet. If society endeavors to make this relationship the focus of education, then it has fully understood its responsibility to the symbiosis between students and their milieu. The reason why this relationship is not fully understood is that school governance is primarily motivated by political interests, not by the educational needs of students. As long as this situation remains, both society and education will deteriorate.

Shanker has also argued that the educational system in the United States needs basic reform because "we have a system that is failing because so many kids are not getting anything out of it. Of all the children who remain in schools until they graduate from high school, only 20 percent can write an adequate letter that requires persuasive arguments. What I would like to see is a totally different institution, an institution in which teaching is not lecturing. The teachers' job is not to talk to kids, but to connect them with a learning experience together to solve problems."[6] There can be no doubt that Shanker is a disciple of John Dewey in this line of thinking. His philosophy of education mirrors Dewey's philosophy of progressive education which emphasized the importance of utilizing a student's experience in building an education that has a real and practical application to human conditions.

From this perspective Shanker recognizes the part that teachers have played in the problems education has been facing. He argues, "We are trying to hire 2.2 million teachers. Unless we are going to pay top dollar to 2.2 million people, we are not going to be able to attract and retain our fair share of talent and

---

5. Abraham Maslow, *Motivation and Personality* (New York: Harper and Row, 1970), p. 6.

6. The AFT, "Albert Shanker, President of the American Federation of Teachers" *The American Teacher* (October 1990) 58: B-3.

officials will continue to lower standards and hire unqualified people just to fill the classrooms."[7]

Shanker has further stressed that it is not the quantity of teachers that would make a real difference in the quality of education in the country, but the quality of those who are attracted to a career in the classroom. He also argues that just as it is important to recognize the physical needs of students in the way Abraham Maslow explained it, it is equally important to recognize the human needs of the individuals society hires to teach its youth. If a relationship is broken between recognizing the needs of students and recognizing those of teachers, then an educational system becomes dysfunctional with severe consequences for all involved.[8]

Shanker suggests that to improve this Catch-22 situation, the public must take an active interest in seeking ways of promoting and preserving the quality of teachers. He believes that the the production process in schools is so ineffective that one has to come to the conclusion that there is something inherently wrong with this model. He states, "It is very similar to the automobile situation in which it is not the worker or just the tail fin or the stereo set or some other minor thing that was wrong, it was the system itself that was wrong."[9]

Shanker elaborates on this aspect of his philosophy by saying that most people in public education do not see the handwriting on the wall. He believes that public schools now function like the traditional automobile factory. They operate on the basis of the assembly line mentality, with each worker responsible for a specific and detached aspect of the automobile, without having any knowledge of the other parts that make up the product they spend one-third of their life working on.

To change the school system so that the education it provides serves the needs of students, the United States must change the psychology of the assembly line production it clings to. The problem that the country faces in its approach to education is that it cannot do without the public school system because public schools have been the backbone of the educational system since the days before the Industrial Revolution of the nineteenth century.

The thinking by former Presidents Ronald Reagan and George Bush to divert public funds toward private education takes away from the efforts that must be directed at finding ways to improve what once served this country well. Shanker has persistently argued that a key factor in not effectively responding to the crisis in public education is that the local school board is obsessed with activities designed to ensure maximum political benefits for its members.

Shanker, therefore, argues that the strategy to restore quality instruction in public schools must include efforts to restore the caliber of both teachers and methodology. The first can be accomplished by improving the conditions under which teachers are employed and serve. These conditions must include salaries,

---

7. Ibid., p. 4.
8. Ibid., p. 3.
9. Ibid., p. 4.

benefits, and freedom to make site-based decisions without first seeking and waiting on the approval of the politically sensitive school administration.

The second can be accomplished by making education relevant to the needs of students as a condition for teaching them to understand the needs of society. If this functional relationship is established, it makes it possible to see the symbiotic relationship of education from the perspective of its importance to both students and society. If this relationship is made a fundamental operative principle of the educational process, then it is quite possible to define, seek, and provide efficacious education in a practical manner.

In expressing his philosophy Shanker seems to accept John Dewey's position as it relates to student experience and the educational process. Dewey views education as a scientific method by which one studies the world of reality, gathers data, understands value systems, and comprehends natural phenomena so that he or she can understand conditions of human existence and self. This basic approach requires the ability to utilize cumulative experiences as a true basis for knowledge. Dewey calls this education. The fundamental question that Dewey poses is: How should the young become acquainted with the past in such a way that the acquaintance becomes a potent agent of appreciation of the living present?[10]

Shanker sees the answer to the question in a comparative setting. Arguing that since 1945 the Japanese have utilized Dewey's model to improve the quality of their education by making it relevant to the needs of both students and their society, Shanker says, "The Japanese are very good at this approach to education. They have produced an educational system which has taken the education of the Samurai and applied John Dewey's philosophy to it by way of Douglas MacArthur.[11] This is the reason why Japan has a system of education that gives the masses what used to be given to a very small number of people."[12]

Like Dewey, Shanker believes that meaningful education is based on experience. Also, like Dewey, he believes that not all experience leads to education because "experience is mis-educative if it has the effect of arresting or distorting the growth of further experience."[13] Shanker concludes that the school and society must work together in creating an environment that provides maximum and diverse educative experiences for all students.

However, Shanker sees a major problem in efforts to forge a new partnership between the school and society to improve education. The disintegration of the nuclear family has created far-reaching problems whose impact on education and society has yet to be fully discerned. The phenomenon of single-parent families has compounded not only socioeconomic problems, but

---

10. John Dewey, *Experience and Education* (New York: Macmillan Publishing Company, 1938), p. 23.

11. Douglas MacArthur (1880-1964), supreme commander of U.S. forces during the Second World War, arranged the surrender of Japan on August 14, 1945. He served as military governor of Japan from 1945 to 1952. During that time Japan adopted some features of American education.

12. The AFT, "Albert Shanker, President of the American Federation of Teachers," *The American Teacher* (October 1990): 58: B-3.

13. John Dewey, *Experience and Education*, p. 25.

also academic ones. Equally serious is the problem of working parents. Both of these phenomena do not always lend themselves to the type of home environment that gives students a foundation conducive to their educational development. Increasingly students are left home alone, and some parents show no interest in their schooling. As a result, their school work often suffers, and the school is blamed for not motivating students to learn.

Shanker is at his best in presenting components of his philosophy when he discusses what he considers a lack of commitment by the federal government to quality education. He has been quite candid in discussing what he regards as a lack of sound policy and direction on the great part of former President Gerald Ford vetoing the education legislation that Congress passed while he was in office. Expressing unhappiness about Ford's action, Shanker could no longer restrain himself in 1976, saying, "As far as Mr. Ford is concerned he has also told us of his plan for the future because under the budget for the first time he is required to make projections on spending for the next five years. Between now and five years from now he proposes to increase average federal spending by $120 billion. How much of that amount will go toward education is not specified. This shows that out of the $120 billion he could not find a dime for the school children of this country. If he did he could have said so. Where does this lead this country?"[14]

The point that Shanker wanted everyone, including the federal government, to understand is that any government that shows a lack of interest or foresight in the ongoing development of education for its own people will pay the ultimate price. As president of the United States from 1913 to 1921, Woodrow Wilson (1856-1924) fully recognized this truth, saying, "Without popular education no government which rests on popular action can long endure."[15] Shanker wanted Ford to understand that without an effective education plan built into national policy, the educational process has little meaning to either the students or the nation itself. He concluded that no matter how hard local authorities tried, if they did not have support and encouragement at the federal level, those efforts would yield limited and fragmented results. This awareness constitutes a fundamental principle of democracy.

This is the background from which Shanker understood Wilson to suggest that democracy is always in danger when the national government does not encourage the development of education. About this belief Shanker added, "We have found now for eight years that policies of high interest and tight credit, and the highest unemployment since the Great Depression do not remain problems isolated in private business, but sooner or later, if unattended, it strikes at the public schools. Now we must do something about it, and 1976 is the year."[16]

Shanker wanted it known that the union he led was not going to stand by and watch education suffer under the pen of a president who failed to demonstrate

14. The AFT, "Albert Shanker, President of the American Federation of Teachers."

15. William van Til, *Education: The Beginning* (Boston: Houghton Mifflin Company, 1974), p. 422.

16. Albert Shanker, "Ford's Educational Policy," *The American Teacher* (September 1976) 6:B-2.

an understanding of the need to have a vision of the future by his failure to articulate a clear policy on education. Although in this regard Shanker appears to address the inherent political implications of education, rather than philosophical concepts, he is quite consistent in discussing essential elements of his philosophy on education.

Shanker is equally at his best when he presents his beliefs about early childhood education. On December 17, 1974, he and the AFT executive council adopted a comprehensive philosophical position paper outlining their views on early childhood instruction. The paper began by stating that the public schools were facing a serious resource crisis, a crisis that was diminishing their ability to provide quality educational programs.

The crisis was being caused by a combination of factors that included declining enrollment, inflation, a shortage of financial resources to support teachers, the absence of an effective national educational policy, budget cuts, political inaction, and flaws in accountability.[17] The conclusion Shanker and the AFT executive council reached was that the problems created by a combination of these variables could not be resolved in isolation, but only through considering them all at once because they were interrelated.

The paper went on to argue that America's children were being educated by teachers who were inadequately trained and whose academic preparation was lacking in comprehensiveness and depth. The reason for this situation was that the government deliberately decided to replace properly qualified teachers with poorly qualified teachers in order to save money. The school administrations were faced with a choice of hiring properly qualified teachers who demanded higher salaries commensurate with their qualifications or poorly trained teachers who were paid low salaries. In choosing the latter course of action school districts did great damage to the education of students, the extent of which will not be undone for years to come. This situation forced the properly qualified teachers "either to accept the limitations of the current crisis or to search within the crisis for opportunities to move forward by developing a school program which will ensure the best possible educational interests of all the nation's children."[18]

The paper concluded that in being thrust into this situation the properly qualified teachers were assuming the responsibility of seeking solutions to educational problems that were not of their own creation. The paper made its point that the importance of early childhood education lay in its being the foundation of all educational success. If this part of education was weakened, then success in education, which is closely associated with success in society, is seriously debilitated.

The attainment of early childhood education often leads to the attainment of other forms of education, such as graduating from high school and enrolling in post secondary vocational and professional courses of study. Shanker and the AFT concluded that to avoid costly remedial education later on, the nation must

---

17. The AFT, "Early Childhood Education: A National Program," December 17, 1974, AFT Files, Washington, D.C.
18. Ibid.

make early childhood education a solid foundation. This can be done in two ways. The first is to assure that teachers are properly trained. The second is to provide an adequate social environment for children so that they do not encounter traumatic experiences that often inhibit educational success.[19]

Shanker and his executive council suggested two directions that the country must take. The first was to initiate research on the importance of the early years to children's future learning. This approach, when combined with the growing desire of many working parents to both have a career and raise a family, would suggest the importance of expanded early childhood education. Such research would show that the individual child develops as much as 50 percent of his or her mature intelligence from conception to age four. Another 30 percent develops between the ages of four and eight.

The second direction was to identify and enrich children whose intellectual development was neglected either by an impoverished home or a social system that was poorly equipped to provide them with the necessary motivation and resources, or by an educational system that was poorly equipped. This was the thinking behind the Johnson administration's initiation of the Head Start program. In 1974 the need for most parents to work underlined the importance of early childhood education as a much needed national program. In 1972, 5.5 million children under six years of age had mothers who were working or in need of work.[20] By reforming Head Start to take into account conditions that now exist, it is quite possible to improve the intellectual level of children so as to lay the groundwork for success in their educational efforts later on.

Shanker and his executive council went on to argue that in the face of these developments, the character of public schools must be altered to accommodate the growing need for early childhood education. This endeavor would not require the allocation of substantial facilities such as buildings because the declining birth rate has resulted in a corresponding decline in enrollment. This development, in turn, has resulted in a considerable number of underutilized school buildings and qualified teachers without employment. They then suggested that the federal government must embrace expanded early childhood education and day care service and that the responsibility for their implementation and administration should be placed with the public school systems.

The reason for this suggestion was that "unless national effort in these areas is perceived as a federal responsibility, there is little likelihood that a comprehensive approach can be developed. Without federal guidance such efforts would inevitably remain fragmented, diffused, and ineffective. The way to ensure that the federal effort is comprehensive and well planned is to insist that the prime sponsor for all early childhood education and day care programs receiving federal financial aid be the public schools."[21] In articulating their position Shanker and the AFT executive council presented a rationale that seemed to prod

---

19. Ibid.
20. Ibid.
21. Ibid.

the Ford administration to reappraise its educational policy. They called the attention of the federal government to their view that:

At present an effective national day care effort is marred by competition for public funds among public, private non-profit, and private profit-making entities. No comprehensive program is likely to grow or succeed under these circumstances. It is impossible to set and enforce protective standards with regard to health codes, licensing of personnel and quality of educational programs when there is such a complexity of multi-sponsored programs.[22]

Shanker and his executive council advanced their position that a concentrated and coherent public commitment must be made to guarantee that day care centers provide the kind of education that is consistent with recent theory utilized to initiate the Head Start program. Care must be exercised to make sure that the proliferation of day care centers run by private organizations carry out their responsibility in proper ways. They suggested that some of these programs are haphazard at best, even dangerous for the children and those who work with them. A collection of unregulated and unplanned services, often without educational value, could not accomplish any specified objectives. The purpose of formulating a national policy would be to eliminate day care programs that did meet minimal health and educational criteria. This would require "broadly extended federal effort monitored through both federal regulations and local standards enforced in local public schools"[23] to be effective and show results.

In concluding this component of their philosophy, Shanker and his executive council argued that it would be a fair and reasonable procedure in a democratic society for public funds to be administered through public institutions. If this procedure were adopted as a national policy, it would mean that establishing criteria for the certification of all educational personnel, assessing educational programs, determining the qualifications of teachers, assessing the needs of students, and evaluating the effectiveness of facilities and staff would all have to be done on a national level.

Although the cost of introducing and implementing this program would be considerable, it would serve the best interests of the country in the long term because the educational products of the program would benefit students. Besides, the executive council argued, if implemented properly, this program would yield high returns. For reasons of accountability this program would best be handled by public schools. Although Shanker wanted it known that this philosophical position was the result of collective action, it was quite clear that it was his personal position as well.

In 1979 Shanker produced a paper entitled "Meeting the Challenge," in which he outlined his view of the relationship existing between the economic position of teachers and the effectiveness of educational programs. He argued that the more teachers are secure economically, the more they produce and the higher the quality of their work. Therefore, the nation has an interest in ensuring the

---

22. The AFT, "Early Childhood Education: A National Program," October 20, 1976, AFT Files, Washington, D.C.
23. Ibid.

economic security of teachers because the educational benefits that flow from it extend to students and ultimately to the country. The nation cannot expect teachers to address the needs of the country if the country did not recognize and meet their needs.

But Shanker was not optimistic about the government efforts to improve the economy of the country by providing for the socioeconomic benefits of teachers. This is why he wrote, "Economic recession, runaway inflation, forced school closures, cutbacks in public services, and unemployment are not good news for teachers. On every front our ability to overcome adversity has been challenged. Cries from every political sector to balance the federal budget at the expense of social programs promise to put teachers in recurring legislative battles in the years to come unless the situation changes drastically."[24] Shanker has persistently argued that the strength of the educational system cannot be sustained on a weak economy. Therefore, efforts directed at seeking to strengthen the economy must be related to national educational policy because the two are intertwined.

Shanker argued that to combat these problems teachers needed to increase their involvement in national policy. The most effective means for doing this was to increase the membership of the AFT. Shanker also advanced his thinking that teacher unions must affiliate themselves with other labor organizations because they are struggling for common goals such as the improvement in working conditions. Shanker concluded this element of his philosophy by advancing his thinking that the AFT's effectiveness in organizing for political action depended upon its ability to perform and produce in the classroom. Shanker advised teachers to remember that performance rests with themselves, as does the quality of the collective leadership they need.

This leadership would make it possible to demand action from the government to confront problems and search for solutions, not just rhetoric. He also urged the AFT's members to emerge from the educational crisis of the Nixon-Ford years stronger in projecting the value of their profession, clear in their understanding of the objectives they sought to accomplish, stronger in the convictions that motivated them, and united in promoting the unity they needed to carry out their agenda. He further urged teachers to endeavor "to build a thriving organization on the foundation of the strength of the past and forge bonds with new conditions. Together we will meet the challenge of the 1980s."[25]

SHANKER ON FREEDOM OF TEACHERS

As one who subscribes to Dewey's philosophy on the various implications of freedom, Shanker has based his thoughts on this critical aspect of human experience on an article in the charter of the AFT itself. This states:

---

24. Albert Shanker, "Meeting the Challenge" (position paper on education), September 1979, AFT Files, Washington, D.C.

25. Ibid.

Since teachers must be free in order to teach freedom, the right to be members of organizations of their own choosing must be guaranteed. In all matters pertaining to their salaries and working conditions they shall be entitled to bargain collectively through representatives of their own choosing. They are entitled to have the schools administered by superintendents, boards or committees which function in a democratic manner.[26]

Shanker regards freedom as a fundamental condition for human self-actualization. He feels that it must be absolute and total. He has argued that for teachers freedom cannot be restricted if they are to fully discharge their professional responsibility. This kind of freedom must include the right to formulate theory on both teaching and learning, to test it by empirical evidence, and to take risks with new ideas and methods.

Like Dewey, Shanker sees a wider dimension of freedom, especially when it comes to learning. Dewey explained the importance of the freedom to learn by saying, "The only freedom that is of lasting importance is freedom of intelligence, of observation, and of judgment exercised in behalf of purposes that are intrinsically worth while."[27] In beginning his own graduate study of philosophy at Columbia University, where Dewey did most of his work from 1904 to 1930, Shanker began to articulate his own ideas on freedom. From his study of Immanuel Kant's (1724-1804) philosophy, especially his *Critique of Pure Reason* (1781), Shanker understood the essence of human freedom in ways that make the human being a unique product of creation.

In his treatise Kant outlined three of these ways. The first is that doing one's duty fully is far more important than seeking happiness, but that only duty that comes from the free expression of thought and action is of a truly fulfilling nature. Duty and freedom are, therefore, interrelated. The second way is that human beings must develop an empirical way of predicting events based upon past experience. Without the freedom to apply reason and logic, prediction becomes mere speculation.

The third way in which human beings become unique products of creation is that the freedom of thought and action must be related to the development of a set of moral values which society must reinforce in its social institutions, like schools. Without a sense of morality, that is, the ability to distinguish what is right from what is wrong, human beings are no better than any other living species.[28] They cannot become the unique product of creation that they are intended to be.

---

26. Quoted in William van Til, *Education: The Beginning*, p. 124.

27. John Dewey, *Experience and Education* , p. 61.

28. Kant would consider an individual who commits crime to lack moral values and society must remove him because his behavior threatens the proper functions of national institutions. Although contemporary society considers morality, like religion, as private and individual, it still expects its members to abide by moral conventions that preserve its integrity.

From this perspective Shanker began to see the freedom of movement in thought in relation to the freedom of movement in teachers' intellect. He saw the freedom of social values and moral imperatives of a nation as the fundamental tenet for being human. Like Dewey and Kant, Shanker understands that the problems of education and society are not resolved until these dimensions of freedom are applied and made functional. Human freedom, in its broadest sense, must become part of an effort to solve problems. Because freedom of thought is action consistent with the need to resolve social problems cannot be forced, solutions to institutional problems cannot be forced either. This is the reason Shanker and the AFT have advocated the principle of collective bargaining to allow for the unrestricted expression of freedom of thought in order to address all relevant issues in negotiations between school boards and teachers.

In applying Kant's and Dewey's philosophy, Shanker has operated under his belief that solutions to educational problems are possible only when these various aspects of freedom come into focus. These aspects make it possible to pose pertinent questions in the process of inquiry. It is a distinctive quality of being human. These aspects of freedom make it possible to interpret old definitions within the context of new situations. They make it possible to examine all issues from all possible perspectives. They make it possible to see all dimensions of the human spirit from all sides of an issue. This is why Dewey concluded that without freedom of thought and action, human existence and its ability to overcome adversity are severely restricted. He also concluded that without freedom it is equally "impossible for a teacher to gain knowledge of the individuals with whom he is concerned."[29]

As a teacher and member of professional organizations, Shanker has subscribed to Dewey's and Kant's thinking that without freedom, a student's ability to be creative and independent is seriously thwarted. Without freedom the student will not grow and develop. For the student, "freedom of movement is also important as a means of maintaining normal physical and mental health and growth. Freedom varies from individual to individual."[30] Shanker understands that freedom from restriction is critical to the development of individuality. He sees individuality as being critical to the process of formulating purpose, of developing relationships between human action and consequences.

Once a student understands that he has a right to exercise his freedom of cognition as part of his learning, he develops the ability to assert his unique personality in order to discern impulse from desire, to make a distinction between emotion and rationality, between reason and intuition, and between logic and mere speculation. As an adult member of society he will also understand these relationships between using dictatorial means and resorting to dialogue to resolve conflict. This shows that freedom as a component of the educational process is an essential element for the stability of society because it is based upon efforts to assure happiness for all concerned.

---

29. John Dewey, *Experience and Education*, p. 62.
30. Ibid., p. 63.

Shanker understands Maslow's position that freedom from fear is as equally important to students as freedom from want.[31] He goes on to argue that the elimination of conditions that inhibit freedom must become the first order of business in the educational process. This begins with the first day of kindergarten and ends with the last day of university education. It lends itself to providing an ideal environment for learning. Both the kindergarten child and the graduate student have fears that must be eliminated: the fear of whether or not his or her teacher agrees with the interpretation of concepts discussed in class, the fear of being evaluated inaccurately, the fear of how classmates may react to his or her ideas, and the fear of offering the wrong interpretation of concepts studied in class.

These are all very real fears in the life of all students, and they restrict their freedom to learn. The only way to eliminate them is for the teacher to assure his or her students that their search for truth within the climate of learning is the only real basis of freedom and that he or she will not pass judgment on their exercise of freedom in interpreting concepts.

Indeed, Shanker sees the concept of freedom as having application to human conditions in real and demonstrated ways. In September 1974 he stated that the lack of economic freedom was hurting teachers in their ability to effectively discharge their responsibilities. He concluded, "When the interest rates come down where the average middle income person, the teacher, can afford to buy a home again,"[32] the concept of freedom would have its ultimate meaning. In this context Maslow's concept of the hierarchy of needs has application to teachers as it relates to freedom from want as a condition of fulfilling his or her obligation to students and, thus, to society. The lack of economic freedom for teachers robs them of other forms of freedom as well, such as academic and professional freedom. The lack of these forms of liberty creates a social and political environment from which oppression of both individuals and society emerges.

Shanker also sees the lack of economic freedom for teachers as having a direct national impact that may be detrimental to the interests of the country. In 1974 he explained, "It is disastrous that we have got hundreds of thousands of teachers who are unemployed. We have 1.5 million students in college who will become teachers within the next few years. This means that there will be an unemployed teacher for every one who is employed. If this situation is allowed to continue it will mean not only the loss of freedom for teachers, but it will also deprive the country of its freedom to plan the economic future with confidence. Economic decline and the rise in inflation will reduce our ability to overcome adversity. This loss of freedom will have a detrimental effect on the country as a whole."[33] Shanker concludes that this collective loss of freedom robs the nation of vital resources it needs to make progress.

Shanker's understanding of the reality of freedom is evident in a variety of ways, including teachers' involvement in politics. In 1974 he explained the need

---

31. Abraham Maslow, *Motivation and Personality*, p. 37.

32. The AFT, "Albert Shanker on Freedom of Teachers," *The American Teacher* (September 1974) 6: 15.

33. Ibid., p. 16.

for teachers to become involved in politics as a way of securing their freedom: "The problems are great, but we are stronger than we have ever been. Our numbers are greater. Support from labor is at an all-time high. For the first time in history we are recognized as a major national power in education, labor, and politics by the newspapers and magazines. This success is the culmination of a long, hard struggle in which our greatest problem is to convince teachers of the powerful role they can play in gaining their freedom to ensure the adequate practice of their profession."[34]

Shanker urged teachers to remember that the strength of their influence as members of a professional organization lay in numbers and in the strategies they utilized to gain the kind of freedom that would allow them to pursue goals and objectives without failure and reprisal from the school administrations and from the courts. This is why he encouraged teachers to become members of the AFT. Without a broader definition of freedom, Shanker reminded teachers, they could not have academic freedom so crucial to educational success and job satisfaction.

An important dimension of freedom that Shanker thinks is critical to education is the freedom of students from detractors. On June 5, 1975, Shanker argued before a congressional committee on education that "child development programs, free from detractors, should be available to all children whose parents desire to utilize this service. It should not be restricted on the basis of means tests, income scales, or other criteria that prevent students from utilizing a highly desirable and crucial public service. Denial of this kind of freedom to children carries a costly national price."[35]

Shanker has suggested that the absence of detractors makes it possible to extend a unique opportunity to students so that they exercise their freedom in not only selecting their course of study, but in determining their actual interest in a career. Shanker also sees freedom as a major factor that "contributes to the intellectual development of young children. Within the past twenty years the work of educators like Benjamin Bloom, J. McVicker Hunt, Jerome Bruner, and Jean Piaget has pointed to the crucial importance of freedom in early childhood education and intellectual development of students."[36]

Shanker sees an increasing phenomenon relative to the concept of freedom, and that is the number of women who work outside the home for economic or personal reasons. He warns that unless American society makes appropriate plans for the future, children who are now growing up will pay the price of social maladjustment. He urges all concerned--politicians, parents, civic leaders, educational administrator--to make sure that adequate arrangements are made for children whose parents work outside the home, that their freedom of emotional stability and intellectual development is fully protected.

Shanker points out, "The need for child care is greater today than it has ever been before because large and growing numbers of women have to work outside

---

34. Ibid., p. 15.
35. Albert Shanker, "Public Schools and Preschool Programs: A Natural Connection" (testimony presented before the Committee on Education), June 5, 1975, AFT Files, Washington, D.C.
36. Ibid.

the home. They are being forced to give up their freedom to choose between staying home to look after their children and leaving their children without the care and attention they need to earn an income. Mothers on public assistance have also been forced to give up the exercise of their freedom of choice regarding the essentials they need to sustain their families. This absence of freedom also carries a costly national price tag."[37]

Shanker argues that since the exercise of freedom of choice requires the application of reason, it demands the acquisition of education to make it possible. Once individuals fail to exercise reason, society loses. This is why, in presenting his argument for the promotion of economic freedom for all people, Shanker cites statistics to show why the country must initiate new plans for the future in order to ensure that the various dimensions of educational freedom became operative. From 1948 to 1973 the number of working mothers grew from 18 percent to 44 percent. In 1975, 26 million children had working mothers. Of these, six million were under the age of six.

In the same year 12 million children lived in a household headed by a female, or what has predominantly become known as the single parent family. In those families the median income was $6,195 per year if the mother worked outside the home and $3,760 if she did not. During the same period 5 million children were living in divorced family situations where various forms of abuse, combined with the denial of their basic rights, may have caused emotional problems that could last a lifetime.[38] The conclusion that Shanker reaches from these figures is that the nation that loses its freedom because it denies its citizens their freedom denies itself the opportunity to build a national character that is a prerequisite in ensuring its own progressive development.

During the presentation of these figures Shanker expressed his belief that it is quite possible to find solutions to the problems they have created. He suggested that a new child development legislation, such as the act passed by the Congress in 1971, would provide a springboard for national action to resolve these problems. Shanker explained,

> We believe that at this time the use of the public school system must be the prime sponsor. This factor is not adequately understood because even in 1971 it was not yet clear that the schools were available to administer a program that would serve even more children than they were already responsible for. But it is now clear that careful planning, coordination, recognizing the reality that educational freedom of the students all combine to lead to the conclusion that this kind of freedom leads to the freedom of the nation. Therefore the task of bringing about freedom of any dimension of education is a national responsibility.[39]

Shanker has tried to put his beliefs into action. His observation of conditions of 1975, a time when national policy should have been directed at combining the interests of students and parents with those of the nation to shape

---

37. Ibid.
38. Ibid.
39. Ibid.

a future different from the past, has been a catalyst for the realization of early childhood education. He has argued that fragmentation of effort and application of service would only inhibit efforts to create a national purpose. This is why he argued, "We believe that putting the responsibility in the schools as an act of recognizing academic freedom is the best way to create an educational program than can grow."[40]

Shanker has also operated under the influence of his philosophy that much of the mental and intellectual development of the child during the early years of his or her life has to do with social, emotional, and physical growth. Intellectual development in later years is merely an extension of the development that took place early in life. When these factors are combined with proper nutrition and good environment, a child has a greater chance of becoming an asset to his or her society. Behavior patterns that are often detrimental to his or her own social and emotional growth are eliminated as a child learns early to behave as a responsible citizen. Shanker cited the report of the U.S. Office of Child Development, which indicated in 1975 that early intervention must be initiated in problematic areas of children's educational efforts. This would increase the likelihood that they develop positive attitudes about themselves so as to have a positive attitude about school and society.

Shanker has expressed serious concern about the conditions that he says robs children of their freedom,

> Hundreds of thousands of handicapped children are living in state warehouses under what has been rightly called institutionalized child abuse. Child abuse and neglect are understood as growing problems among all social and economic classes. Teenage alcoholism and drug abuse are growing problems. One out of nine children will be in juvenile court before they reach the age of eighteen. Suicide is now the second leading cause of death for young Americans between the ages of fifteen and twenty-four. Children represent forty percent of the population and yet they receive only ten percent of the national budget allocated towards health care. Less than one percent of Revenue Sharing money has been spent by states and local authorities on children. It is not hard to see that any one of these conditions or a combination of any of them will deprive the children of their basic freedom to acquire the essential services they need to be themselves.[41]

Shanker reached two philosophical conclusions regarding these disturbing statistics. The first is that any society that subjects its young to abusive conditions of any kind destroys the very essence of its own future. Such a nation must realize that sooner than later it will pay a costly price in the crime, violence and nonproductive behavior many of these children will exhibit as adults.

The second conclusion is that the cost of failing to solve the problems society encounters in its poor treatment of children is enormous. For children their loss of freedom means limited opportunities and experiences that can lead to

---

40. Ibid.
41. Ibid.

a happy and fruitful life later. For society this loss of exploration means expensive compensatory or punitive programs to deal with increased crime and penal institutions. It has become an accepted truth in contemporary society that those who were victims of abuse as children often become abusive as adults. It has been reported that over 75 percent of prison convicts were abused and/or learning disabled children. This vicious cycle must be stopped if the nation is to work toward a better future.

In 1975 Shanker suggested that the United States was utilizing inappropriate solutions for its social problems. It was spending $4 billion annually on trying to rehabilitate juvenile offenders and $400 million on early childhood educational programs. He went on to argue, "We know that in a school system serving over 45 million students, there are instances of success and failure. But we believe that we should avoid the limited program of the poor and begin with programs open to all children as a practice of national freedom. Programs for the poor only are often poor programs."[42]

Shanker concluded his call for good early childhood education by suggesting that, if accepted, the process must be initiated at the national level and the programmatic responsibility must be placed in the public schools. This is the only way that the public will support it, and without public support the program will not be successful. Former U.S. Senator Walter Mondale, a Democrat from Minnesota, was so impressed with Shanker's views that in 1975 he sought his advice on the structure and content of the bill on early childhood education he planned to introduce in the Senate. Shanker was pleased with this recognition and effort by an influential national politician.

LEGAL PROCESS, FREEDOM, AND SHANKER'S PHILOSOPHY

In 1974 Shanker and the AFT had an opportunity to move from discussing theoretical precepts to practicing their belief that freedom for all teachers is the practice of freedom for the country. When the U.S. Supreme Court was considering *La Fleure v. Cleveland Board of Education*, they decided to make their views known. This was from the desire not to influence the decision of the Court, but to inform the public about the issues that were in dispute between the litigants in a number of cases that were pending before the judiciary. In this section four examples are cited to show that Shanker has adopted a new strategy in applying his philosophy when he argued his position on various issues of freedom in a number of cases that held serious implications for teachers.

The first example addresses the right of pregnant teachers to teach. The second addresses the right to hire and fire and due process regarding teachers. The third looks at the principle of collective bargaining and the right to select negotiating representatives. The last example deals with academic freedom relative to teachers' choices of educational materials. These four examples arise from situations that the American legal system had not addressed before. They

---

42. Ibid.

gave Shanker the opportunity to formulate a strategy for dealing with them and to articulate on a national level the AFT's position on them. They also served to add cohesion to the union.

Like most school boards across the country, the Cleveland Board of Education had long maintained a policy requiring termination of female teachers' employment at a fixed stage of their pregnancy. Recognizing the need to influence change in that policy, the AFT executive council decided to provide an *amicus curiae* brief as a friend of the court. The brief argued that because that policy was arbitrarily imposed, it denied female teachers their basic freedom to make decisions about childbearing. Therefore, the policy was a violation of Fourteenth Amendment rights. Using the philosophy that the executive council had developed under Shanker's guidance, the AFT made three points for the Court's consideration.

The first was that in developing regulations that mandated the termination of female teachers at a predetermined stage in their pregnancy, the Cleveland Board of Education was acting without any regard for the preference and physical condition of the teachers, as would have been outlined in a certification written by a woman's physician testifying to her inability to discharge her responsibility. Therefore, the board of education was acting in an arbitrary manner in imposing conditions of service. This was a violation of the women's freedom to decide for themselves.

The second point was that the regulations were an infringement on the exercise of a fundamental right of teachers to engage in collective bargaining before policy was developed and implemented. The third point was that the classifications made in the regulations jeopardized women's access to equal employment opportunities without any substantial state interest beyond limiting the freedom of female teachers to be involved in the process of making professional decisions.

That the decision of the Supreme Court paralleled the AFT position[43] shows the logic found in Shanker's philosophy. This is the logic that the Supreme Court used in reaching its decision that the Cleveland school board had failed to show any compelling interest and reasons for formulating its policy the way it did. The Court went on to say that to deny a mother the rights and freedoms to make decisions about her pregnancy was a denial of the rights and freedoms that other individuals were exercising.[44] The court further stated that the policy was also a denial of due process under the Fourteenth Amendment. The AFT was particularly pleased with the Court's opinion that the rights and freedoms of women everywhere, and of women teachers in particular, must be protected in accordance with the principles of collective bargaining.

Shanker had learned an important lesson early in his term of office as president of the AFT: a clear articulation of philosophy was essential to enable him and the organization he led to address national issues they considered important. Slowly the period of confrontation and resorting to strikes was giving way to the application of reason and logic to resolve the conflicts that emerged

---

43. *La Fleure v. Cleveland Board of Education*, 39 L. Ed, 2nd 52 (1974).
44. Ibid.

between them and the boards of education. He also knew that the application of logic was impossible without formulating a clear philosophical position on which to base such an argument. The success of any philosophical position lies in the ability to be persuasive and diplomatic. Throughout his term of office Shanker has never lost sight of this basic principle. The success he has enjoyed as both a union leader and a strong advocate of teachers' rights rests squarely on his recognition of this principle.

The precedent for the success of this strategy came two years earlier in 1972 in two cases that were decided by the Supreme Court on the same day. They were *Roth v. Board of Regents of California* and *Perry v. Sindermann*. Both cases involved the extent to which procedural due process was applied to teachers who were not tenured. At that time David Selden, then president of the AFT, and his executive council supported the position that due process is intended to protect all people, including teachers who were not tenured, and that termination of these teachers' employment without due process is a denial of their equal protection. Through its general counsel the AFT presented an impressive argument. Up to this point it was generally taken for granted that untenured teachers could be dismissed at will because they were not entitled to a hearing at which to present their case if they were not hired at the beginning of the new school year.

Aware of the implications of its performance, the AFT based its argument on its philosophy that the very nature of the teachers' work was such that it was entirely possible that unfounded suspicions often served as a reason for dismissing untenured teachers. Unless these teachers were entitled to due process, there was a substantial danger that the termination of their employment would be based upon clearly illegal reasons, such as their political association or lifestyle.

The AFT further argued that to ask the teachers to appeal to the board of education about decisions it had reached was analogous to asking a patient who had been treated by Dr. Jekyll to seek a second opinion from Mr. Hyde. The Supreme Court ruled in favor of the AFT position, saying that to allow school boards to terminate the employment of untenured teachers without due process would be to sanction the violation of their Fourteenth Amendment rights.[45]

The next important case was decided in 1967 while Shanker was still president of the UFT. He had developed a philosophy of collective bargaining that stressed two critical elements. The first was that parties to it would gain more than by arbitrary and unilateral action. The second element was that dialogue was a prerequisite of democracy. Shanker also knew that the principle of collective bargaining was not fully accepted by the boards of education as a constitutional right that teachers could exercise.

The boards did not consider the National Industrial Relations Act of 1933 and the National Labor Relations Act of 1935, popularly known as the Wagner Act, as a constitutional basis for collective bargaining. Although President John Kennedy's Executive Order 10988, issued on January 17, 1962, did much to

45. *Roth vs. Board of Regents of California*, 408 U.S. 564 (1972), *Perry v. Sindermann*, 408 U.S. 593 (1972).

encourage collective bargaining, the boards of education did not seem willing to operate under its provisions.

Shanker and his executive council decided that the courts must compel the boards to respect collective bargaining. In 1966 they brought suit against the board of education in Chicago, the city in which Margaret Haley and Catherine Goggin had been active in forming teacher organizations more than sixty years earlier. It was a city that persistently refused to recognize the principle of collective bargaining. When arguments were presented in the state circuit court in 1967, the AFT had done its homework. It established certain critical facts relative to the dispute. It presented to the court the fact that the Chicago Teachers Union was waging a campaign to prevent the Illinois Education Association from exercising authority as the teachers' representative body because it had adopted negative attitudes toward the AFT, because its members had placed their sympathy with the board of education, and because it had expressed a bias against teachers' unions in general.

The AFT wanted to hold elections for purposes of selecting a bargaining representative committee. While this was happening, a taxpayers' suit was initiated, arguing that the board of education could not legally extend recognition to any organization that did not show proof that it was representing the group it claimed it was representing. This scenario between teachers and the school board had not been seen before. The school board had not fully recognized how much things had changed and did not learn fast enough to grasp the essence of how things were now expected to be done. Events were moving so rapidly that the board of education did not realize that collective bargaining was now an applicable principle in negotiating contracts with teachers.

In the maze of confusion that was unfolding the AFT presented two critical positions relative to the suit. The first was that the board's refusal to operate by the principle of collective bargaining was a violation of the teachers' Fourteenth Amendment rights because it was dictating conditions of their employment. The second point was that the board could not negotiate terms with any organization that did not represent the teachers. Thus, *Chicago Division of Illinois Education Association v. Board of Education of the City of Chicago* became a landmark case regarding the AFT's philosophy of collective bargaining. After all the arguments had been presented, Illinois Circuit Court Judge Cornelius J. Harrington ruled that the board of education could legally extend representation only to a collective bargaining agent selected by the teachers themselves.

That Harrington's ruling was upheld by the Illinois Appellate Court strengthened the AFT position. That the appellate court rejected the board's argument that collective bargaining violated constitutional restraint[46] shows the accuracy of the logic the AFT had applied in presenting its arguments. The appellate court concluded, "The Board cannot require legislative authority to enter into a collective bargaining agreement with a collective bargaining agency selected by its teachers. We hold that such an agreement is not against public

---

46. *Chicago Division of Illinois Education Association v. Board of Education of the City of Chicago*, 222, N.E. 2d 43 (Ill. App. Ct. 19) (1967).

policy."[47] This means that the board was required to enter into collective bargaining only with a representative agency selected by the teachers themselves. Therefore, collective bargaining under this ruling extended constitutionally protected freedom to teachers.

In 1963 Paul S. Finot, a tenured teacher at John Muir High School in Pasadena, California, decided to exercise his personal freedom and civil rights by wearing a beard. When Finot appeared at an important school function in his neatly trimmed beard, he was reassigned to a different responsibility. The school authority issued an ultimatum to shave or be terminated in spite of the fact that Finot was a tenured teacher and was regarded as a highly successful teacher.

After considering his options Finot declined to shave his beard. He was immediately reassigned to teach homebound students with seven preparations for grades 10, 11, and 12. Finot complained that this action was a violation of his personal freedom and civil rights because it was initiated for the sole purpose of coercing him to change his personal appearance by forcing him to shave his beard. He also argued that his freedom of association with other teachers had been taken away. The principal stated that a school policy that prohibited students from wearing beards and mustaches was also applied to teachers.

Carl Megel, then president of the AFT, and his executive council concluded that the case was important to teachers across the country. They decided to direct Finot's suit to its conclusion. It took four years of careful preparation based upon a philosophical strategy that stressed the thinking that questions of personal appearance and dress were of no interest to the state and that they remained outside the control or regulation of the board of education because Finot had the freedom and right to dress as he pleased. When the California Court of Appeal ruled unanimously in *Finot v. Pasadena City Board of Education* in 1967, it sustained the AFT's philosophy, adding,

> On the record before us with the complete absence of any actual experience at the high school involved as to what the actual adverse effect of the wearing of a beard by a male teacher would be upon the conduct of the educational process there, beards as such cannot constitutionally be banned from the classroom and from the campus. A beard is a man's expression of his masculinity and wisdom, an emulation of such a beard is a show of a great man as John Muir himself, Socrates, or Abraham Lincoln. Restraint of personal freedom may not be used to limit First Amendment freedom.[48]

This case laid the foundation for *Tinker v. Des Moines Independent School District* in 1969.

Regardless of these court rulings the boards of education did not appear to understand the message that the courts were trying to convey relative to the various rights they were addressing. H. Keith Sterzing, a political science

---

47. Ibid.

48. *Finot v. Pasadena City Board of Education*, 58 Cal. 520, Cal. Ct. App. (1967).

teacher at John Foster Dulles High School[49] in Sugar Land, Texas, was suddenly dismissed in February 1968 without prior notice following complaints made by some parents about how he was teaching a course on race relations. A brilliant and capable teacher, Sterzing tried to bring a balanced and unbiased curriculum to his students. This included reading an essay by the controversial Benjamin Spock on racial discrimination, an article by B'nai B'rith on prejudice, and a paper on anthropology by the John Birch Society.

Sterzing brought suit and argued that he was only trying to show his students all sides of a controversial issue and that his dismissal was a violation of his right to academic freedom. As soon as Shanker learned of the case, he and his executive council decided to support Sterzing, basing their action on their philosophical argument that the principle of academic freedom must not be violated if students are to receive a balanced education. The case dragged on through the courts, and when they ruled in 1975 in Sterzing's favor, the board of education decided to settle out of court by agreeing to pay him $40,000 in back pay plus the expenses he had incurred.

In a statement he issued following this settlement, Sterzing said that while he was pleased that his long drawn-out case had reached a conclusion, there were two major unresolved questions. The first was: Would the school board be held responsible for the costly, arbitrary, and unconstitutional action it took against him? The second question was: How much longer would it be before all state and local professional teacher organizations developed a strategy for action based on a philosophy designed to sustain their position on critical educational issues?[50]

In spite of this remarkable success Shanker and his AFT did not rest and enjoy the fruits of their labor. Instead, they looked for new opportunities in their continuing crusade to find solutions to the many problems that education was facing. For example, in 1975 they decided to work with the Boston Teachers' Union and the Massachusetts Federation of Teachers in defining an educational policy to resolve the problems the city was facing regarding busing. What came out of the strategy was a philosophy that worked for the people of Boston, a troubled city that was enduring the agony of racial conflict.

Shanker found himself once again playing the role of mediator. He stressed two elements in the conflict. The first was that the continuing racial conflict would paralyze the educational process and the institutional functions of the city to the extent that in the end there would be no winners, only losers. The second was that the only way to resolve the conflict was through dialogue and understanding, rather than through confrontation; through the application of human reason and logic, rather than through emotional outburst; and through persuasion, rather through coercion.

The AFT worked with segments of the community to preserve the educational interests of the students and to disseminate information about the

---

49. Named after John Foster Dulles (1888-1959), U.S. secretary of state from 1953 to 1959. Dulles was born in Washington, D. C.

50. The AFT, "Teacher Wins $40,000 Award for Fighting Firing Since 1968," *The American Teacher* (June 1975): 59: 4.

availability of employment opportunity for both racial groups.[51] The major component that made this strategy a success was its cooperative approach to the problems of racial strife. The strategy worked, as Boston seemed to move toward resolving its problems.

SUMMARY AND CONCLUSION

This chapter has presented components of Shanker's philosophy on education as it is related to specific rights of teachers. Those who argue that Shanker has moved from the radical position he took as president of the UFT to a more moderate position point out that experience has tempered him over the years. This experience has made it possible for him to expound a philosophy that has allowed him to establish a national climate of dialogue pertaining to issues endemic to education.

Indeed, Shanker has recognized that national policy and action evolve from ideology, rather than from any action unrelated to philosophy that would provide justification. One reason Michael Dukakis lost the presidential election to George Bush in 1988 was his failure to formulate a vision rooted in a philosophy that lent itself to policy. Over the years Shanker has learned the value of having a philosophical base as a method for dealing with critical issues without having to resort to strikes to get the point across.

In relying on philosophical justifications Shanker has learned that the power of persuasion yields much more positive results than does confrontation. In May 1993 Shanker outlined the basic elements of his views by saying, "My general philosophy of education is that it must be available to all students on an equal basis. How to achieve this is a product of dialogue. Above all else we must provide an education that seeks to enhance an understanding of values. We must encourage education that is based on scientific experimentation and logical thinking in seeking justice. The key issue of American society is always how to maintain a social system which stays together to preserve a certain amount of unity and at the same time valuing itself not to destroy diversity. The balance between these is the central principle of freedom of all people because it is the strength of the American society."[52]

One can see that this is not the philosophy of a radical. The reason Shanker has become more effective as president of the AFT is that he strongly believes in democratic principles and process. Shanker has never lost sight of this critical factor. In his holistic or systemic approach to problems in education in the United States, Shanker is closer to the philosophy of Georg W. Hegel (1770-1831), who believed that the historical sequence of events represent various phases in the development of the individual human being and the society of which he or she is a member.

For Shanker these historical events began to influence his cognition and behavior as soon as he assumed the office of president of the AFT. He has never

---

51. The AFT, "Human Rights and Community Relations," *The American Teacher* (September 1975): 6:24.
52. Albert Shanker, interview with author, in Washington , D.C., May 17, 1993.

been the same since that time. Chapter 6 discusses Shanker's position on critical issues that the United States presently faces.

6

Where He Stands: Albert Shanker's Position on Issues

Affirmative action must not operate to restrict considerations to minorities and women only. Job requirements must be applied uniformly to all candidates.

Albert Shanker, 1975

Where one stands on issues helps to find solutions to problems of society.

Albert Shanker, 1993

SHANKER AND THE THEORY OF TEACHER INVOLVEMENT

In his discussion of teacher involvement in the administration of education as a method of seeking solutions to the problems of education, Joel Spring advances theories that may explain the reasons for Shanker's involvement in social and educational issues. In discussing the concept of teacher empowerment Spring argues that a change of attitude has been taking place since 1970 and that teachers now demand a meaningful role in providing input on educational issues. They are, after all, the ones in the proverbial trenches fighting the war to educate young people.[1]

From the time that Shanker assumed positions of influence and responsibility, both as a teacher and as president of the UFT, he became conscious of the fact that teachers must be free to express their opinions on the many issues that are related to education. These include the curriculum, the administrative system, teacher empowerment, and student activities.

---

1. Joel Spring, *Conflict of Interest: The Politics of American Education* (New York: Longman, 1993), p. 76.

Shanker believes that although teachers are at the bottom of the hierarchy when it comes to making decisions about the conduct of their schools, they must come forward and articulate their views. It is for this reason that Shanker has forcefully expressed his opinions on this matter based upon a clear comprehension of the issues at hand. In this regard he is very deliberate in going further than merely expressing his opinion; he makes an earnest effort to inform and advise. It is in this regard that Spring's theoretical ideas come into play relative to Shanker's position on certain issues.

Spring suggests that school administrations have throughout the years refused to share power with teachers. This means that "within the corporate-like school hierarchy, teachers are at the bottom of the chain of command and the objects of power from above. Teachers' unions have attempted to provide an antidote of the corporate model of school organizations, and beginning in 1970, the teacher power movement has become an important element in the politics of education."[2] Spring concludes that there are two aspects of what he identifies as teacher power. The first is direct involvement in politics, educational and none educational alike. Teachers need to be involved in order to influence the passage of state and national legislation favorable to their profession.

This involvement is why, in 1976, the AFT endorsed the Carter-Mondale ticket as a means of reminding the government that it had a responsibility to the constituency that had supported it. But before offering that endorsement, the AFT made its position clear on a number of issues critical to education to make sure that its support required Carter to accept its concerns as part of the Democratic election platform. Since the election campaign of 1976 both the AFT and the NEA have been actively involved in national politics in order to ensure that their members would, in return, benefit from the implementation of policies formulated and promoted by those seeking public office, policies they clearly helped to define.

The second aspect relates to what Spring identifies as efforts made by teacher organizations to develop relationships with both the educational bureaucracy and the public. Because teacher organizations have found themselves in direct competition with educational administrators for influence on the conduct of education, they have designed a strategy to enhance their reputation among members of the public in order to enlist public support of their views on education. He argues that teacher organizations have utilized this strategy to make sure that the members of the public fully understand and are well informed so that they will place their trust and support in teacher organizations when educational issues are being discussed in a political forum, such as a state legislature.

Spring concludes that the conflict that often arises between educational administrators and teacher organizations can easily be resolved if members of the public have a complete understanding of the issues in dispute. He says, "In recent years the introduction of site-based management has increased tensions between administrators and teachers. Site-based management involves some sharing of power. Many school administrators object to the implementation of

---

2. Ibid., p. 77.

policy relating to procedures and the idea of sharing power over site-based management."3

This attitude compelled the American Federation of School Administrators (AFSA) to place an advertisement in the *Education Week* of April 3, 1991, trying to persuade members of the public to accept its view that site-based management, if implemented in the way teachers were advocating, would give control to teachers who have no idea about the finer points of school administration, and that all the teachers want is to promote their own political agenda. This is the kind of distortion that Spring says teacher organizations cannot allow to go uncorrected. This type of propaganda demands them to take a position, not in the interest of seeking political influence in and of itself, but in order to ensure effective and farsighted educational management.

Recognizing that teacher organizations were gaining considerable influence under provisions of collective bargaining, the AFSA argued that in Dade County, Florida, which was a pioneer in site-based management, student academic achievement did not improve as a result of implementing ideas of site-based management. The AFSA did not, however, say how academic achievement would improve as a result of implementing traditional administrative policies, which administrators were fully responsible for developing. As a result of this campaign, public opinion in Florida began to shift in favor of administrators and against teacher organizations because the latter had failed to explain their own position on the issues. This does not mean that the position of teachers was wrong, it simply meant that because they had not explained it, the public had no opinion on it.

SHANKER ON PUBLIC PERCEPTION OF HIMSELF

As soon as Shanker assumed the presidency of the UFT, he recognized that the success of his objectives would be determined by the public perception of him as a national leader as well as by his efforts to shape the character of the organization that he led. By the time he assumed the presidency of the AFT in 1974, Shanker had decided to shape the public perception of him in order to generate support for his programs. It is for this reason that he began to write a series of articles entitled *Where We Stand*,4 in which he presented his thoughts and feelings on various issues that American education and society were facing. Shanker knew that the public attitude toward him was generally negative because some people thought that he was self-serving and promoting his own political agenda.

This perception of Shanker was expressed to the author by a college instructor in June 1993, saying, "Shanker is clearly a very influential union leader. He seemed to conduct himself in order to promote his own political agenda. But I must confess that after reading the series of articles he has written,

---

3. Ibid., p. 78.
4. These articles and the author's interview with Shanker in Washington, D.C., in May 1993 are the main sources for this chapter.

entitled *Where We Stand*, I have come to realize that he is a national leader who has the interest of education and the American society at heart. I now believe that Shanker has mellowed with time. The series of articles shows the mind of a scholar and researcher. I have now come to admire and respect him deeply."[5] Slowly the articles began to shift public opinion about him and the AFT from a negative perception to a positive one. By 1993 Shanker had become a leading spokesman on critical educational issues. But the road to this recognition and acceptance has been very difficult and tenuous.

In May 1993 the author asked Shanker to explain the background of his articles and what he hoped to accomplish in writing them. He took the opportunity to review the events and circumstances that influenced him to write them, saying:

> Back in 1968 I led four very long and bitter strikes. Before these strikes started I took the view that I did not care what the general public thought of me as long as the members of the organization I led liked me. After all, I was a union leader and the members of the union were the ones I should worry about. However, after these four strikes the newspapers portrayed me in such a negative light that I became worried that the public would reduce its support of the public schools if they thought the leader of the teachers was some crazy guy[6] who was always closing schools down, a power-hungry person. So, I tried to get articles published in newspapers and magazines dealing with educational issues. At first none of the papers and magazines wanted to take my articles because they said, "No, you are a union leader, you are writing these articles to promote your political agenda, but what do you know about education? You are merely promoting strikes." I then knew the extent of the negative perception the public had of me and I decided to change it to enable us to carry out the task we had before us.[7]

Shanker then concluded that the only way he could convince the public of his good intentions was to show that as a leader of a teachers' union, he was also a person and an individual who thought about issues carefully, who read a great number of books and was able to master and present good and logical arguments. Gradually the newspapers and magazines provided him space every week, beginning in December 1970, so that he could express his views on issues the country was facing, especially those involving education. Shanker knew at that

---

5. A college instructor during a conversation with the author in Flagstaff, Arizona, June 12, 1993. The instructor declined to be identified because, he said, "I do not wish to appear to contradict myself. But I believe I am being honest to myself in recognizing that one can be wrong in judging another person. During the past decade Shanker has developed as a professional person from leading strikes to articulating logical positions on issues. That is why I have come to admire and respect him.

6. See also Timothy Noah, "The Fiery Unionist as Educational Leader: Albert Shanker," *The New Republic,* June 24, 1993, for similar views of Shanker in his early days as the leader of the UFT and the AFT. The confession that he expressed to the author shows the maturity of a national leader.

7. Albert Shanker, during an interview with author, Washington, D.C., May 17, 1993.

point that he was moving from being defensive to being offensive in the struggle for favorable public opinion.

Shanker's newspaper exposure through the syndicated weekly column entitled *Where We Stand* gave him a golden opportunity to express his position on various educational and social issues. He knew that the series would enable him to reach, in a responsible manner, a large number of people across the country. This cross section of the American population included members of Congress, former national presidents, the current state and federal administrations, teachers, parents, and people from all walks of life. They read the series because Shanker was expressing his opinions on these issues in a way that compelled their support and admiration. In 1993 Shanker told this author how the column had been received, saying, "In my travels internationally sometimes I meet a prime minister or president and he would tell me, 'I usually agree with you, Albert, but that piece you wrote three weeks ago I thought it was terrible.'"[8] This indicates that the series has a wide distribution and interested readership.

What seems to please Shanker the most is that although some readers of the column disagree with him on the various issues he has addressed, they read the articles with great interest and reflection. In time his readers began to change their perception of him from that of a fiery union leader who was leading strikes that closed schools to that of a statesman who was articulating clear and logical positions on an array of educational and social issues. This also means that the series has had an international readership of considerable size. This has forced Shanker to read more and to think of how to present issues in a manner that is intelligent, coherent, and responsible.

In order to project himself as an intelligent, logical, and responsible individual, Shanker attempts to examine all issues critically to ascertain what the relevancy and points of view are. From this perspective he has presented his views in a balanced manner to accommodate all possible positions. Those who have argued that "Shanker is outside the mainstream of issues in American society because he represents the radical approach to problems"[9] have not seen this side of him. Shanker explained the reason for the overwhelming success of the *Where We Stand* series and what it has done for him: "The need to get down to two or three points of the issues which are powerful and persuasive and can be understood very readily, which you have to have when you write a short piece like that, provides a very important opportunity for shaping one's way of thinking because in the world of reality one is constantly faced with the need to express one's views on national and international issues. Where one stands on issues helps to find solutions to problems of society. Finding solutions to problems of society determines national character."[10]

---

8. Ibid.

9. A college instructor during a conversation with author, in Flagstaff, Arizona, July 7, 1993.

10. Albert Shanker, during an interview with author, Washington, D.C., May 17, 1993.

During his term of office as president of the AFT, Shanker has grasped that ability to think critically and to articulate his views based upon a clear understanding of human issues. In January 1990 Ernest Boyer, president of Carnegie Foundation for the Advancement of Teaching, concluded that Shanker's ability to think has made him an unusual national leader. Boyer concluded, "I think it is fair to say that he continues to be one of the most creative thinkers in education."[11] The ability to think is the reason why Shanker believes that opinions must be educated ones, as "emotion has no room in the application of logic to engage in debate or collective action to seek solutions to problems of society."[12]

When this author asked Shanker to explain what he has gained from the series, he readily responded, "I have gained tremendous knowledge as a result of the series. I do intense research on each particular piece before I write it so that I bring something new for the reader to think about. This is not an easy task, but it is one that has to be carried out if one must make a contribution to the search for solutions to problems. One cannot merely think in abstract terms because man does not live in abstract terms. He lives in the practical reality of his environment and constantly struggles with issues of survival, of happiness, of conflict, of security, of having good relationships with other human beings, of perceiving values in a larger social context, and of determining what is right and what is wrong."[13]

Shanker concluded that these are the elements that make human beings different from other living species. In this context he believes that "one needs to master a few sharp sentences to make a point. In this context the series has been a very good experience for me, and I think that it has been very good to the AFT in terms of presenting a thoughtful and positive image of both myself and of itself. This adds to the responsibility and influence of the organization."[14]

WHERE HE STANDS: SHANKER'S POSITION
ON ISSUES FACING THE NATION

Among the issues that Shanker has addressed is his confidence in the public school system. Writing in July 1974 while he was still president of the UFT, Shanker reminded Americans that the public schools were doing better than some people would have them believe. One must remember that a number of publications came out beginning in 1964 arguing that the American public schools were slowly becoming an endangered species. Among those who were most critical of the public schools and who demanded their abolishment was Ivan Illich, who argued in his *Deschooling Society* in 1971 that the only approach for public schools is to abolish them because they have become so bureaucratic and selective in the kind of education they offered.

---

11. Ernest Boyer, "On Shanker," *USA Today*, January 9, 1990.
12. Albert Shanker, interview with author, Washington, D.C., May 17, 1993.
13. Ibid.
14. Ibid.

Illich also argued that the public schools have moved away from meeting the educational needs of all students to serving only those of the rich and the privileged. He went on to argue, "Many students, especially those who are poor, intuitively know what the schools do for them. They school them to confuse process and substance. Once these become blurred, a new logic is assumed: The more treatment there is, the better are the results, or, escalation leads to success. The pupil is hereby 'schooled' to confuse teaching with learning, grade advancement with education, a diploma with competence, and fluency with the ability to say something new. His imagination is schooled to accept service in place of value. Medical treatment is mistaken for health care, social work for the improvement of community life, police protection for safety, military poise for national security."[15]

One reason for Illich's discontent with the public schools was his belief that they were initially founded on the basis of total equality among all students. But in real practice the public schools are now being run by politicians who seek to subvert the educational process in order to make maximum political gain. He went on to argue, "Equal educational opportunity is, indeed, both a desirable and a feasible goal, but to equate this with obligatory schooling is to confuse salvation with the church. School has become the world religion of a modernized proletariat, and makes futile promises of salvation to the poor of the technological age. Two centuries ago the United States led the world in a movement to disestablish the monopoly of a single church. Now we need the constitutional disestablishment of the monopoly of the school."[16]

Illich was most vocal in his criticism of the public schools and in his call to abolish them when he discussed his position that, within the context of the schools, "neither learning nor justice is promoted by schooling because educators insist on packaging instruction with certification. Learning and the assignment of social roles are melted into schooling. Yet to learn means to acquire a new skill or insight, while promotion depends on an opinion which others have formed. Learning frequently is the result of instruction, but selection for a role or category in the job market increasingly depends on mere length of attendance."[17]

Illich pointed out that half the population of the world has yet to set foot in a formal school, but he failed to discuss the vastly changing world of technology and communication so critical to the survival of the modern world which is dependent upon formalized instruction. One must therefore take Illich's arguments as coming from a social anarchist who, while knowledgeable about education in general, did not seem to see its value in meeting the conditions and needs of the world today. His position that the educational process has been subverted by the politicians to suit their own ambitions is the rationale as to why it must be reformed. Illich seems to ignore important facts about adversity in the human global condition.

When the heating or cooling system fails one does not destroy the house. When the light goes out one does not abandon the house. When a car breaks

---

15. Ivan Illich, *Deschooling Society* (New York: Harper and Row, 1971), p. 1.
16. Ibid., p. 15.
17. Ibid., p. 16.

down, one does not set it on fire, one takes it to a mechanic. When the sun goes down, one does not curse the darkness; one lights the candle. The very fact that the educational process has many flaws does not mean that we should close down the schools. This is exactly the reason why Horace Mann and others like him initiated fundamental reform. They did not suggest closing the schools. How could Illich, an educated man himself, suggest closing down the schools from which he gained national prominence?

To substantiate his argument Illich even quotes Fidel Castro as saying that by 1980 Cuba would not need formal higher education because life experience itself would become the best form of education.[18] But Illich does not discuss the enormous socioeconomic problems that Cuba has found itself in during the past two decades. Even Castro himself did not know that in August 1994 the people of Cuba would stage a demonstration against the social malaise that, in recent years, has become their lot. Jonathan Kozol, another critic of the public schools and author of *Death at an Early Age* (1967), described *Deschooling Society* as "a dangerous book."[19]

The literature that Illich used as a basis for his own argument and conclusion include George B. Leonard's *Education and Ecstasy* (1968), George Dennison's *The Lives of Children* (1969), John Holt's *How Children Fail* (1964), Jonathan Kozol's *Death at an Early Age* (1967), Herbert Kohl's *The Open Classroom* (1970), and Daniel Fader's *The Naked Children* (1971). These authors had found A. S. Neill's *Summerhill* (1960) quite appealing in discussing radical approaches to educational innovation because they felt that education was not keeping up with the extent of change that was taking place in the world.

William van Til explains the emerging thinking among these radical writers, saying, "They challenge the curriculum which seems to be more concerned with preparing students to fit into a society which to them is rapidly becoming obsolete than with developing individual self-realization and improvement."[20] Everett Reimer's *School Is Dead: Alternatives to Education* (1971) was perhaps most critical of the radical writers of Illich's period in his assessment that the public schools were doing more than a good job in their efforts to educate America's youth and that while reform was needed, flaws in the educational process were no reason to suggest abolishing the schools.

By 1974 Shanker felt that the criticism leveled by these critics against the public school system was itself a discredit to public education. He decided to respond and argued that those who faulted public schools "are espousing elitist and anti-democratic views in calling for the elimination of formal schooling. It is astonishing to see so many educational elitists who themselves were of modest social origins, and who owe their present status in society to the opportunities offered by the most openly accessible educational systems in the

18. Ibid., p. 10.
19. Ibid., p. 188.
20. William van Til, *Education: The Beginning*, p. 81.

world, but are quick to deprecate the schools as far as other people's children are concerned."[21]

Shanker cited the Coleman Report of 1966 which concluded that for children whose families and neighborhood were educationally disadvantaged, it was important to replace that environment, which has a negative effect on the learning process, with an educational environment conducive to educational achievement. This could be done by starting the educational process early in the life of the students.[22]

Shanker concluded that instead of advocating an end to public education, these radical critics should direct their effort toward seeking improvement because since the days of the reform movement of the nineteenth century, the public schools had been the reason for the success of American democracy. Shanker went on to add,

> Our schools have always been a whipping boy for disgruntled theorists. When the Russians launched Sputnik I, our schools were blamed. When we beat the Russians in the race to the moon, the schools received no praise, but were chided instead for not eliminating poverty. The critic who at one time condemned the schools for neglecting the most intelligent students who will be our nation's future leaders attacked them a few years later for concentrating on the more intelligent children while neglecting those at the bottom because he argued that society is not run by the most intelligent individuals but by the ordinary persons.[23]

Recognizing how critical it was for him to convince the public that his position on educational and social issues was not merely an expression of personal opinions but a documented and substantiated response, Shanker designed a strategy of documenting his views by quoting from authoritative writers on the particular subject he was discussing. This is why, arguing for the preservation and improvement of the public schools, he quoted Daniel Tanner, professor of education at Rutgers University, who published an article entitled "Retreat from Education" in the January 1974 issue of *Intellect: The Magazine of Educational and Social Affairs*, as saying: "When the liberal academician declared that schools make no difference for other people's children, while demanding the best schools for their own, they are acting to destroy our democratic ideals."[24]

Aware that what he wrote would have a profound impact on the public perception of him and the issues he discussed, Shanker carefully thought out what he was going to write in the future. In this manner he was shifting the public perception of him as a so-called radical union leader who was leading strikes to one of a mature and seasoned national leader who understood critical issues and who contributed solutions to problems. An opportunity to do just

---

21. Albert Shanker, "Where We Stand: The Public Schools Are Doing Better Than Some Would Have Us Believe," July 7, 1974, AFT Files, Washington, D.C.
22. Ibid.
23. Ibid.
24. Ibid.

that came in November 1974 shortly after he had assumed the presidency of the AFT.

The mayor of New York City, Abraham Beame, announced that the city was facing a budget deficit of $430 million. Beame stated that this was caused not by budget miscalculations, but by new and unforeseen circumstances that included economic stagnation and inflation. Beame proposed two solutions to the problem. The first was to ask the federal government to bail out the city. The second was to initiate considerable budget cuts and massive reductions in city programs and personnel, including education.

Shanker studied the situation closely during the next two weeks and discovered some disturbing facts. He learned that while the cost of running the city had gone up by 9 percent, revenue had actually declined by 11 percent. The cost of city service had risen by over $100 million over the previous quarter, most of which went toward the influx of welfare recipients who had become victims of a recession that had caused the loss of 8,000 jobs.

The elimination of these jobs reduced the deficit by only $135 million. The city's schools were suffering through drastic cuts in programs, finances, and personnel. While this was happening, Congress was considering a trade bill that would grant the Soviet Union most favored nation status. This meant that the United Sates was going to lend money to the Soviet Union at 7 percent interest. At the same time Americans were paying 9 percent interest on their home mortgage.[25]

Shanker felt that he now knew the facts of the crisis sufficiently well to suggest possible solutions. First, he did not think that cutting programs and reducing personnel constituted a viable option. A loss of 8,000 positions would further complicate the problems of recession and inflation and would make recovery efforts very difficult. This would hurt the economy further. Shanker then suggested a long-term solution, saying, "Greater federal aid on a regular basis is a matter of on-going government policy. It is an absolute must. Clearly there is no justification for the current situation in which thousands of city employees are fired. If the federal government had provided adequate aid for public services all along, this deplorable dislocation would not have occurred."[26]

Shanker then directed his remarks to the situation that teachers faced, arguing, "If there is one truth that has emerged from the mess we are in, it is that the problem of employees in the public and public sectors are intimately connected. Unemployment in the private sector leads to unemployment in the public sector. The needs, interests, and problems of the wage-earners in both groups, public and private, are inseparably linked."[27] To solve the problem Shanker called for greater communication between employees in the private sector and those in the public sector. In making this call, he refrained from blaming Mayor Beame for the crisis, but criticized the Ford administration for failing to see the situation as a result of a failing national economic policy.

---

25. Albert Shanker, "Where We Stand: Federal Aid To Cities," December 15, 1974, AFT Files, Washington, D.C.
    26. Ibid.
    27. Ibid.

This position was quite consistent with the position that Shanker had taken three months earlier when he argued, "The administration's approach to the problems of inflation over the last five years has imposed unequal sacrifices on different segments of our population. If tax loopholes are plugged $30 billion could be raised. Instead of unemployment and a lower standard of living, the nation could enjoy full employment, decent health care, and smaller classes in the schools."[28]

Shanker went on to argue that the economic policy of the Ford administration had led to budget cuts and the preservation of high interest rates. Shanker concluded that this situation, in turn, increased unemployment. While the current 5.4 percent unemployment rate sounded low, it was misleading because it was concealing the fact that among the young minority population the unemployment rate was actually between 24 and 50 percent.[29]

Shanker went on to stress that as long as inequality remained a factor of national life, the country could never live up to its full potential. The only way to resolve the problem would be to initiate a new policy that could begin with the federal government. One way in which the federal government could start this process would be to guarantee low interest rates to low-income people who would like to purchase homes. He concluded, "With millions unemployed the government seems more willing to pay unemployment and welfare costs than to pay for hiring people to train the young, help the sick, and improve health facilities, and assist those in our schools and colleges."[30]

Early in his term of office as president of the AFT Shanker decided to address a highly controversial issue that he thought was paralyzing national efforts to educate all young Americans: bilingual education. When it was introduced for the first time in 1974 under provisions of the Education Act, bilingual education was intended to assist those students whose first language is not English so that they could make a smooth transition to English. This educational strategy would lessen the adverse effects of an educational environment with which they were not familiar. This effort would make it possible for those students to make a connection between learning English and learning in their own language. But there were individuals who felt that the introduction of bilingual education was bad for education because it would take away the concept of the melting pot.

Among these individuals was columnist Stephen S. Rosenfeld, who wrote in the *Washington Post* on September 27, 1974, "It is not clear how educating children in the language and culture of their ancestral homelands will better equip them for the rigors of contemporary life in the United States."[31] Rosenfeld went on to argue that bilingual education would weaken the students' link to common American values so essential for national unity and purpose. He concluded that those who were promoting bilingual education, including the members of

---

28. Albert Shanker, "Where We Stand: The Ford Administration's Policies," September 22, 1974, AFT Files, Washington, D.C.
29. Ibid.
30. Ibid.
31. Stephen S. Rosenfeld, "Bilingualism,"*Washington Post* , September 27, 1974.

Congress who had supported it, were indirectly promoting an environment of ethnic tension and conflict. He, therefore, urged the abolishment of bilingual education.

Recognizing that "the American taxpayer, while accepting the existence of cultural diversity, still wants the schools to be the basis of an American melting pot,"[32] Shanker argued that multicultural and bilingual education must be viewed not as a course of social conflict or ethnic tension, but as a national enrichment.[33] He then argued that bilingual education must not be a substitute for teaching English as a second language.

Rather, the two must supplement each other to make sure that the student whose first language is not English is introduced to a learning environment that will help him or her gain the skills needed to ensure the success of his or her educational endeavor. Shanker concluded, "Bilingual education should provide a comfortable and rapid transition for the foreign-language student."[34] It is not surprising that within a few years bilingual education had been accepted as a viable national educational feature.

The controversial issue of quotas began to emerge at the same time that affirmative action programs became part of a national effort to eliminate past discriminatory practices against minorities. By 1975 affirmative action was seen by some as a means to increasing ethnic minority representation in employment. But it was also seen by others as a form of what became known as reverse discrimination, meaning that affirmative action programs were discriminatory against whites.

The confusion that resulted from the need to implement affirmative action placed the entire program in doubt. In January 1975 Shanker addressed these issues, saying, "Affirmative action must not operate to restrict consideration to minorities and women only. Job requirements must be applied uniformly to all candidates without regard to race, color, sex, religion, or national origin."[35] Shanker cautioned those who were too enthusiastic in implementing affirmative action policies that hiring by quotas would hurt both the individuals concerned and the program itself.

In 1975 the crisis caused by the racial integration of schools in Boston was peaking. The attention of the nation was fixed on what the federal courts were doing to implement the integration order. In that crisis Judge Arthur Garrity took the center stage as he tried to bring the two sides together in an effort to resolve the crisis. Shanker saw the dispute from a much broader political perspective. He recognized that in the two most recent presidential elections of 1968 and 1972, both won by Richard M. Nixon,[36] "the traditional coalition of

---

32. Albert Shanker, "Where We Stand: Bilingual Education, Not Why, But How," November 3, 1974, AFT Files, Washington, D.C.

33. Shanker stressed this view during an interview with the author on May 17, 1993.

34. Albert Shanker, "Where We Stand: Bilingual Education, Not Why, But How."

35. Albert Shanker, "Where We Stand: Strong Voice Against Ethnic Hiring," January 12, 1975, AFT Files, Washington, D.C.

36. In 1968 against Hubert Humphrey and in 1972 against George McGovern.

liberal labor unions and minority groups fell apart on a number of issues."[37] He argued that Nixon's conservative policy inhibited his ability in articulating a national policy to assure the development of all segments of American society.

Shanker concluded that the disunity among labor unions and minority groups was traumatic for the country in two key ways. First, the Watergate scandal destroyed the Nixon presidency because Nixon lacked confidence in his ability to communicate with the people. Second, in order to please the conservative right, Nixon appointed conservative jurists to federal courts, moving the Supreme Court to the far right and in a way that did not serve the interests of all Americans.

Compounding this problem was the fact that the crippling effects of the recession caused a spiraling inflation that robbed the people of their ability to,plan and their confidence in the future. In addition to all these problems educational programs were left facing a major crisis not seen since the Great Depression. This national climate was the root cause of the integration crisis confronting the nation.

Casting the school desegregation crisis in Boston into the context of these events, Shanker observed, "School districts are making a serious effort to bring about equal opportunity for all children of various ethnic groups to intermingle and to share a common learning environment. The school districts need not be required to be organized by or measured by ratios or quotas of white students to black students. What the courts ordered in Little Rock in 1959 is quite different from what the courts have ordered in Boston."[38]

However, Shanker concluded that from Little Rock to Boston the country had still not learned the importance of providing equality of educational opportunity to all students as a crucial step toward providing equality of opportunity in society. The responsibility for the success of both racial integration and education lay squarely on the shoulders of parents, local authorities, and politicians.

Shanker advanced his belief that if all parties concerned understood the need to exercise this responsibility fully, and in the best interest of the educational development of all students, then the federal courts would not intervene. Reminding the parties in this conflict of the basic difference between the crisis in Little Rock and that in Boston, Shanker quoted columnist William Raspberry, "Little Rock was firmly rooted in the *Brown* decision that ruled that a school system may not maintain schools open only to whites or to only blacks. In Boston the argument is that it is not enough to maintain a school system that is identifiably white or black on the basis that a large number of children who attend it are the same race."[39] By putting the issue of racial integration in schools in a historical perspective, Shanker was able to delineate the elements of the crisis in a manner that the public could understand.

---

37. Albert Shanker, "Where We Stand: Little Rock, 1959, Boston, 1974," January 26, 1975, AFT Files, Washington, D.C.
38. Ibid.
39. Ibid.

The people involved in the crisis knew back in 1970 when the courts started that they faced a major situation comprised of issues that included the political process, the economy, and education. They struggled to find solutions in an increasingly difficult environment. By 1975 the question of merit pay for teachers was generating considerable debate. The thinking behind the debate was that good teachers should be paid more to provide incentives and to help ineffective teachers improve their performance. While this issue had first surfaced some fifty years earlier, it took on compelling dimensions in 1975 because education was going through a period of severe testing and disarray. Those who supported the idea thought that the conditions in 1975 demanded an approach to the concept different from that of fifty years earlier.

Instead of merely giving his opinion on another critical national issue, Shanker studied the existing literature on the subject of merit pay so that he would base his position on actual knowledge of the facts at hand. His research led him to an article written by Herbert Meyer entitled "The Pay for Performance Dilemma," which was published in the Winter 1975 issue of *Organizational Dynamics: A Quarterly Review of Organizational Behavior for Professional Managers,* a publication of the American Management Association. Meyer had worked in personnel research for General Electric for some twenty years. As a professor and director of the Industrial and Organizational Psychology Program at the University of South Florida, Meyer concluded in the article that only a small percentage of the workers, even those considered good and productive, supported the idea of merit pay because it was not easy to define merit.

For this reason Meyer argued that merit pay could not be applied with consistency in all areas of professional performance. For example, is merit in teaching English to be defined in the same way as merit in teaching athletics? Meyer argued that merit pay was a wrong incentive for teacher productivity because when financial reward superseded the satisfaction from professional performance, then the profession itself would lose its meaning. He concluded that applying the concept of merit pay would have a negative effect on the attitudes and the professional development of the workers.

Meyer argued that what he would prefer was a system that recognized the professional competency and importance of all teachers. Instead of rewarding some teachers on the basis of a questionable system, the nation must think of raising the salaries of all teachers to help them have a sense of higher professional productivity for the good of the country.

Applying Meyer's line of thinking Shanker argued that if the idea of merit pay was bad for the worker in industry, it was also bad for the teacher. He went on to suggest that if the supervisor would succeed in convincing the employees that they were as good as they believed they were, he would have accomplished his goal of seeking improvement in their self-esteem as a result of improving their performance.[40] He went on to argue that throughout the years school board members and administrators across the country had made themselves popular by

---

40. Albert Shanker, "Where We Stand: Why the Idea of Merit Lacks Merit," March 2, 1975, AFT Files, Washington, D.C.

urging that schools adopt the practices of private enterprise in education, a notion that was rejected in the nineteenth-century reform movement.

Now some people were promoting the assumption that school boards and administrations know best about educational issues, but they overlooked the fact that this actually hurts the self-esteem and the professional competency of teachers. This psychological strategy initiated to control the thought processes among teachers is what led to the conflict with merit pay. This is the kind of thinking that Shanker rejected as he argued that the idea of merit pay actually lacked merit and must be abandoned.

In March 1975, right in the midst of a deep recession, President Gerald Ford and the Congress, uncertain about what to do to revive the economy, considered the possibility of a tax rebate. They thought that this would stimulate the economy because it would increase the purchasing power of both individuals and businesses. Shanker felt that the issue was too important for him not to be involved. As interest in the idea of a tax rebate seemed to grow among employers, members of the public, the Congress, and President Ford, Shanker conducted a study of all the relevant aspects of the issue in six cities[41] to make sure that he fully understood what was at stake so that he could explain his position to the union and the country.

The study led Shanker to the conclusion that the idea of a tax rebate would not improve the economic situation of either the workers or the teachers. He went on to observe, "The Congress and the President have virtually ignored the plight of city and state governments and school districts across the country. Some school systems, like local and state governments, are maintaining essential services by raising taxes. If Washington's inaction compels local governments to raise taxes while the federal government is reducing taxes it would mean merely shifting fiscal responsibility from one local government to another. In most cases school systems are unable to increase taxes sufficiently to maintain services. Giving taxpayers $200 will do little to make up for the loss of jobs or the loss of purchasing power, nor will it be enough to generate a sustained upswing in the economy."[42]

Shanker also suggested that what was needed was for the federal government to release public works and construction funds and to initiate full funding of the Comprehensive Employment Training Act to the tune of $5 billion, instead of the $1 billion President Ford intended to request. He also suggested that the law be amended so that some of the money could be used to avoid laying off and dismissing public employees. The reason for this suggestion was his position that "if the federal government acknowledged the need to provide such a relief to individuals, it must recognize the urgency of extending aid to schools."[43]

To be successful this program would require something more than just a tax rebate, it would require careful planning and cooperation at all levels of

---

41. These were Bismarck, Detroit, Seattle, New York, Cleveland, and Washington, D.C. He selected these because they were affected more adversely than other cities.

42. Albert Shanker, "Where We Stand: Much More Than a Tax Rebate Is Needed," March 30, 1975, AFT Files, Washington, D.C.

43. Ibid.

government. Not only did President Ford accept Shanker's proposal, but also he utilized Shanker as consultant on how it could be implemented. Did this mean that Ford and Shanker, two national leaders who hardly agreed on anything, were about to enter a period of cooperation? That was not to be, as Shanker persuaded the members of the organization he led to reject Ford at the polls in 1976, contributing to his losing the election to Jimmy Carter. Differences of opinion and philosophy between the two men were too great to be reconciled by a single event or issue.

In 1972 the country was faced with a new, serious, and destabilizing issue, educational malpractice. Up to that point a considerable number of decisions on education were being made by the courts. The cases decided dealt with school integration, free speech for both teachers and students, school finances, and due process for students. Since the *Brown* decision the courts focused on the constitutional rights of both students and teachers. But in 1972 a new direction had been taken that would open the door to a vast amount of educational litigation based not on constitutional considerations, but on what was clearly an emerging line of thinking: malpractice.

In November of that year the case of *Peter Doe v. San Francisco United School District* was filed in a California Superior Court. Immediately the case became the subject of a number of articles in journals of education throughout the country because how it would be resolved would determine the character of education in the country. It would have a profound effect on how teachers would conduct themselves in relation to their efforts to educate their students. Among these articles were two that attracted national attention. The first was written by Gary Seretsky, "The Strangely Significant Case of Peter Doe," which was published in the May 1973 *Phi Delta Kappan*. The second article, "Can a Student Sue the School for Educational Malpractice?" was written by David Abel and published in the November 1974 issue of the *Harvard Educational Review.*

The two articles referred to the action taken by Peter Doe, who was an eighteen-year-old white high school graduate. Doe's IQ was determined by the San Francisco School District to be normal. During the thirteen years that he was in the public schools in the city Peter showed that he was an average student who did not encounter any serious academic or disciplinary problems. His attendance record was considered regular. He advanced through the educational system until he was awarded a high school diploma. At different times during his years of schooling Peter's parents expressed to school officials their concern over what they considered to be Peter's difficulty in reading. But the school officials assured them that Peter was reading at the average level and did not show unusual problems.

Soon after his graduation from high school Peter was having serious problems filling out application forms for jobs. Two private reading specialists tested his reading skills independently and both came to the same conclusion that he was reading at the eighth grade level. This was not adequate enough to enable him to fully function as an adult in society. Peter and his parents decided that he needed private tutoring in reading. Peter eventually showed considerable improvement in his reading skills. They then decided to sue the school district on the basis of two considerations.

The first was that if Peter made progress in improving his reading skills as a result of private tutoring, then he should have made that progress as a regular student in the San Francisco School District. To them this meant that the school failed in its responsibility to educate him properly. The second consideration was that the school officials repeatedly told his parents that Peter did not encounter unusual problems in reading and so did not require any remedial instruction to improve his skills.

In filing the suit Peter and his parents asked for damages in the sum of $500,000 for his loss of earning capacity because, they argued, he was undereducated. They also asked for another $500,000 in punitive damages as well as the cost incurred in engaging a private tutor. In dismissing the suit the California Superior Court ruled that even if the facts of the case were accurate, they did not constitute sufficient grounds to rule in Peter's favor. There was no universally accepted definition of proper education and of malpractice in which the responsibility of the school was made clear and the test of its educational responsibility to the student was known to the parties.[44] Using the arguments that Abel and Seretsky had made in their articles on the case, Shanker established a line of thinking that he used to advance three reasons to show why the concept of educational malpractice must be eliminated from the educational issues that schools were struggling with.

The first reason was that "teaching processes are not yet understood adequately. There is as yet no model of competent educational practice comparable to that which exists in medicine or law. Abel and Seretsky suggest that the San Francisco School Board might well argue that a victory for Doe would lead to a flood of litigation."[45] The second reason was Shanker's belief that if the concept of educational malpractice were accepted, it would "divert huge sums of money from meeting the educational needs of students to the coffers of lawyers and insurance companies."[46]

The third reason was that while malpractice suits were designed to seek improvement of professional practices, when applied to education they might actually lead to the adoption of poorer practices because schools might require rules that were too rigid and procedures that would restrict the rights of both students and teachers to engage in academic freedom.[47] Therefore, the issue of educational malpractice came to an end, with Shanker advancing reasons to support his position that it must not come into the picture to affect the educational process.

In 1975 the problems caused by the recession and those of the declining economy combined to force city governments to take unconventional measures to stop themselves from going bankrupt. In New York the situation was

---

44. It is common for states to initiate follow-up action in cases in which they have an interest by passing legislation to cover future cases. That the California state legislature did not initiate such an action shows that it did not think that the Peter Doe outcome required any legislative action.

45. Albert Shanker, "Where We Stand: Dangers in the Concept of Educational Malpractice," April 20, 1975, AFT Files, Washington, D.C.

46. Ibid.

47. Ibid.

deteriorating rapidly even though Mayor Beame received considerable financial aid from the Ford administration. In an effort to find solutions to the fiscal problems the city was facing, the city council and the mayor began to consider investing pension funds in projects they thought would yield profit.

The retirement systems across the country were controlled by boards of trustees who were responsible either to the employees or to the employers. In New York City it was these trustees who were considering the request from the mayor and the city council to invest the pension funds in what Shanker considered questionable projects in order to make profit and save the city from going bankrupt. Since this investment amounted to gambling, the trustees were not allowed to gamble. Therefore, the mayor and the city council were considering the implementation of a plan of action that would be illegal.

Upon learning of the decision to consider this high-risk method of bailing the city out of its financial mismanagement, Shanker took the high ground in opposing this method of seeking solutions to the fiscal problems the city was facing. He argued, "This consideration clearly does not deal with what would happen in case of default. As trustees the city could not concern itself with the question involving the overall human impact of the default, the national or international economic repercussions, or what would happen to the city schools and its services."[48] From this line of argument the city government now came to realize how risky the proposed plan was. The employees made it known that they opposed the plan. The city was, therefore, forced to abandon it.

In 1976 the country faced another controversial issue that Americans had not encountered before. This was a decline in college entrance examination scores. The decline occurred on a number of major test instruments including the Scholastic Aptitude Test (SAT), the American College Testing Program (ACT), the Minnesota Scholastic Aptitude Test (MSAT), and the Iowa Tests of Educational Development (ITED). Because many people regarded this unprecedented decline as a national crisis, a fundamental question was raised as to why. In an effort to pinpoint the cause of the decline two schools of thought emerged. The first was that the decline was caused by some serious defects that were present in the tests themselves. Those who belonged to this school of thought argued that the tests themselves were not designed to measure what students knew and, therefore, were irrelevant to the educational achievement of students.

The second school of thought was that the quality of the students had declined sharply because the students no longer pursued their educational quest with the same enthusiasm as did students of previous generations. Those who subscribed to this way of looking at the problem attempted to identify a number of factors that had caused the decline.

Among these factors were a general decline in morale as a result of the Watergate scandal; the recession which robbed students of their ability to plan the future; and the decline in the economy, which hurt students' motivation to prepare for the future in an increasingly hostile socioeconomic environment.

---

48. Albert Shanker, "Where We Stand: Federal Protection for Public Pension Funds Is Needed," December 14, 1975, AFT Files, Washington, D.C.

Finally, those who shared this line of thinking argued that the general breakdown in the traditional nuclear family structure created serious emotional problems for students and also eroded away the emotional support system that they needed to succeed in their educational socialization.

Recognizing how important it was for the country to focus on the controversy, Shanker once again undertook a review of the literature to discern the real causes for this decline and what could be done to address it. His first real find was a study conducted in 1976 by Annegret Harnischfeger and David E. Wiley entitled "Achievement Test Scores Decline: Do We Need to Worry?" The second was a position paper written in the same year by Leo A. Munday, vice-president of ACT, whose responsibility was to conduct ongoing research and develop test items. The article was entitled "Causes of the Decline in Test Scores."

Shanker digested both articles, which agreed upon the causes for the decline. The first was an increase in student absenteeism throughout the country. Shanker stressed, "No matter how good the curriculum may be, students who are not present will not learn from it."[49] Although the articles made no specific suggestions about how to improve attendance, it was recognized that if the country is to eventually depend on its young, it must encourage in them the discipline and commitment to attend school.

Also among the causes identified were the following: The general lack of interest in formal education was a global phenomenon, material comfort was having an adverse impact on students' pursuit of education; the belief among some students to participate in professional athletics was forcing them to abandon their studies; society was not demonstrating the tangible benefits of a formal education; the thinking that one could become successful financially with little or no education compelled many students to give up their studies; the drug culture was having a devastating effect on students' ability to plan the future in terms of educational prerequisites. The reality of these causes suggests that the country was going through a cultural change that was not altogether positive in its influence on young people. Western culture was, and is, emphasizing short-term, immediate gratification.

The second cause for the decline in test scores was that many parents left their children alone without adequate care and guidance. While it has been recognized that both parents often have to work to provide their children a comfortable life style, it is equally recognized that leaving children alone can have a devastating and indelible impact on their education. The third major cause was a change in values that placed more emphasis on material comfort than on educational success. In 1988 an ABC-TV documentary entitled "America's Kids: Why They Flunk," hosted by Barbara Walters, reached these same conclusions. Shanker suggested that only through cooperation and collaboration, rather than through trying to apportion blame, could the nation find solutions to the problems. His position on this issue helped to put the search for solutions into a

---

49. Albert Shanker, "Where We Stand: Decline in Test Scores, a Cause for Concern," March 14, 1976, AFT Files, Washington, D.C.

proper perspective for the stockholders in education, who are ultimately the entire nation's population.

If Shanker had thought that differences between himself and President Ford over policy were serious, he soon realized in 1981 that differences between himself and President Ronald Reagan were even more serious. The Reagan administration introduced what has been referred to as Reaganomics, sometimes called "trickle-down economics" and what George Bush called "voodoo economics." As introduced by Reagan's budget director, David Stockman, Reagan's economic plan entailed essential elements of the philosophy of the Republican party that Shanker disagreed with. In the spring of 1982 Stockman announced to the American people that taxes for the wealthy would soon be reduced drastically to stimulate the economy. According to this philosophy, cutting taxes for the rich would increase investment and savings, create more jobs, and lead to greater productivity.

For this to happen the federal government would have to cut programs, including education, in order to reduce spending because of reduced revenue. In September 1982 Horman Ture, Reagan's undersecretary of the treasury, traveled all over the country to generate support for Reagan's policies and programs. He supported cuts in government spending that Reagan had initiated. Among these new cuts was a 12 percent reduction in federal aid to cities. Reagan, who campaigned for the presidency in 1976 and 1980 and for reelection in 1984 on an anti-government platform, did not think that the federal government should have any role in extending financial aid to the local districts for educational purposes.

When state, county, and city governments indicated that they could not absorb the cut that Reagan was imposing, Ture suggested that they raise taxes to meet their budget and provide police, fire, education, and other services. These developments brought Shanker into the scene because he believed strongly that Reaganomics could have dire consequences for public education. He quoted a joke from columnist William Rasberry to illustrate the implications of Reaganomics, saying, "It is like a man waiting for the delivery of his new car. He gets a note from the salesman saying 'This is to notify you that we have shipped the car you ordered. In order to reduce the weight and so lower your shipping costs, we have removed the wheels and the motor. You would have to buy these elsewhere.' Maybe David Stockman or some other Reagan administration officials can explain how the federal tax cut will result in savings, investment, jobs, and productivity."[50]

Shanker acknowledged that Ture "is aware of the trap set for the poor person in a poor area. Where the poor need services most they will get them least. These cuts will make Reagan look like a good guy for the rich because he cuts taxes while state and local officials look like bad guys because they raise them."[51] It is not surprising that Reagan and Shanker remained distant and did not have any cordial interaction because Shanker characterized Reaganomics as an

50. Albert Shanker, "Where We Stand: A Sharp Look Inside Reagan's Tax Plan," May 15, 1982, AFT Files, Washington, D.C.
    51. Ibid.

unmitigated national disaster.[52] He could not understand why Reagan was acting in the way he was. It is known that the Republican philosophy espouses the view that when the wealthy are secure in their position, they will benevolently provide service to the rest of the population. There is no evidence to substantiate this philosophy in the history of the United States. Some would call it a delusion. That is why Shanker strongly disagreed with it.

In 1986 the educational services in public schools were experiencing a major crisis. This was caused primarily by the attitude of the Reagan administration and by provisions of the Gramm-Rudman legislation, requiring the federal government to cut spending in order to balance the budget. This crisis meant that school districts found it hard to allocate funds for equipment that teachers needed to carry out their duties. When the situation became even more critical, Shanker commissioned a study of the situation in the New York City schools. He discovered some disturbing facts.

One high school was struggling to make its only VCR work. One English teacher who wanted to show a videotape to illustrate scenes from *Hamlet* used a cardboard strip to make it work. But during the afternoon, after the VCR had been used a few times, it failed to operate. While this was happening, Shanker found that in one school the principal spent 80 percent of his school's budget of $42,837 for basic supplies, primarily administrative forms. In another school the principal decided to repaint administrative and staff offices, leaving the classrooms in a dilapidated state.[53]

Unable to make any sense out of this situation, Shanker sought answers in his accustomed manner. He reviewed the literature to understand it better. He read an article entitled "We Have Set Up a Special Account to Finance Teachers' Bright Ideas," written by Barbara Novatis, an elementary school teacher in the Farmington public school system in Michigan. It was published in the July 1986 issue of *The American School Board Journal*. In the article Novatis discussed three creative ways used by teachers to make the most out of limited educational equipment.

The first related to a speech pathologist who compiled tapes on listening skills and rearranged them for use in several grades. The second was about an elementary school media specialist who began a pilot program to develop thinking skills by having children in advanced grades work in groups to develop reading skills. The third was about eight elementary school teachers who attended a week-long training seminar on using concrete objects such as rods and blocks, rather than traditional rote and drill,to teach mathematics.

Shanker argued that in the face of dwindling resources principals must utilize common sense to maximize usage of the materials available for the benefit of students. He concluded, "Had the ideas that Novatis discussed been more widely implemented, the chances are that one New York City school may have had a good deal less than $33,000 worth of new forms, but teachers would

---

52. Albert Shanker, "Where We Stand: Reagan Takes Short Cuts to Disaster," April 28, 1982, AFT Files, Washington, D.C.

53. Albert Shanker, "Where We Stand: School Priorities Need Balance," August 2, 1986, AFT Files, Washington, D. C.

probably have made sure that their students had functioning microscopes for their laboratory work and a map on the wall that indicated that Rhodesia is now called Zimbabwe, and an English teacher that I know would not have had to spend valuable class time trying to bend a piece of cardboard into the right shape to make the VCR work. Hamlet deserves a lot better deal than this."[54] Although Shanker did not hope to solve this serious problem by what he said, it helped the schools become more sensitive and careful about how they used the limited resources available to them.

The strained relationship that developed between Shanker and Reagan over policy extended into the term of office of the Bush administration. At the beginning of his administration in 1989, George Bush announced that he wanted to be known as the education president. During the next two years, however, he did little to show Americans what he intended to do to fulfill his pledge.

When White House aides[55] told him that his failure to live up to his vow was having a negative effect on his popularity among voters, Bush decided to do something he believed would have a dramatic impact on the public perception of him as being pro-education. On April 18, 1991, he released *America 2000: An Education Strategy,* which Lamar Alexander, Bush's secretary of education, called "a bold, complex and long-range plan to move every community in America forward to the national education goals adopted by the President."[56]

President Bush wanted the American people to know some things about his proposed reforms in education. Arguing that the reforms would affect the 110,000 public and private schools in the country, Bush claimed that the reform plan would bring "change in every American community, change in every American home, change in our attitude about learning."[57] His claim was a reminder of what Herbert Hoover said at the beginning of the Depression in 1929: that the period of economic prosperity was right around the corner and it would bring two chickens in every pot and a car in every garage. Like Hoover, Bush had no idea of the extent of the political problems he was facing due to an absolute lack of understanding.

In a state of excitement, Bush said, "As a nation we now invest more in education than in defense. If standard tests and report cards tell parents and voters how their schools are doing, choice gives them the leverage to act."[58] The centerpiece of Bush's reform plan for both public schools and private schools was to provide federal financial aid so parents could have a choice of where they sent their children to school, public or private.

---

54. Ibid.

55. One such aide was John Scully, Bush's advisor on education. In 1992, when Bush ignored his advice on ways of improving education, Scully endorsed Bill Clinton for president. For details see Dickson A. Mungazi, *Educational Policy and National Character: Africa, Japan, the United States, and the Soviet Union* (Westport, Conn.: Praeger Publishers, 1993), p. 171.

56. Lamar Alexander, "A Message from the U.S Secretary of Education", in *America 2000: An Education Strategy* (Washington, D.C.: U.S. Department of Education, 1992), p. i.

57. Ibid., p. 11.

58. Ibid., p. 22.

Bush's proposal of school choice for parents using federal financial assistance took many people by surprise, including Shanker. As the reform plan became known, it was clear that there was nothing new except Bush's idea of extending public funds to private schools. This is the idea that Shanker disagreed with strongly. In November 1992, six months after Bush released the plan, Shanker argued, "The Bush administration has never kept secret its infatuation with giving public funds to private schools as the key to educational reform. What is surprising is how far the administration is willing to go to undermine America's common school tradition in the name of private school choice."[59]

Reminding Americans that America was built upon the introduction of the public school system as intended by the reform movement of the nineteenth century, Shanker urged Americans to reject Bush's reform plan because it was intended to abolish public schools. In 1992 his educational reform in doubt and his economic agenda in disarray, Bush did not know that his days as president of the United States were numbered.

During the presidential election campaign in that year Bill Clinton, Bush's Democratic opponent, put out an extremely well written document entitled *Putting People First: A National Economic Strategy for America*. In it he argued, "My national economic strategy for America will put people first at every stage of their lives. We will overhaul America's public schools to ensure that every child has a chance for a world-class education."[60] This was all Shanker needed to support him.

The American voters also believed that his was a better plan for the country than Bush's. Clinton won the election. It would be erroneous to conclude that Shanker's support helped Clinton win the election. However, that about one out of eight delegates to the Democratic National Convention was NEA or AFT member made a difference in the nomination process. It goes without saying that Clinton's anti-private school choice position endeared him to teachers, who, in turn, helped get him elected. Some people, however, note that after winning the presidency Clinton enrolled his daughter, Chelsea, into a private school. Many Americans recognized Clinton's *Goals 2000: Educate America,* which he designed "to promote long-term direction for the improvement of education and lifelong learning"[61] as more meaningful than Bush's *America 2000*.

SUMMARY AND CONCLUSION

The discussion in this chapter has presented Shanker as a national leader who knew that the position he held compelled him to play an active, effective, and constructive role in seeking solutions to educational issues that were and are unavoidably interrelated with national problems. This leads to two conclusions

59. Albert Shanker, "Where We Stand: Bush's America 2000 Plan, A Feast for Private Schools," November 15, 1991, AFT Files, Washington, D.C.
60. Bill Clinton, *Putting People First: A National Economic Strategy for America* (Little Rock, Ark.: Bill Clinton for President Committee, 1992), p. 15.
61. U.S. Department of Education, "Clinton Sends Congress *Goals 2000: Educate America* (Washington, D.C., March 21, 1993).

about that role. The first is that in playing that role Shanker knew that he must rise above the peripheral level of a union leader to exert appropriate national leadership consistent with the demands of a leader who placed the interest of the nation above that of his own and the organization he led. This is an essential characteristic of a statesman. For Shanker the strikes to force school boards to recognize the demands of teachers were replaced by dialogue that mirrors democratic principles.

The second conclusion is that before he expressed his position on the various critical issues facing the nation, Shanker made sure that he fully understood both sides of the arguments. He then initiated a thorough study of the issues through a review of the literature, which enabled him to understand what was being said about these issues. When he expressed his position, Americans perceived that he was giving them a well thought out position. In this regard Shanker has proven to be more than a knowledgeable leader of a national organization, he is a national leader who has the best interests of the nation always in mind.

7

Shanker's Relationships with Other People and Organizations

To talk about independence of an isolated professional association is to show a lack of wisdom.

Albert Shanker, 1975

Seeking solutions to problems of society must be initiated in the context of developing relationships that one must have with other people and organizations.

Albert Shanker, 1993

SHANKER'S PHILOSOPHY OF LEADERSHIP AND RELATIONSHIPS

Writing on the essentials of effective leadership and the nature of relationships that a good leader must have with leaders of other organizations, Adam Curle presents elements of theoretical considerations that are applicable to Shanker. Curle writes, "The concept of awareness includes, as an indispensable element, the sense of social environment, sensitivity to social injustice, empathy with the suffering, and the general capacity to relate warmly to other people. Unless the action of a leader is free of negative emotion, and the particular manifestations of his leadership are associated with a sense of belonging and identity, his leadership is competitive materialism. In this setting institutional power alone cannot afford protection against rapacity and exploitation."[1] Curle goes on to argue that the importance of these attributes of effective leadership determines the nature of the relationships that the leader has with other people and organizations.

Curle reaches the conclusion that these relationships in turn determine the character of the institution that one leads. This institutional character intimately

---

1. Adam Curle, *Education for Liberation* (New York: John Wiley and Sons, 1973), p. 60.

affects the kind of service it provides for its members. For this to happen Curle suggests that a leader needs to understand three basic elements of leadership if he or she is to be effective. The first is that he or she must recognize the need to develop a personality that makes it possible to be sensitive to the values of those around him or her. This requires respect for democratic principles.

Curle goes on to argue that acquiring sensitivity must lead to action consistent with the objectives of the group. The second element is that a leader must demonstrate complete knowledge of the issues so that they can be approached with a clear understanding of all relevant arguments or positions. This indicates that a leader must rise above the level of debate among the members of the organization he or she leads to articulate positions on issues that serve their needs.

The third attribute of leadership that Curle says is critical to develop is that a leader must demonstrate flexibility and not be too rigid. He or she can do this without showing a lack of resolve. Curle believes that this makes it possible for "the learning relationships to serve as a good model for relationships in the wider world, one in which understanding, nurturing, and care replace the impossible barriers of hierarchical freedom in learning and the flexible relationships which it depends on to involve a relearning of the concept of self."[2]

Curle argues that this form of learning is far more important than the process of gaining knowledge. It involves a system of communication of feelings and ideas about human relationships so critical to seeking solutions to problems of human existence. Human relationships, based on clear lines of communication, become the basis for promoting those values that members of an organization consider important. An agenda for action has meaning only in this kind of environment. It is the responsibility of the leader to nurture it so that he or she has ideal relationships with the followers in the organization her or she serves.

Curle cautions that the acquisition of these three basic components of effective leadership does not guarantee the successful operation of an organization. They merely make it possible to establish an optimal basis of communication, which is absolutely necessary to create a learning environment that "has all these attributes which help establish the prerequisites for the growth of awareness."[3] This awareness becomes a critical foundation required for sensitivity and understanding. Curle raises the question of what awareness does to the leader, the organization, and the society.

Curle provides the answer when he concludes, "The more aware we become, the more we recognize the limits of awareness. The more we become aware of others, the more we see them in terms of their similarities to or differences from ourselves. But greater awareness shows us glimpses of what cannot be described in these terms and which we therefore cannot fully grasp."[4] What Curle seems to suggest is that awareness is vital to the success of relationships that members

---

2. Ibid., p. 6.

3. Ibid., p. 64

4. Ibid., p. 65.

of an organization have with their leader and with one another. These relationships cannot, therefore, be taken for granted.

The challenge of leadership is to recognize the contradiction that often emerges in the importance of awareness of human limitation in comprehending critical dimensions of institutional operations and the fact that a leader cannot be autocratic in taking a position under the notion that only he or she is right. Curle suggests that because, in general, politicians are excellent at autocratic behavior, they are less sensitive to human limitations, including their own. They do not, therefore, recognize that their opponents may be right and that they may be wrong.[5]

Rather than taking the position that he or she only knows the truth, a good leader must always accept responsibility for errors in judgment or opinions on critical issues. A fundamental question must be posed: How does a leader function in a democracy that takes great pride in the values of its institutions and still play a decisive role in seeking solutions within an environment of conflicting political ideologies? Curle offers a possible answer when he suggests that a leader cast in this kind of environment must follow the path of Edmund Burke (1729-1797)[6] and Thomas Hobbes (1588-1679),[7] and not Niccolo Machiavelli (1469-1527).

Because Machiavelli remains an important subject of study, a word or two needs saying about the implications his political philosophy poses for leadership in a modern world. Recognizing similarities in the theories of leadership of Hobbes and Burke, and differences between their theories and Machiavelli's, one needs to understand the effect of political behavior in the types of environments in which they functioned. The main differences lay in accepting the effects of democratic principles and of dictatorial behavior in the conduct of leadership in seeking to fulfill objectives. This is why Machiavelli argued that the leader must use any means, no matter how wicked, to strike down his opponents and to make his followers obey him. Machiavelli believed that the practice of democracy has serious flaws that limit efficiency in both designing and implementing policy. He argued that it shows weakness in a leader if a group cannot always agree on what must be done.

These are the ideas that Machiavelli took into consideration in writing the *History of Florence* and *The Art of War*. In these books he outlined suggestions

---

5. An example of this occurred on October 4, 1993, when Boris Yeltsin, president of Russia, authorized the armed forces to storm the Russian parliament because deputies had expressed opinions different from his own regarding constitutional matters. Yeltsin abolished democratic principles in a way that made him a dictator, a serious contradiction to his claim that he is trying to build democracy.

6. Edmund Burke, a British social reformer and political thinker whose *A Philosophical Inquiry into the Origins of Our Ideas of the Sublime and Beautiful* (1750), has been recognized as an authority on social issues.

7. The author of *Leviathan or the Matter, Form and Power of a Commonwealth, Ecclesiastical and Civil* (1651), Thomas Hobbes offers political theory to resolve conflict.

for what the leader must do to sustain power. Along with *The Prince*,[8] these books have also made it possible for Machiavelli to be considered the father of modern political science. But if one examines the seemingly endless political disarray that has remained a legacy of Italy it is questionable as to whether Machiavelli deserves that dubious honor. The son of a famous jurist and a member of an old Tuscan family, Machiavelli was educated primarily through tutoring and private study. He became a leading figure in the Republic of Florence after the powerful and influential Medici family was driven out in 1498. For fourteen years Machiavelli served as the chief secretary to the Ruling Council of the Republic, giving him an opportunity to formulate his political philosophy.

But with all his power and influence, Machiavelli's days were numbered. When the Medici family returned to power in 1512, Machiavelli lost his position of prominence. Were it not for the action taken by Pope Leo X, whose reign lasted from 1513 to 1521, to minimize the effect of his arrest, torture, and imprisonment, Machiavelli might have lost his place in history. What makes Machiavelli controversial is his belief that it is more important to sustain the power base of the leader than it is to serve the needs of the people. He does not recognize the truth that when sustaining the power structure becomes the primary objective of the leader, the institutions and the people in them endure agony, suffering, and underdevelopment. Even when leaders such as Nicholas II (1894-1917) of Russia and Louis XVI (1754-1793) and his colorful wife, Marie Antoinette (1755-1793),[9] of France attempted to utilize a paternalistic approach to critical issues, they only succeeded in increasing discontent and possible insurrection.

In recognizing the attitudes that Curle believes made both Hobbes and Burke unusually great and progressive thinkers on political leadership, one recognizes a characteristic that made them authors. This was their unwavering belief in democratic principles. In applying these principles to Shanker's relationships with other people and organizations, one must discuss three specific groups with whom he interacted. These are the NEA, African-Americans, and the general public. These relationships were determined by the nature of the issues that had to be resolved in the course of carrying out his responsibility to the AFT. A brief discussion of these three examples will illustrate the extent to which

---

8. Although Machiavelli completed writing this book in 1513, it was not published until 1532, five years after his death. In it Machiavelli argues that a leader need not worry about the views of his subjects in his efforts to accomplish certain objectives because the end justifies the means. In short, Machiavelli was suggesting that the leader must make no apology for resorting to dictatorial means to accomplish his objectives.

9. Shortly before the French revolution started in 1789, Marie Antionette wanted to know why the people were unhappy with her. "Because they do not have bread," was the answer. "Let them eat cake," she responded. This situation is similar to the one a national leader might face today if he is told that the homeless are starving because they do not have hamburger and he responds, "Let them eat prime rib." He might seal his own fate. That is exactly what Marie Antionette did.

Shanker has been committed to the values and principles that have made his term of office unique in the labor movement, especially the AFT.

SHANKER'S RELATIONSHIPS WITH THE NEA

Since he assumed the educational leadership in 1958, Shanker has believed that the strength and the quality of American education lie in the strength of teacher organizations. He, therefore, endeavored to improve the socioeconomic condition of teachers as a prerequisite for seeking improvement in the quality of education.[10] During the formative years of his leadership Shanker could be described as obsessed with this perceived necessity. His zeal was such that he was prepared to call for or lead strikes to see this need actualized.

Although he has mellowed with experience and time, Shanker still believes in the importance of sustaining the socioeconomic status of teachers as a springboard for national development. In 1993 he explained how important this was to the author: "The socioeconomic aspects of education must be the means to make efforts dedicated to developing the intelligence needed to run a democratic society. The development of education to make this possible is one of the greatest challenges America has ever faced."[11]

Shanker's view that the socioeconomic position of teachers must improve if effective methods for seeking solutions to national problems are to be found seemed a departure from the conventional approach of trusting school boards to determine what was appropriate for teachers. This has created an environment of conflict between Shanker and the NEA. In 1962 William G. Carr, executive secretary of the NEA, argued that for the UFT, led at that time by Shanker, to resort to strikes in order to prevail was damaging the teaching profession. Carr went on to argue, "Industrial practices cannot be copied in a doctrinaire manner in public education. Such tactics do not represent values that can be taught to American public school children."[12] There is no question that Carr was trying to restore the NEA to a respectable level after its humiliating defeat in the collective bargaining elections of 1961.

The cause of conflict between the AFT and the NEA was the question of whether or not teacher organizations should resort to political methods to address educational problems. This dialectic is as old as these two organizations. On the one hand, since its founding in 1857, the NEA had held steadfast to its position that teacher organizations must not resort to strikes because this runs contrary to the basic principles that teaching rests upon. Conversely, since its inception in 1916, the AFT has operated under the belief that the only way to restore quality to American education is to elaborate and protect the rights of teachers. Shanker has explained that the AFT position is that collective bargaining, though

---

10. Albert Shanker, interview with author, Washington, D.C., May 17, 1993.
11. Ibid.
12. William G. Carr, "The Education of William G. Carr," 1962, NEA Files, Washington, D.C.

political in practice and process, yields results that are beneficial to education.[13] That Timothy Stinnett, a member of the NEA, agreed with the AFT's position on this issue suggests that there may be a growing segment within the NEA that wants to revise its no-strike position.

As the conflict between the two organizations escalated in 1962, each organization entrenched itself. The AFT began to supply its members with information on what the NEA was doing that appeared to be contrary to the interests of teachers. What Carr considered to be a Machiavellian approach to a growing national controversy led him to react: "Some labor leaders may be planning to use their considerable economic and political power to affiliate all public school teachers with a white-collar union."[14] Carr concluded that in its effort to discredit the NEA, the AFT had actually declared war on his organization and that this was a very serious crisis.

Carr also saw the AFT's action as "an assault on professional independence. The AFL-CIO program, as defined by its leadership, would, if successful, destroy the NEA and its state and local affiliates."[15] He urged teachers to reject this attempt by labor unions in order to preserve the professional integrity of the organization they were members of. He also reminded teachers of the differences between a professional association and a union, which he said was always associated with politics, which is not the business of education.

In making his argument against the AFT, Carr attempted to persuade the NEA to accept his position that as part of the AFL-CIO council the AFT had opposed the practice of using taxes to support public education. He further suggested that if every teacher in the country became affiliated with it, the entire teaching profession would be forced to live and operate under repressive conditions much like those behind the Iron Curtain.

In its own way the NEA was accentuating the strained relationship at a time when both organizations needed to cooperate in order to direct their efforts toward seeking solutions to the problems that education and they were facing. These included a decline in teachers' morale, a crisis in domestic and foreign policy, and the dissipation of family values. These issues affected teachers more than any other segment of American society. Efforts to find answers could only become truly successful within an environment of cooperation, not through one of conflict and competition.

By the time Shanker assumed the presidency of the AFT, the issues dividing the NEA and the AFT had become very complex. A big gulf had formed between them. In 1978 the controversy over political activity and professional conduct was highlighted in the Allan Bakke case. In 1977 Allan Bakke, a white student, brought suit against the medical school at the University of California at Davis. He argued that he was discriminated against when he was twice denied admission to the medical school. It became a landmark case in what became known as reverse discrimination. White applicants have since argued, as a result of the

---

13. Albert Shanker, interview with author, Washington, D.C., May 17, 1993.
14. William G. Carr, "Response to the AFT," 1962, NEA Files, Washington, D.C.
15. Ibid.

findings of the U.S. Supreme Court in favor of Bakke, that they have been discriminated against because of their color and ethnicity.

Because of the university's efforts to meet the requirements of affirmative action, the medical school reserved 16 places for minority students out of a pool of 100 selected students. The admission of the eighty-four white students was based on a variety of academic criteria that Bakke argued were higher than the criteria used to admit minority students. When all the arguments were heard, the U.S. Supreme Court ruled 5-4 in *Bakke v. Regents of the University of California* that Bakke's rights had been violated by the denial of his admission to the medical school. It ordered the school to admit him.

Although most civil rights organizations, women's groups, and the NEA opposed Bakke's suit on the grounds that if he succeeded, the precedent would be a setback for gains made by minority groups and women, Shanker saw this in a different light. He shocked many by providing an *amicus curiae* brief supporting Bakke's position. He argued that Bakke's suit was grounded on educational and professional principles and that the opposition from civil rights organizations and the NEA was politically motivated.

Shanker noted that in its ruling the Supreme Court seems to have widened the gulf separating the NEA and the AFT. The implication of both Shanker's position and the Supreme Court's decision included the subtle emergence of new thinking that the principle of "collective bargaining was no longer regarded as a right that belonged to groups."[16]

To understand Shanker's relationships with the NEA and their effect on education in the United States, one needs to understand the relationship between the NEA and the AFT in terms of its historical development. Writing in 1960 Myron Lieberman, a periodic contender for the AFT leadership, concluded, "Essentially there are two basic issues which divide the two organizations. One is the fact that the NEA has no restrictions upon administrator membership. The other is the AFT's affiliation with the AFL-CIO."[17] The fact of the matter is that the relationship between the two organizations in 1960 was not as seriously strained as it has progressively become, beginning in 1972.

The formation of the AFT was closely associated with the belief that it would fill a gap that the NEA was not willing or able to fill. This was the need to safeguard teachers' interests on issues of job security, salaries, tenure, academic freedom, and individual rights. If the NEA had sought to include these important matters in its original charter in 1857, it is doubtful that the AFT would have moved in the direction it did. William van Til concludes that this is the reason why members of the NEA were also involved in promoting the AFT agenda.[18] They had found the original agenda and objectives of their own organization seriously lacking in meeting the needs of teachers in a vastly changing world.

---

16. Marjorie Murphy, *Blackboard Unions: The AFT and the NEA, 1900-1980* (Ithaca, N.Y.: Cornell University Press, 1990), p. 265.

17. Myron Lieberman, *The Future of Public Education* (Chicago: The University of Chicago Press, 1960), p. 231.

18. William van Til, *Education: A Beginning* (Boston: Houghton Mifflin Company, 1974), p. 109.

As the AFT continued to grow, conflict and competition began to permeate the interaction between the two organizations. In 1918, when the membership of both was about 10,000, there was a feeling of cooperation. But by 1960, when the NEA had 713,000 members and the AFT had 60,000 members, the relationship between the two organizations became more strained because NEA members thought that the AFT was gaining in membership by attracting some of its own members by claiming to obtain better conditions of service for teachers.

The NEA also felt that the AFT was slowly, but steadily replacing it as an organization that represented the political and socioeconomic interests of teachers in ways that had not been tried in the past. In 1974 van Til described the kind of interaction that was emerging between the two organizations as a result of these developments, saying, "With respect to size the NEA remained Goliath and the AFT remained David. But the AFT's gains were disturbing to the NEA supporters. Although the NEA still heavily outnumbered the AFT in membership throughout the 1960s, the speed of growth of the teachers' unions in big cities and in some suburbs threatened the NEA's controlling position."[19]

The differences in position between the two organizations were so paralyzing that they tried to reconcile and even considered a merger. That the AFT made the offer of the terms for the merger indicates its willingness to settle the differences. The AFT's conditions included a clause that upon implementing the unification NEA members would be free to exercise their right not to be affiliated with the AFL-CIO and hence would not pay any affiliation fees. The position of the NEA, however, was that this term was unacceptable because it still left open the possibility of affiliation with labor.

The NEA also argued that a united national organization for teachers would be much stronger and more effective in seeking the fulfillment of its agenda if it operated outside the affiliation and influence of the labor movement, which the AFL-CIO represented. The reason advanced for this line of thinking was that an independent organization would not need affiliation to carry out its own agenda because it would be quite large, powerful, and influential in its own right. The NEA further argued that this would mean the clear articulation of the wishes of teachers and the goals of the organization, bringing more benefits to teachers all across the country.

In 1974 Larry Sibelman, the AFT vice-president, understood the NEA position perhaps better than any other official in his union when he discussed it, stating, "The NEA felt that affiliation with other unions through the AFL-CIO would constrain the organization from pursuing its goals since they would need to conform or fall into line with general AFL-CIO policies and decisions."[20] When the AFT indicated that it was unable to meet the conditions that the NEA stipulated, the NEA abruptly withdrew from the merger discussions, arguing that no matter what proposals the AFT offered as a compromise, it was unwilling to consider them because of its present affiliation with the AFL-CIO, and that this

---

19. Ibid., p. 110.
20. Larry Sibelman, "A Philosophy of Splendid Isolationism: The NEA vs the AFL-CIO," *The American Teacher* (October 1974): p. 25.

would have to change before further talks could be undertaken. This is a condition that the AFT has said it is unwilling to consider. The climate of conflict between the two organizations was exacerbated when the NEA denied the AFT allegation that it was anti-AFL-CIO and thus anti-union.

As one studies the conflict between these two, one is led to the conclusion that the NEA failed to comprehend the value that the AFT placed on its affiliation with the AFL-CIO. The NEA did not understand that from its founding the AFT recognized that if the conditions of service for teachers were to improve, it must affiliate with labor. This did not take away the professional component of its mission. When one considers the substandard pay, the vulnerable position the teachers were in, and the political and vindictive actions of school boards and school administrators, it becomes evident that affiliation with labor was an absolute necessity in protecting the interests of teachers.

Although organized workers, including teachers, have not always been represented by the AFL-CIO, it has demonstrated complete understanding of the plight of teachers and other employees. Sibelman concluded, "These are people who themselves have an immediate empathy with the aspirations of other working people because they are workers. Union members best understand the benefits derived from improved and expanded social services because they are directly affected. Where but to the AFL-CIO will public employees turn for support of their needs?"[21]

In March 1975 Shanker decided to respond, not in words as the NEA had done, but in deeds. At a joint session of the New York State United Teachers and the American Federation of Teachers held in New York City, Ralph Lloyd, a member of Shanker's executive council, said, "Shanker brought the 2,000 applauding delegates and guests to their feet by unveiling a major plan for national, state, and local governments to correct an economic situation which looks impossible."[22] In the glare of this publicity Shanker outlined five sources of direct and indirect federal assistance that would be needed to upgrade education. The first was to pay the states for the increased costs of welfare caused by inflation and economic decline. The second was to establish a federal bank to make low-interest loans to state and local governments and school boards.

The third was to create new public service jobs that were did not replace existing jobs. The fourth was to increase revenue-sharing funds and make them available to education agencies. The fifth was to release all federal funds impounded for education, public works, and construction of new school buildings. Shanker stated that the AFT would not allow Congress to use the income tax reduction as an excuse for holding back federal aid to education because this would force an increase in local taxes. He added, "As soon as that tax reduction is passed all of us have to march on Washington. If you have $30

---

21. Ibid.
22. Ralph Lloyd, "New York Teachers Don't Want War with the NEA," *The American Teacher* (April 1975): 6: 17.

million to give away, you better have $5 or $10 billion for the public schools of this country."[23]

Shanker then directed his remarks toward James Harris, then president of the NEA, who had sent a letter to the New York teachers attacking Shanker for continuing the affiliation with the AFL-CIO. Harris also accused the AFT of a gross distortion of NEA policies and programs and argued that the members of his organization were independent professionals. He urged the AFT to allow its members the same independence by withdrawing its AFL-CIO affiliation because it inhibited their ability to exercise their freedom of thought and action.

Shanker criticized the NEA's failure to protect the economic interests of teachers. Deploring Harris's action as a waste of time and money in attacking the AFT, Shanker responded, "Teachers cannot be independent because our jobs depend upon the prosperity of other people and their jobs. What does independence mean for teachers? It means isolation. It means being alone. Teachers live from the profits and productivity of other people. To talk about independence of an isolated professional association is to show a lack of wisdom because we do not have a nickel to bargain for unless everybody else is working and prosperous."[24]

Shanker argued that because the success of the teaching profession depends upon its relationships with other people and organizations, it was essential to strive to maintain those relationships in order to provide the kind of education students need to function in society. Although, since 1975, the AFT has called for continued efforts to bring it and the NEA together to coordinate their strategies to improve the quality of education, those efforts have yielded no tangible results. Hopefully this will change in the foreseeable future as unification talks continue to be conducted.

Although Shanker has actively been involved in educational matters since 1958, he assumed new prominence in 1980 during the presidential election campaign. Ronald Reagan, a conservative Republican candidate, repeatedly argued that American education was encountering major problems because teachers were not taking their responsibility seriously. Shanker took exception to this attitude, making it very hard for the two leaders to develop the type of interaction needed to solve problems together during the period that Reagan served as president.

In 1987 the National Board for Professional Standards (NBPS) was formed to create national certification standards for teachers. However, teacher organizations, including the AFT and the NEA, saw this move by the Reagan administration as a threat to the position of teachers and the overall status of education. But, in spite of their common concern about Reagan's failure to understand the real causes of the problems facing education, the NEA and the AFT did not find a common ground for improved dialogue and political cooperation.

---

23. Albert Shanker, "The Financial Crisis in Public Schools," 1975, AFT Files, Washington, D.C.
24. Ibid.

The formation of the NBPS was a direct result of the concern that many individuals began to express in 1981 that Reagan's policy was likely to weaken education and cause a deterioration in the position of teachers. In 1983 Alan Pifer, president of the Carnegie Foundation, wrote an article that was published in *Education Week.* In it he sounded an alarm about the effect of Reagan's educational policy, saying, "There lies nothing but increasing hardship for ever-growing numbers, a mounting possibility of severe social unrest, and the consequent development among the upper class and business community of sufficient fear for survival of our capitalist economic system."[25] In the same year the National Commission on Excellence in Education echoed that alarm in its report entitled *A Nation at Risk.*

Joel Spring suggests that this concern was the reason why the Carnegie Corporation developed a foundation to fund means of improving "the status and skills of teachers through a system of national certification."[26] Shanker fully supported this effort because he believed that it would bring about much-needed improvement in education and it would help Reagan realize that he was pursuing wrong policies. But Mary Futrell, then NEA president, opposed the Carnegie initiative because she thought that it would take away the responsibility that she believed belonged to the states and that there would not be a proper method for implementing the proposed plan at the national level.

The increasingly strained relationship between Shanker and Harris in 1975 resurfaced between Shanker and Futrell in 1983. A decade later the AFT and the NEA were still far apart in their positions on national policy. The two organizations do not seem to recognize that in a democratic society it is not always in the best interest of the people they serve to try to merge. This stems from the need to have a healthy dialogue in which the participants represent diverse perspectives. Given the societal need for the constant presence of divergent thinking in educational matters, both the AFT and the NEA have been trying to forge a merger because they believe that it is in the best interest of the people they lead and the society they serve.

This is why, according to the minutes of an NEA meeting held on November 1, 1993, representatives from the NEA and the AFT concluded a constructive meeting on a variety of issues that are related to the possibility of a merger of the two organizations. These issues included the structure, governance, and operations of each organization. That Shanker and Keith Geiger, the new NEA president, agreed at that meeting that cooperation to improve public education and the plight of America's children was a major impetus for the merger negotiations suggests the critical nature of the move. At the conclusion of the meeting the two sides issued a statement, saying:

> Too many children in this society are poor and unhealthy, exposed daily to violence unimaginable just five years ago and unable to benefit from schooling. We want to find ways to work together along with parents and

---

25. Alan Pifer, "When Fashionable Rhetoric Fails," *Education Week,* (February 23, 1983), p. 6.

26. Joel Spring, *Conflict of Interest: The Politics of American Education* (New York: Longman, 1993), p. 13.

other concerned citizens to get children ready to learn and to provide them with an education that will help them grow. There is a lot that needs to be done to improve the quality of American public education. Members of both our organizations have a commitment to improving education and the lives of children and it makes sense for us to join forces on these issues, instead of expending talent and resources in battles with each other.[27]

Shanker and Geiger characterized the meeting as "honest and thorough" and decided to hold other meetings in the future. The knowledge that at that time the AFT had 820,000 members and the NEA had 2.1 million members became a critical factor in the negotiations between the two organizations. A merger would represent a considerable change in the situation facing teachers. Meeting on April 27, 1994, the NEA board of directors outlined some similarities between it the AFT that may make it possible for the two organizations to merge. "The NEA believes that voucher plans would lead to racial, economic, and social isolation of students, and weaken or destroy the public school system. The AFT believes that a strong public school system is essential to our democracy. It will dedicate itself to oppose politically all efforts to use public moneys for private schools."[28]

SHANKER'S RELATIONSHIPS WITH AFRICAN-AMERICANS

The enactment of the Civil Rights Act of 1964 was considered a major milestone. It was, and is, an unprecedented national recognition that all Americans must be treated equally. It was also believed, at the time, to be the ultimate solution to the problem of social injustice that African-Americans and others felt was overtly expressed when Rosa Parks was ordered to give up her bus seat to a white male passenger in Montgomery, Alabama, in 1955.

The Civil Rights Act of 1964 was also considered to be the quintessential panacea for racial conflict in the United States. It was more comprehensive in its provisions than the civil rights legislation of 1875 and 1957. In the Civil Rights Act of 1964 Americans thought that their nation had at long last found a permanent solution to the problems of inequality and injustice. They optimistically and prematurely believed that the country could now look into the future with great expectations and excitement, putting the past behind them in order to concentrate on making the future the best that it could possibly be.

In 1965, when Americans thought social utopia was within reach, a violent riot erupted in the Watts area of Los Angeles caused by discontent that stemmed from unfulfilled community expectations. This was a prelude to equally violent eruptions and Detroit in 1967. What had gone wrong? Americans had thought the Civil Rights Act of 1964 was an instrument for eliminating racial

---

27. "The NEA and the AFT Continue Merger Talks" minutes of the NEA-AFT merger talks, (November 4, 1993, Washington, D.C. Courtesy of Janice Truitt).

28. The NEA and the AFT: A Policy Position Comparison" Minutes of the NEA Board of Directors, (April 27, 1994, Washington, D.C. Courtesy of Janice Truitt).

inequality. They discovered that old practices die hard, but they believed that the country was embarking on a new era of changed racial attitudes. They soon found out that racial prejudice was entrenched and emerging in new and profound ways. They mistakenly thought that the country had adopted a new idealism that would ensure national development, only to find that the era of goodwill that the Civil Rights Act of 1964 was expected to create had actually never materialized. They thought that racial integration would bring all ethnic groups together in cooperation to create a new society with shared values. They learned that racial conflict remained the modus vivendi of the nation.

Americans had also believed that the Civil Rights Act of 1964 would make it possible for all people to trust one another, only to find that distrust and suspicion had even intensified. They thought that the Civil Rights Act would help extend the concept of equal economic opportunity to all people, yet they discovered that the country continued to grow apart. This is precisely what the Otto Kerner Commission of 1968 took into account when it reported that the United States was moving in two opposite directions, that African-Americans were being impoverished at the same rate that white Americans were getting richer. The Kerner Commission warned, "What white Americas have never fully understood, but what the Negro can never forget is that white society is deeply implicated in the ghetto. White institutions created it, white institutions maintain it, and white society condones it."[29]

Jonathan Kozol's *Death at an Early Age* (1967) showed the extent to which black youth felt isolated and alienated from the socioeconomic life of the country. The book was also an account of a generation lost in the shuffle of social disintegration and the malaise it endured in a rapidly disintegrating urban environment. Marjorie Murphy concluded that the educational process, considered the salvaging instrument of a society in dire straits, was seen in a negative light because "teachers were perpetuating a racist class-based system of education."[30] While this was happening, black organizations were conducting intense self-examination.

As a result of this exercise several black groups adopted a more militant and confrontational position on the issue of race. For example, Stokley Carmichael, who later changed his name to Kwame Toure,[31] the chairman of Student Nonviolent Coordinating Committee, concluded that seeking racial integration should not be part of the objectives of African-Americans. The Congress of Racial Equality (CORE) acquired a new level of popularity among African-Americans as a result of its insistence that society recognize the need for minority groups to aggressively demand their rights. Both the National Association of the Advancement of the Colored People (NAACP) and the Urban League were compelled to reexamine the traditional relationships they maintained with liberal whites.

---

29. Quoted in Henry Hampton and Steve Fayer, *Voices of Freedom: An Oral History of the Civil Rights Movement from the 1950s Through the 1980s* (New York: Bantam Books, 1990), p. 398.

30. Marjorie Murphy, *Blackboard Unions: The AFT and the NEA, 1900-1980*, p. 232.

31. After Kwame Nkrumah of Ghana and Sekou Toure of Guinea.

The Black Panther party, led by Eldridge Cleaver, Huey Newton, Bobby Seale, and H. Rap Brown, began to advocate black power in a way that frightened most white Americans. The violent confrontation that erupted in Oakland between the members of the Black Panther party and the police was indicative of how seriously strained racial relationships had become. When put together, these events show that in spite of the hope for improved social relationships expressed by the Civil Rights Act of 1964, the United States was heading directly toward further major racial conflict unless all segments of the society made a concerted effort to resolve the issues that deeply divided them.[32]

Indeed, by 1965, only one year after the passage of the Civil Rights Act, observers concluded that the failure to establish clear lines of communication between Africa-Americans and white Americans was having an adverse effect on the needed dialogical interaction between them. Americans recognized that the future of the country was in doubt unless they came to an understanding of the real problems that divided them and then cooperated in seeking solutions.

The decade between 1955 and 1965 saw the Reverend Milton Galamison conduct a series of workshops on racial communication and understanding on behalf of the NAACP. In the process Galamison was able to convince school officials that African-Americans and white Americans could establish lines of communication by identifying issues that were adversely affecting relationships between them, such as inequality in educational opportunity, the unrepresentative character of the political process, deteriorating community facilities, and wide differences in socioeconomic opportunity.

Galamison's efforts began to show results in 1967 when CORE and the UFT thought that they understood the importance of easing tension between the races. But when given an opportunity to do so, they actually expressed opposing points of view on the issues of community involvement in the educational process. CORE demanded an active role in those schools with a black majority. The UFT felt that such involvement must be based on the application of professional principles, which it argued it represented, and that because CORE was a political organization, it lacked professional knowledge on educational issues.

Recognizing the potential for conflict if lines of communication remained closed, Albert Shanker suggested a meeting between the UFT and CORE. Although the two sides did not fully resolve their differences, they were able to establish the principle of dialogue as a basis for further understanding and communication. Shanker learned a very important lesson about human behavior, which was that once one begins to listen to a different point of view, even if one disagrees with it, one helps to build a sense of confidence and ability in conflict resolution. In doing so one also puts in place the elements of the democratic process which is so crucial in human interaction. While this gave him confidence to face other problems in the future, Shanker knew that he had not yet surmounted the challenge of his leadership calling. The test of his ability to do so was yet to come.

---

32. Quoted in Henry Hampton and Steve Fayer, *Voices of Freedom: An Oral History of the Civil Rights Movement from the 1950s Through the 1980s,* p. 399.

That challenge came in 1968 when Shanker faced an issue that would determine the nature of relationships he would have with African-Americans. During the previous year McGeorge Bundy submitted a report on behalf of the Ford Foundation urging the establishment of community boards to supervise the operation of schools under the principle of local control. In the Ocean Hill-Brownsville district of New York black parents formed a committee in accordance with Bundy's recommendations.

Shanker and the UFT, however, saw Bundy's recommendation as a threat to the guidance they thought teacher organizations should exert on the conduct of the educational process. They therefore opposed the recommendation. In 1968 Mayor John V. Lindsay and the city board of education supported Bundy's recommendation, bringing them and Shanker into direct conflict. Strained relationships were thus formed, with African-Americans and Mayor Lindsay in support of the idea of local community involvement in school administration and Shanker, the UFT, and the school board in opposition.[33] This development meant that Shanker and the African-Americans were at odds about the issue of local control of schools. How could they resolve the conflict?

As the dispute continued the African-American community in Ocean Hill-Brownsville felt that the UFT and the board of education were using it as a pawn in the political game they were playing. In turn the UFT felt that the school board was dictating conditions of service for teachers. Mayor Lindsay felt that the UFT was usurping authority that did not belong to it in order to promote its union agenda. In April 1968 the board of education in the Ocean Hill-Brownsville district decided to make certain changes in its school staffing by removing thirteen teachers and five assistant principals from their positions. This was done because it supposedly suspected them of working against the principle of community control advocated in Bundy's report.

When Shanker's suggestion that a hearing be held before the teachers were removed was rejected, the UFT felt compelled to call a strike to begin May 8, 1968. Compounding the problem between the parties was the fact that Rhody McCoy, the superintendent, did not make any arrangements to transfer the teachers involved to other schools. Without reassignment the teachers were out of a job although McCoy maintained that he had not dismissed them. In effect, McCoy was refusing to accept responsibility for the fate of the dismissed teachers. McCoy was not aware that his school district had reached an agreement with the UFT that specified that matters regarding teachers' security, promotion, grievance procedures, and personnel questions must be resolved through negotiation to prevent the UFT from resorting to a strike to protect their members.

The UFT had always regarded the involuntary transfer of teachers as an action inconsistent with the provisions of the agreement because history indicated that school officials made such transfers "as political punishment for activist teachers who defended the principle of unionism."[34] McCoy considered

---

33. Marjorie Murphy, *Blackboard Unions: The AFT and the NEA, 1900-1980*, p. 240.

34. Ibid., p. 241.

the attitudes and action of the teachers in question to be detrimental to the new experiment with decentralization under the principle of local control that Bundy had recommended and Mayor Lindsay was now trying to implement. As summer vacation got under way in June 1968, the Ocean Hill-Brownsville school controversy had not been resolved. Shanker and the UFT took advantage of the vacation to study the situation closely to ascertain if a new strategy should be initiated to resolve it in favor of the de facto dismissed teachers.

Both Shanker and Lindsay were aware that if the crisis was not resolved to the satisfaction of the parties, not only would the educational process be seriously disrupted at the beginning of the fall session, but that also Shanker's relationships with African-Americans would be irreparably damaged. Shanker knew that he could not lose the support of a constituency he needed to carry out his educational crusade. He also knew that he could not continue to disagree with Mayor Lindsay, a Kennedy Democrat whose views were basically in alignment with Shanker's philosophy. Like Shanker, Lindsay felt that the public schools must be strengthened. He believed in collective bargaining and teacher empowerment. Neither Lindsay nor Shanker wanted to see a prolonged conflict between them that could have an adverse effect on other important programs.

Following their analysis Shanker and the UFT reached three conclusions. The first was that it was fortunate that CORE and the African-American community it represented and the UFT were not in conflict because of race: any conflicts between them resulted from differences in their respective political ideologies and philosophies of education. Because race was not a factor, it was quite conceivable that they could resolve the conflict.

The second conclusion was that the demand made by the Ocean Hill-Brownsville school board for local control was quite consistent with the general UFT philosophy of professional autonomy which it had been trying to promote as an essential operational principle for teachers. Therefore, the conflict between the parties could also be resolved to their satisfaction. The third conclusion was that the UFT was not opposed to the idea of decentralization because the larger the administrative bureaucracy was, the less efficient it was in meeting the educational needs of students and the professional goals of teachers.

Shanker's ability to see issues from their proper perspective was due to his ability to adopt a procedure that made his leadership appear unique. This has been explained in the previous chapter as his propensity to study issues thoroughly in order to make sure that he is fully informed about all pertinent facts of the situation. In the Ocean Hill-Brownsville controversy this strategy meant two things. The first is that Shanker lent his support to the principle of decentralization and cooperated in the implementation of the Bundy-Lindsay plan. In return, the Ocean Hill-Brownsville school board restored the dismissed teachers to their positions. As a result, the UFT and CORE shared the same side of the controversy, and McCoy was placed in a very difficult situation from which he could not effectively discharge his role as superintendent.

The second thing is that Shanker recognized that resolving the controversy would make it possible for the school district to receive additional federal funds to carry out its educational programs. The amount of the funds would be determined by the extent of support the school board received from members of the community and professional organizations. To receive this support the board of education knew that it had to formulate an effective program. This required a fiscal incentive to make it possible for all the parties to recognize that they had a substantial interest in solving the controversy.

The understanding and cooperation that were needed between the Ocean Hill-Brownsville school board and the AFT meant that a strained relationship must surely have developed between Shanker and McCoy. Before the summer of 1968 was over McCoy had been reassigned to the Brooklyn School District. Because the UFT teachers went on strike over a dispute about salary, working and teachers' rights, McCoy quickly hired 400 hundred "scab" teachers to replace them. In taking this action McCoy apparently was not aware that the UFT would regard his action as a direct violation and an affront to the principle of collective bargaining. This behavior only inflamed emotions and accentuated the conflict between him and Shanker.

The conflict edged closer to a confrontation when a few UFT teachers threatened physical violence toward the teachers McCoy hired to replace them. Marjorie Murphy concluded on this crisis:

> The more the UFT teachers felt uncomfortable in the community the more they appealed to the authorities in the central office. It was a stand-off between two groups, a feud that centered on an angry and disappointed but united black community exercising its power against teachers whom it perceived as holders of absolute control over the system. Both the teachers in their quest for collective bargaining and the African-American community in its quest for community control hoped for a new educational system that would give them and public school children a sense of empowerment.[35]

While this was happening the relationship between Shanker and McCoy deteriorated so rapidly that communications between them ceased. However, the relationship between Shanker and the African-American community improved considerably. It seems that Shanker played his cards well. But while Shanker recognized the fact that decentralization was good for community involvement in education, he remained unwilling to give up the principle of political action, which he has maintained to this day as a prerogative of teachers. It was not possible for him to reverse a principle and practice that had yielded results that could easily be measured in terms of benefits to members of the unions.

In this position Shanker was merely articulating a fundamental philosophical position that teacher organizations must exist if professionalism is to pervade the nation's schools. The fact that the African-American community understood this position helped to improve the understanding of the importance of the principle. While these developments were unfolding, the NEA was watching the drama from the sidelines, unable and unwilling to be involved in a controversy that had so many ramifications for the conduct of education and the society it serves. It is not surprising that when the issues were finally resolved, the African-American community came to identify itself first with the UFT and

---

35. Ibid., p. 244.

second with the AFT, leaving the NEA on the outside wondering what step to take to restore its increasingly tarnished image.

One way in which the NEA tried to improve its image was to elect Mary Futrell, an African-American teacher, as president. By articulating a position that demonstrated sensitivity to the issues in dispute, Futrell made the search for solutions to the growing lack of credibility a top priority of her term of office. This meant that the talk of merger between the AFT and the NEA had, for all practical purposes, come to an end. In 1990 Shanker discussed the events that changed the nature of interaction between him and the African-American community, saying, "I did not oppose community participation or even community control. I am against what in those days was called total community control, which means that we can do anything we want and people do not have any civil rights or human rights. To me the civil rights movement was a movement for racial integration and for the elimination of racial segregation."[36] In 1993 Shanker reiterated this line of thinking to the author, saying, "Seeking solutions to problems of society must be initiated in the context of developing relationships that one must have with other people and organizations; otherwise a person in a responsible position becomes a dictator."[37]

Throughout his term of office as president of the AFT Shanker has remained an ardent supporter of the African-American community. He has fully supported the objectives of Jesse Jackson's Poor People's Campaign, the Rainbow Coalition, and People United to Save Humanity. There are two critical elements that one sees in the relationships that Shanker has had with African-Americans.

The first is the ability of the African-American community to demonstrate a clear understanding of the issues critical to their development and to put them in the context of seeking solution s through dialogue. The second is Shanker's ability to exhibit a sound knowledge of these issues and to recognize them as essential in seeking solutions that satisfactory to all parties. If all segments of the American society embrace those two basic elements when approaching problems of national development then solutions can be found. Shanker clearly embraces the principle found within the acronym TEAM (together everyone achieves more).

SHANKER'S RELATIONSHIPS WITH OTHER INDIVIDUALS

In addition to the relationships he has had with the NEA with the African-Americans, Shanker has also had involvement with other organizations and individuals as necessitated by the office that he has held. These relationships determined not only Shanker's behavior and that of the AFT, but also to some extent the nature of both American society and education. This section provides a sample of these relationships and the impact they've had. On July 14, 1985,

---

36. Henry Hampton and Steve Foyer, *Voices of Freedom: An Oral History of the Civil Rights Movement from the 1950s Through the 1980s*, p. 496.

37. Albert Shanker, interview with author, Washington, D.C., May 17, 1993.

Shanker appeared on C-Span to discuss certain critical issues that he saw affecting the country, especially as they related to the increasing responsibilities placed upon teachers. Among these were how to handle increasing class sizes. He felt that this was having a seriously adverse effect on the quality of instruction.

On that same day Ray Callahan, professor of education at Washington University in St. Louis, wrote to compliment Shanker on that presentation, which he had just watched. Callahan went on to say, "How refreshing to hear someone talk about ideas in education. You asked for ideas in regard to the problem of numbers in our high schools. Let me try out a specific proposal. Let every freshman entering high school have a chance to select one small seminar in a subject of his or her choice. The class would meet for two hours a week for the entire academic year. I would suggest a maximum of six to eight students in each seminar. This arrangement would be repeated in the sophomore, junior, and senior years with a proviso that the student select a different subject each year. The advantage for the student is that confidence in contact and face-to-face relationships in teaching would increase."[38]

Callahan went on to outline the advantages to the teacher saying, "Each teacher would have one small class in his or her major field of interest. This would give every teacher a chance to get very well acquainted with a few students each year. If you ever get to St. Louis, please plan to have dinner with us."[39] There is no question that Callahan admired the work that Shanker was doing and that Shanker was moved and encouraged by this show of support. The suggestion that Callahan made in response to Shanker's invitation to offer ideas indicates the need to confront the the many problems that society faces.

Today American schools are handicapped by an array of problems related to large classes. These include students who bring weapons to school, the illegal distribution of drugs, and sexual harassment and promiscuity in the midst of an AIDS epidemic. These take place in school in large part because teachers do not know all the students by name when classrooms are bursting at the seams. Now that Callahan and Shanker have provided an example of how dialogue can begin on an important aspect of education, it is necessary to direct national resources to find solutions to these problems before they create other serious problems for the nation. How long can Americans as a society afford to wait before they consider the suggestions from two professionals who are privy to the escalating crisis impacting American public school system?

On January 16, 1986, Edward A. Wynne, executive secretary of For Character, a school recognition program sponsored by the University of Illinois, wrote a letter to Shanker, stating, "Can we obtain your council's support in organizing and conducting a national conference on the operation of school recognition and incentive programs?"[40] In requesting Shanker's assistance Wynne went on to outline what he and his organization had in mind, saying,

---

38. Ray Callahan, to Shanker, July 14, 1985, AFT Files, Walter Reuther Archives of Labor and Urban Affairs, Wayne State University, Detroit.

39. Ibid.

40. Edward A. Wynne to Shanker, January 16, 1986, AFT Files, Walter Reuther Archives of Labor and Urban Affairs, Wayne State University, Detroit.

"There has been an increasing tendency for school recognition programs to identify such programs they feel must be conducted by federal and state education departments. The programs present an opportunity to apply the insights of educational research and the American tradition of wholesome competition among students in our public and private schools. It is certain that other institutions are now assessing the desirability of sponsoring such programs. We would want to organize a conference to introduce the program."[41]

Wynne then asked Shanker to advise him and his organization on a number of questions, the answers to which they needed to know in order to plan the conference: "Is the overall idea of a conference constructive? What are some general ways the ideas can be improved and refined? Apart from the U.S. Department of Education are there other possible sources of funds to be pursued? Are you willing to provide on-going advice? Are you willing to be listed as an official advisor to the conference? Would you be willing to attend the conference?"[42]

These questions show two things. The first is that Wynne and his organization had a great deal of faith and confidence in Shanker, so much so that they turned to him for advice. The second thing is that the success of the conference they were planning would depend on careful and deliberate thinking and the consideration of all pertinent aspects.

The idea of recognizing special talent and achievement in education was quite consistent with Shanker's views of what a nation and its institutions must do to promote the potential that he felt always existed in its people. This is why Shanker stated his belief that "the socioeconomic aspects of education must be related to efforts that must be directed at developing the intelligence needed to run a democratic society, and that if a nation fails to develop this talent it is limiting its own ability to plan the future."[43]

This indicates that Shanker fully understood the need to support any efforts made in planning the proposed conference. From this correspondence Shanker came to appreciate what other individuals and organizations were doing to promote education as a prerequisite in promoting the development of the country.

On March 11, 1986, William D. Smith, superintendent of the Alsip Elementary School in Worth, Illinois, wrote a letter to Shanker, enclosing a three-page article he had written and asking Shanker to consider it for publication in the guest section of *The American Teacher*. It was entitled "Teaching: Not Just a Job, but a Profession." The article stated:

> Education is in tough times. Public confidence is dwindling. Fiscal restraint is the name of the game. Enrollments are declining. Test scores are down. The bottom line is that teachers are very susceptible to being captured by the fear of the times, a depressive mood that makes the job of teaching seem less and less important and promising. We in education tend to be captured by the routine, the mundane and the problems so that teaching becomes just

---

41. Ibid.
42. Ibid.
43. Albert Shanker, interview with author, Washington, D.C, May 17, 1993.

a job. If we believe that education is the key to a successful life, then certainly the teacher is the key factor in that quest. Be proud of your profession. You have a right to be. No one stands taller than the one who stoops to help a child.[44]

Smith, who had thirty-three years of experience as a teacher, principal, and superintendent, also taught graduate courses in education at St. Xavier College in Chicago. This placed Smith in a position to know the problems that education faces. Shanker was impressed by Smith's clear articulation of the issues he saw as critical to education and by his ideas of what must be done to resolve them.

On the same day that Smith wrote to Shanker, Ellen Meyers, director of communications at Impact II, an organization founded in New York City in 1979 to reward and recognize public school teachers for creative work, wrote to Shanker to invite him to appear in a segment of a video that her organization was planning to produce. The informational materials that Meyers enclosed with her letter stated, "Over 1,200 teachers have received Impact II grants in the past six years. These are developer grants which assist teachers in packaging their programs for other teachers. They are also adopter grants for those teachers interested in other teachers' programs so that they take new ideas to be creative. These grants provide on-going support to programs that are of continuing value to other teachers."[45]

Shanker was impressed by the innovative ideas that he saw among members of the teaching profession across the country. That they wrote to share these ideas with him was equally impressive. He would never decline an invitation to participate in any program that he saw as being designed to promote the development of education for the benefit of the country. He honored their request.

On March 19, 1986, Morten Botel, chair of a search committee in the graduate school of education at the University of Pennsylvania, wrote a letter to Shanker to make an unusual request saying, "The Graduate School of Education at the University of Pennsylvania is now searching for a successor to Dell Hymes who is to retire as Dean in June 1987 after twelve productive years. As chairman of the search committee appointed by President Sheldon Hackney, I am writing to seek your suggestions for an outstanding candidate. Not only would we appreciate your nominations and comments, but also any supporting information that you might have."[46] Botel went on to outline the character of the school and its mission, saying, among other things, that its intellectual life revolved around two basic functions. The first was the importance of professional education and research. The second was disciplinary and interdisciplinary research in various aspects of education.[47]

---

44. William D. Smith, "Teaching: Not Just a Job, But a Profession," (draft article sent to Albert Shanker with a letter dated March 11, 1986), AFT Files, Walter Reuther Archives of Labor and Urban Affairs, Wayne State University, Detroit.

45. Ellen Meyers to Albert Shanker, March 11, 1986, AFT Files, Walter Reuther Archives of Labor and Urban Affairs. Wayne State University, Detroit.

46. Morten Botel to Albert Shanker, March 19, 1986, AFT Files, Walter Reuther Archives of Labor and Urban Affairs, Wayne State University, Detroit.

47. Ibid.

Botel's letter suggests two things that indicate the kind of relationships that Shanker has had with others. The first is that Botel and his search committee did what most university search committees rarely do: they placed their total trust and confidence in someone outside the university setting in seeking help to fill a need. The second is that Shanker has acquired such a national reputation as a professional person, people request his advice on a variety of issues that are not necessarily connected to teachers and public K-12 instruction. This is why Botel went on to discuss the type of leadership that Dell Hymes had provided. This points out that Botel associated Shanker with the honed skills of a leader and the knowledge that goes with strong leadership. Botel's letter was more an affirmative statement about Shanker as a national leader and less a request for assistance in filling the vacancy left by a retiring dean.

This is also true about the letter that Kelman Goldberg, editor of *The Journal of Economic Education,* wrote to Shanker on April 1, 1986 to say:

> I am taking the liberty of enclosing a copy of the draft of a paper, "The School Reform Debate," written by Liscot Miller, program officer of the Exxon Foundation. I am also enclosing a copy of some comments on the paper by Michael A. McDonell, president of the Joint Council on Economic Education, and Marilyn Kourisky, professor and assistant dean for Teacher Education at UCLA. These papers will be published shortly in *The Journal of Economic Education.* I am writing to ask if you would undertake a brief (3-5 pages) reply or comment on the issue as raised by Miller. Your role in education and your prestige and influence will help focus further attention on the problems of education. Your suggestions will command respect and effective response.[48]

There is no question that Goldberg wrote this letter in the absolute belief that Shanker would consider it recognition of his keen understanding of the issues that the letter addressed. Indeed, this letter was more about paying tribute to Shanker than it was about asking for his response about the issues it raised.

A compelling piece of evidence to substantiate this conclusion is found in a letter that Mortimer Adler,[49] a leading educator, wrote to Shanker on May 27, 1986. The letter said, "It is necessary for universities to have graduate schools of education in which research is done with regard to the economic, sociological, administrative, political, and historical aspects of educational institutions. But I wish that there were, in addition and quite separate, institutes for the training of teachers which were more like our graduate and professional schools set up to train physicians."[50] Adler than went on to commend Shanker for the kind of leadership he had provided in the development of education and to urge that he

---

48. Kalman Goldberg addressed to Albert Shanker April 1, 1986, AFT Files, Walter Reuther Archives of Labor and Urban Affairs, Wayne State University, Detroit.

49. Mortimer Adler is the editor of *The Paideia Proposal: An Education Manifesto* (New York: Collier Macmillan, 1982), a book that has been widely acknowledged for its clear articulation of educational issues.

50. Mortimer Adler to Albert Shanker, May 22, 1986, AFT Files, Walter Reuther Archives of Labor and Urban Affairs, Wayne State University, Detroit.

remain as accessible in the future as he had been in the past to offer his advice and counsel on various issues the country was facing.

It is quite clear that Adler, who held the position of chancellor of conferences at the University of North Carolina, was expressing ideas that he held in common with Shanker. The purpose of the letter was, therefore, not to inform, but to reflect upon ideas that helped him see the issues from the perspective of a national leader who fully comprehended the essence of what needed to be done in education and the society it serves. That Adler and Shanker had mutual respect and admiration for each other underscores the importance of the relationships that Shanker has had with other professionals.

Busy as he was, and is, Shanker has always found time to respond to the requests that come from all over the country for assistance either in implementing a new concept in trying out new strategies to improve pedagogy. These are the elements that help shape the unique leader that Shanker has become.

SUMMARY AND CONCLUSION

The discussion in this chapter leads to two deductions. The first is that Shanker considered the relationships that he had with other people and organizations as providing a national environment that made it possible to discuss critical national issues from the perspective of well-informed individuals who had the best interest of their nation at heart. As a professional person staunchly devoted to democratic principles Shanker has always believed that there is no single person or organization that can find solutions to the problems of national development. Collective action based upon dialogue provides a climate in which solutions can be found.

Shanker believes that dialogue is the true basis for the salvation of a nation. Without engaging other people in constructive dialogue, the problems of any nation and of human interaction become more complex and resisted to change. Healthy relationships rooted in open communication make it possible to see issues from all their perspectives. Shanker has persistently demonstrated a total commitment to these principles. This is one reason why he has become a major national leader.

The second deduction to be made is that in every situation, from issues raised by the Ocean Hill-Brownsville school district crisis, through the abortive merger negotiations with the NEA, to the correspondence he has had with other professionals, Shanker has endeavored to listen and learn.[51] These two qualities have helped him comprehend issues in a manner that few leaders have attempted to do. In turn, those he has communicated with in his shared effort to find solutions to problems, placed their trust and confidence in him. This is because

---

51. The author saw evidence of this during an interview with Albert Shanker, Washington, D.C., May 17, 1993. Shanker remembered details of the question and answered every aspect of it fully.

he has identified himself with them and their cause. This is the distinct mark of a national leader.

The relationships that Shanker has had with these individuals and organizations were based on the principles of leadership outlined by Adam Curle and were influenced by the philosophical ideas perceived and articulated by Edmund Burke and Thomas Hobbes. Shanker's successful leadership is the result of his respect for and observance of these basic principles.

8

Albert Shanker of the AFT: Summary, Conclusions, and Implications

Albert Shanker understands the problems facing public education better than any other person in the country.

Fletcher L. Byrom, 1989

There is no way we are seriously going to address educational and social problems unless we first know what they are.

Albert Shanker, 1993

THE PURPOSE OF THE STUDY IN PERSPECTIVE

The purpose of this study was to present important aspects of the contributions made by Albert Shanker to the continuing development of education in the United States.When Shanker began his career as a teacher in 1952, working conditions were so difficult that his became a struggle not only to discover himself in a rapidly changing world, but also to help shape a new and better direction toward the future. Shanker's election as president of the AFT in 1974 signaled a change in direction and agenda in the unionization of teachers. To understand why Shanker has conducted the business of the AFT and the agenda he has sought in the manner he has, it is first necessary to know something about the conditions that shaped both the man and the union.

This study, therefore, has attempted to discuss important events relative to the leadership of the AFT since its inception in 1916. It also presented some major developments that took place in the United States from the time of Shanker's birth in 1928 to the present. A discussion of his mission, his philosophy, and the interactions he has had with the AFL-CIO, presidents, governors, African-Americans and other minority groups, women, the NEA, and others helps to explain the kind of man and leader he has been, and continues to be.

THE LEGACY OF THE PAST: HALEY,
GOGGIN, AND THE CTF

Does the man make the time or the time the man? This study adheres to the synthesis found in this dialectic, which is that people can be predisposed to becoming good leaders, but it takes a challenging environment to trigger the risk-taking found in putting one's ego on the line by seeking the role of leader. With this view in mind this study began with a discussion of certain critical events that began to unfold as early as 1902. Two major strikes by workers shook the confidence and optimism that the United States had for in its future, which the Industrial Revolution generated.

The first was the coal miners strike that broke out in May of 1902 raising fundamental questions and doubts about the possibility of creating a new socioeconomic system void of any flaws. The second was the student strike in Chicago in October, which spawned concerns about the legacy of the school reform movement and the objectives that Horace Mann had outlined in introducing the common or public school system.

This national pessimism about the future took seed with the assassination of President William McKinley in 1901. This and other tragic events, coming at the beginning of the twentieth century when great things were expected, led to disillusionment about the ability to create a socioeconomic and political utopia. Many Americans began to wonder if the Industrial Revolution was a curse or a blessing. Many began to wonder if Charles Dickens's characterization of the best of times and the worst of times was a prophecy for the twentieth century.[1] The confusion that gripped the world about new values brought about by the Industrial Revolution translated into a general malaise, which inhibited the ability of the populace to see the future from the perspective of hope and vision. This, in turn, affected their motivation to challenge this collective depression.

For many people the world of tomorrow had been marred by the decline in social, moral and political values. The position of teachers was slowly, but steadily, bringing about the realization that if they did not do something to reverse the trend, no one else would. The very thought that teachers felt that the nation was not motivated to improve its position was quite disturbing. It became the basis for their decision to change things for the better, with education being the catalyst for the optimism that had to be rekindled. In the course of seeking improvement in the conditions under which teachers served, the educational needs of their students took a back seat. This caused the students to express discontent with the administration, not with their teachers.

This was the situation that the schools encountered in 1900. It set the stage for student strikes two years later. In that year the Chicago Teachers Federation (CTF), in a desperate attempt to keep hope of a better future alive, voted to

---

1. In 1859 Dickens published *A Tale of Two Cities*, describing conditions in Europe beginning with the French Revolution. For an interpretive discussion of the implications of Dickens's characterization for the world of 1945 and beyond, see Dickson A. Mungazi, *Educational Policy and National Character: Africa, Japan, the United States, and the Soviet Union* (Westport, Conn.: Praeger Publishers, 1993), p. 129.

provide salaries for Margaret A. Haley and Catherine Goggin, two influential and powerful women in the city's school system, to study the pattern of tax revenue distribution and to suggest ways of locating more funds for the schools in need of financial assistance.[2] These two ladies were also asked to suggest how working conditions for teachers could be improved. At that time the two women shared an apartment that also served as a meeting place for teachers in Chicago. It was the birthplace of teachers' unionization.

This situation dictated that the city's teachers were forced to form an organization out of the need to protect their economic and political interests. Although women were not allowed to vote until the ratification of the Nineteenth Amendment in 1920, Haley and Goggin championed a cause that would later transform both a profession and the country's political system. Slowly teachers began to realize that their future depended largely upon their ability to organize in the pursuit of the objectives they collectively identified with.[3]

Although in 1900 Susan B. Anthony was eighty years old,[4] the spirit she had implanted in women to seek social justice was embraced by the teachers who were struggling for the improvement of the conditions of service as members of a profession that was not respected. In their assigned task Haley and Goggin kept a vigil for the teachers whose fate was being considered by the board of education. They, and other teachers in Chicago, had not received a pay raise in two years. In a system in which they had no pension or other retirement plan, theirs was a struggle for bare survival.

These two women also gained a national reputation for being outspoken members of the Women's Suffragist party in Illinois as well as effective spokespersons for the disenfranchised. In an effort to solicit help for their cause the two women contacted John Fitzpatrick, the labor leader who had expressed sympathy for their struggle. They also initiated contact with Jane Addams, the founder of Hull House in the city. They believed that maximum publicity would generate support for both the women's struggle across the country and that of teachers who were predominantly female.

History has not given Jane Addams the proper recognition that she fully deserves. This is why Willis D. Moreland and Erwin H. Goldenstein[5] paid tribute to this remarkable leader when they wrote, "Jane Addams had the qualities of tolerance, patience, and understanding, which made her so effective in

---

2. "Tribute to Margaret A. Haley and Catherine Goggin," *The American Teacher* (November 1975): 59, 6.

3. Ibid., p. 7.

4. Susan B. Anthony was born February 15, 1820. After her arrest and imprisonment in 1872 for trying to vote, she served as president of the women's suffragist movement from 1892 to 1900. The ratification of the Fifteenth Amendment on March 30, 1870, giving Negroes the right to vote provided women an incentive to intensify their struggle for the same right. Anthony took the center stage in that struggle. She died in 1906, fourteen years before the ratification of the Nineteenth Amendment.

5. The author was privileged to study under the direction of this distinguished scholar at the University of Nebraska from 1974 to 1977.

providing assistance to the poor. She had great integrity and a high degree of intellectual ability which earned her respect in those areas where wealth and privilege and professional   scholarship prevailed. The range of her interests continued to broaden throughout her life as she came to grapple with some of the most serious problems of her times."[6] These qualities are the reasons why Margaret Haley and Catherine Goggin and the teachers in Chicago requested her to come to their assistance in promoting the cause they were committed to.

When Haley and Goggin released the results of their study in 1901, they revealed a pattern of policies that led to the conclusion that these were detrimental to the educational interests of both teachers and students. This was seen as stemming from policies and procedures that inhibited their ability to discharge their respective responsibilities fully. This dysfunctional pattern contributed to the emergence of a climate that led to the strike staged by students at Clarke School and a general deterioration in the relationship between teachers and the board of education. When Haley became ill in 1905, Goggin took over the entire organizational operation and ran it in an efficient and effective way.

A letter that Goggin wrote in October 1905 to Cynthia Leet reveals the admiration that she had for Haley: "The work in the city has been enormous during the last few years and Miss Haley, who always does more than any two women, broke down last spring through overwork, from February until the end of September. She did take a small part in the proceedings of the convention at Asbury Park. In the meantime it is a struggle which takes every bit of time and energy which Miss Haley possesses and everything not absolutely pressing has been eliminated from her work."[7]

But when she recovered, Haley approached her task and duties with a dedication and commitment that surprised many. Her belief that teachers must receive the proper recognition for the work they did in preparing future citizens remained one of the areas of her life that inspired associates. She was willing to pay a high personal price to ensure the success of the cause she led. This dedication was not lost on future leaders of teacher organizations, including Shanker.

When Goggin died in January 1916 an outpouring of grief and condolences were sent to Haley, who felt that she had lost a sister and faithful partner in the struggle for proper recognition and appreciation for teachers. Even a newspaper account of Goggin's life focused on the close relationship that the two women shared as the most important asset utilized in promoting their cause. Haley's decision to publish highlights of Goggin's life had a profound impact on bringing teachers together to support the cause that the two women had launched.

Haley wrote about her friend and associate and the impact Goggin's death had on teachers, saying, "There will be many sore hearts in Chicago at the news of this tragedy. Nothing could happen which could affect the teachers more. She

6. Willis D. Moreland and Erwin H. Goldenstein, *Pioneers in Adult Education* (Chicago: Nelson-Hall Publishers, 1985), p. 153.

7. Catherine Goggin,   to Cynthia Leet, October 15, 1905,   AFT Files, Washington, D.C.

was the most beloved of all teachers. She came in contact with more teachers than any other person in Chicago."[8] Funeral services were held in the city council chambers, and more than 10,000 mourners attended to pay respect to a leader who had given everything she had for the benefit of others.

Tragic as it was, Goggin's death galvanized teachers in Chicago. It brought about the realization that she and Haley had a vision of the future different from the past, a vision worth sharing and pursuing. They decided to strengthen the CTF in order to fulfill the objectives she had relentlessly worked toward. They began to feel that the best tribute they could pay her was to dedicate themselves to the cause she had initiated. Combined with the general deterioration of working conditions for teachers, Goggin's death was the catalyst for the formation of the AFT in the same year as her death.

By all accounts the impact of Goggin's death can best be described as the birth of a martyr. It was a blow to a struggling organization at a time when it was under the control of the infamous Loeb Rule. This policy was named after its author, Jacob Loeb, the politician who was vehemently anti-teacher organizations. This man opposed any political rights for teachers because he believed that they were civil servants who must refrain from any political activity or involvement of any kind. Goggin died four months after the Loeb Rule had been passed, which outlawed the CTF.

The application of the Loeb Rule precipitated a two-year struggle between the Chicago Board of Education and the CTF. Goggin, then suffering from acute bronchitis, was physically spent from the struggle. In December 1915 she retired to a sanitarium in Chicago hoping that her condition would improve. She declined to consider her doctor's suggestion that she move out of Chicago and go to a warmer place to have a better chance at a full recovery. She chose instead to stay close to the cause that gave her life meaning. She occasionally attended CTF meetings. Indeed, she was returning from such a meeting when she was fatally struck by a delivery truck.[9]

Although Haley continued to lead the struggle for teachers, she was overwhelmed by the loss of her dear friend. For a time her leadership was less than effective. She was also subjected to relentless attacks by the members of the board of education. When Loeb called her "Queen of the Lady Labor Sluggers,"[10] she became even more determined to carry out the crusade that she was a part of even though she recognized that Goggin's death had left a void that could not be filled.

One must ask the obvious question: Why were these two women so determined to carry out what appeared to be an impossible task? The answer lies in the working conditions that produced these visionaries. Their style of work and ability to articulate positions suggest a pattern that was typical of women's reactions to the adverse conditions of their day. This ability appears to have

---

8. Margaret Haley, "Tribute to Catherine Goggin, " January 1916, AFT Files, Washington, D.C.

9. The AFT, "Tribute to Margaret A. Haley and Catherine Goggin," *The American Teacher* (November 1975): 59: 18.

10. Ibid., p. 19.

originated from the socioeconomic and political conditions that demanded that women adopt the restrictions imposed by an Anglo-male-dominated society.

Without any real political power this adaptation made it possible for women to define and refine their strategy to achieve their stated objectives. The ability to clearly articulate positions on issues was born out of the harshness of these conditions. This gave them an opportunity to understand who they were in relation to who they should be. The refusal to give up a cause even when the odds were stacked against them helped sustain their spirit to overcome the insurmountable.

There is another important factor to be considered in explaining why women of the Haley-Goggin period showed the type of commitment they did to a cause. This is the feminist element of the CTF, which became a major instrument in uniting the then predominantly all-female teachers. Through feminism the CTF teachers were encouraged to support the leadership of the organization. This broadened the social restraints and professional circle of its members. Underneath it all there was an invisible bond brought about by a common search for a destiny and a future in a hostile social environment. The strategy that Margaret Haley and Catherine Goggin utilized to launch a crusade under adverse conditions later served as a model for Albert Shanker years.

In an editorial in December 1915 the *Milwaukee Evening Wisconsian* described the imperative for teachers to form a union that would protect their socioeconomic interests:

> A teacher is a person who teaches things to people when they are young. However, it would be unfair to accuse her of teaching them what they know when they grow up. She only teaches them what they have forgotten by that time. The teacher comes to school at 8:30 o'clock and when she has gotten enough number of children for a class in her room, she teaches them reading, writing, geography, grammar, arithmetic, music, and cooking. When school is out she stays behind with five or six of her worst students and tries to help them. The job of reforming them later on is not easy. Teachers' salaries are about $30 a month. On that salary the teacher must dress neatly, buy herself things for her work, pay her way to district and state meetings, pay for her costs the three summer months when she earns no salary.[11]

The fact that the editorial was widely circulated in Chicago indicates the need for teachers to form an association or union designed to protect their unique interests.

Two years later the struggle for teachers to strengthen the AFT suffered a serious setback when the Illinois Supreme Court ruled in favor of the board of education, saying, "The board has the absolute right to decline to employ or to re-employ any teacher for any reason and is not required to furnish any reason for its decision because it is free to enter into a contract with whom it chooses."[12]

---

11. *Milwaukee Evening Wisconsian*, (editorial), December 30, 1915.
12. *Chicago Teachers Federation v. Board of Education*, Ill., May 5, 1917.

Although disappointed, the AFT did not lose heart. The decision signaled the beginning of a new phase in the struggle to realize the Haley-Goggin vision.

THE AFT'S STRUGGLE FOR TEACHERS' DEVELOPMENT

Recognizing that the demise of any semblance of teachers rights in Chicago would spell the same demise for teachers all over the country, individuals in other school districts came to the CTF's aid. Writing in *The American Teacher* of June 1917, Abraham Lefkowitz of New York observed, "Our union has aided the Chicago teachers in their fight for the right to organize. It stands ready to support any other body of teachers that is struggling for its professional right to exist. In the struggle of any individual teacher against unfavorable conditions and against invasion of professional privileges the union card bids itself as an insurance worth having. A long struggle is being waged against the imminence of an increase to a 210 day-year and against the lengthening of the school day."[13] Lefkowitz went on to defend the decision of the AFT to fight against the declining purchasing power of the dollar because with their low salaries, teachers would be more adversely affected than any other group of wage earners.

Lefkowitz further urged teachers to recognize that prices and the cost of living had been rising since 1900. The situation, he concluded, contributed to the 1902 coal miners' strike. The outbreak of the First World War in 1914 also contributed to the rise in prices. This affected teachers more than any other group of workers. It was recognized that teachers with stationary salaries suffered more than did other workers. The CTF argued that by pursuing economic policies that recognized the need to assure that teachers were not placed at a financial disadvantage and by preventing waste in local and state governments, they could save enough to restore the full purchasing power of teachers' salaries without adding a nickel to the annual budget.

Although the CTF made a suggestion to the board of education to take positive and immediate steps to resolve the growing pressure on the diminishing financial resources of teachers, there was no response to indicate that the common problems that schools and teachers were facing would be considered. Lefkowitz concluded in a prophetic manner: "The struggle for economic justice will continue as long as necessary."[14] Lefkowitz's words became a reality with the formation of the American Federation of Teachers. To this day the problem of discontent among teachers has not been fully resolved. This is why teachers' associations and unions have added a political dimension to the educational process.

During its formative years the AFT utilized a variety of strategies in its struggle for development. The AFT respected the democratic process and stressed that it must replace the autocratic process used in educational administration that the Illinois Supreme Court had sanctioned. What the AFT wanted to know was

---

13. Abraham Lefkowitz, "The Teachers' Union: Past, Present, and Future," *The American Teacher* 6, no. 6 (June 1917): 87.

14. Ibid., p. 88.

how teachers could be expected to teach democratic values to their students if society failed to respect those same values in its interactions with teachers. The most critical element that the AFT recognized as having an adverse effect on the continuing development of education was the fact that teachers were mere cogs in the educational wheel of a politically fueled vehicle that chauffeured politicians to the seat of the power that they were seeking.

The AFT, therefore, condemned the action of the boards of education in denying teachers their right to freedom of speech and to engage in dialogue in seeking solutions to educational problems. It also urged city governments to have a teacher representative on their respective boards of education to make sure that all points of view were heard when discussing issues affecting teachers. It urged the periodic revision of the curriculum so that the subject matter and the teaching strategy would be coordinated in order to sustain the viability of democratic principles and values. The AFT has always insisted that any system of education must role-model democratic principles to the students it serves.

Recognizing that its survival depended upon the effectiveness of the program of action it adopted, the AFT decided, as Lefkowitz said, "under any and all circumstances it must continue its fight for the protection of teachers against injustice of any kind, to fight for the elimination of the rating system, to fight for a social and just pension, principles of fairness, for scientific salary adjustment, for the democratization of the administration of schools, for reform of the psychological examination of children, for the scientific evaluation of the entire administrative structure."[15]

This was, indeed, an impressive agenda bravely initiated by a young, fragile, and struggling organization that had a better vision for the future than the system that controlled it. The strength in the convictions of its members, their commitment to their cause, and the dedication with which they approached their task left no room for failure. This is why AFT members united in opposing the actions of the courts against the principles that teachers were trying to promote. The AFT realized that it were to continue its crusade if the ideals of democracy must prevail in the educational process.

THE CHALLENGE AND THE TASK

Since its formation the AFT has recognized that its future success lies in the quality of leadership it renders to teachers. From the beginning of Charles Stillman's term of office in 1916 to the end of David Selden's term in 1974, the AFT provided the kind of leadership that lived up to expectations. By 1927 among the challenges that the AFT decided to meet was an increase in its membership. This would allow it to have the wider representation needed to strengthen its position in the struggle it was waging against boards of education. Having thirty-five locals with a total membership of 4,000 in 1927, the AFT realized the need for it to keep growing if it was ever to have a chance at attaining its objectives.

---

15. Ibid., p. 92.

For the next two years the AFT concentrated its efforts on generating a new level of confidence among its members. By 1929 this strategy had yielded some tangible results evident in the number of new locals and its 25 percent increase in members from 4,000 to 5,000. Although Florence Hanson, the AFT secretary-treasurer, reported that year that she was disappointed in what she regarded as a small gain,[16] it was, nonetheless, improvement. Hanson's disappointment came from the fact that the NEA had increased its membership from 8,000 in 1916 to 200,00 in 1929. The AFT concluded from these figures that it must continue to increase its membership if it hoped to attain parity with both the NEA and the boards of education. This task was not going to be easy to accomplish.

At the annual convention held in Chicago in June 1928 the AFT considered eight issues that the delegates believed were crucial to educational development: legal injunctions, an inadequate and unrepresentative school administrative structure, heavy teaching loads and other school responsibilities, a lack of an objective system for negotiating contracts, an ineffective merit and seniority system, wide differences of opinion between itself and the NEA, an inadequate system of communication, and the need to improve curriculum. How the AFT hoped to resolve these critical issues was the great challenge before it, and its members knew it would be hard to achieve.

How did an organization barely twelve years old hope to attain success with these difficult issues? At this convention the delegates voted to make all efforts to resolve each of these issues in a manner that was satisfactory to the AFT cause.[17] That the delegates voted to condemn injunctions as incompatible with democratic principles suggests that the AFT regarded the courts' actions as interfering too much in education and that their situation required political, not legal, interventions.

The collapse of the economy in October 1929 created a situation that compelled the AFT to work even harder at its annual convention that year. Six of the eight issues it had identified and discussed in 1928 were once again on the agenda for debate. The other two issues, legal injunctions and differences of opinion with the NEA, were regarded as so controversial that the convention committee decided that discussion of and action on them were not needed. The convention agenda of 1929 included the employment of married women teachers and international education. Both were considered issues of increasing importance.[18]

While the collapse of the economy and the use of legal injunctions combined to create conditions that made it difficult for the AFT to meet its challenge, its members decided to intensify their efforts to build an organization that would serve the future needs of teachers. This is why in 1939 the AFT identified eight new goals to accomplish in addition to those it established in

16. Florence Hanson to Mary Barker June 19, 1929, AFT Files, Washington, D.C.

17. The AFT, "Twelfth Annual Convention Proceedings, Chicago," June 1928, AFT Files, Washington, D.C..

18. The AFT, "Annual Convention Proceedings, Chicago," 1929, AFT Files, Washington, D.C.

1928: designate funds for the ongoing drive for new membership establish a resource fund for emergencies, such as helping teachers who had been indiscriminately dismissed; organize an effective publicity program; initiate an investment plan in buildings to generate a steady source of income, expand publications[19] as a means of disseminating information about the plight of teachers and education, coordinate activities between locals and the national office; establish regional secretaries and other organizational personnel with responsibilities for coordinating regional programs; and prepare and distribute historical materials about the activities of the AFT.[20]

There is no question that this agenda demonstrates the AFT's confidence in its future and its determination to face any and all challenges in order to fulfill the tasks it knew had to be carried out. This agenda also shows a high degree of confidence in itself as an organization that was operating under its own set of principles and purposes. James Earl Clarke concluded, "Confidence led militant teachers to defend their organization against the continuing attacks by professional educators and schoolmen on teacher unionism."[21]

The decision by the AFT to retain, strengthen, and defend its relationships with labor has remained a thorny issue for the union. It has been an issue that has inhibited the AFT's ability to successfully negotiate a merger with the NEA. Even some of the most ardent supporters of the AFT have questioned the practice of regarding itself as a union. In 1928 John Dewey argued that regarding teacher organizations as unions was inappropriate because it stressed the importance of maintaining an affiliation with the AFL-CIO, which he felt took away from their professional stature.

Suggesting that while their idea of associating a teacher organization with labor was undignified, Dewey went on to defend the AFT, saying, "I long ago came to the conviction that this snobbery is a considerable part of the objections to teacher unions and to their federation with other bodies of working men and women."[22] Dewey argued that the main reason for his interest in and support of the AFT was its demonstration of organizational skills and the objectives it was seeking to accomplish. He rejected the argument that because the courts ruled against them on the grounds that they were public servants, teachers should not be associated in any way with labor organizations and union activity.

From 1929 to 1940 the determination and drive to meet its challenge in seeking its goals received a boost from a number of prominent individuals who decided to join its ranks. Among these was George Counts, who served as AFT president from 1939 to 1942. Counts outlined two major reasons for his decision to join. The first was his belief that the educational and socioeconomic positions

---

19. For a listing of these publications, see *The American Teacher* (October 1974): 54: 27.

20. The AFT, "Annual Convention Proceedings, Chicago," 1929, Washington, D.C.

21. James Earl Clarke, "The American Federation of Teachers: Origins and History from 1879 to 1952" (a Ph.D. diss. Cornell University, 1966), p. 191.

22. John Dewey, "Why I am a Member of the Teachers Union," *The American Teacher* (January 1928): 59: 6.

taken by the AFT and its affiliation with labor were compatible with basic ideals fundamental to a democratic society.

The second was that organized labor and public education were natural allies because both were designed to serve the needs of teachers. Counts, a writer on various aspects of education in the Soviet Union, brought an intellectual depth to the AFT that strengthened its leadership without alienating those members of the public whose support it was seeking.

Jerome Davis,[23] professor of theology and philanthropy at Yale University, believed that because the AFT addressed educational and socioeconomic issues, its impact on society was profound. He became an active member and served as its president from 1936 to 1939. When George Counts succeeded him, the AFT had its second university scholar serving as president. John Childs, a leading authority on education and social justice, said that he believed in the AFT's agenda for action and its objectives because they were directed at seeking improvement in the overall conditions of public schools. He saw this action as a real salvation for the country.

Mike Mansfield, later the powerful member of the U.S. Senate from Montana, stated that he joined the AFT when he was professor because he believed in what it was trying to accomplish. In the same way Paul Douglas, also once a powerful U.S. senator, indicated that he joined the AFT in 1922 because "teachers needed an organization to bolster their economic conditions and to defend their dignity against administrative tyranny."[24]

Among the individuals who gave the AFT support was Goodwin Watson, another prominent educator. Watson advanced six reasons for his support. The first was that the AFT had proved that it was an agent for promoting both social change and education in the best interest of the country. The second was that the AFT was needed to develop a strong national economy. The third reason was that the AFT was candid and forthright in promoting its programs. The fourth was that the AFT was genuinely seeking to eliminate class conflict and racial inequality. The fifth was that in its endeavors the AFT was operating under democratic principles. The sixth reason was that the AFT recognized that the development of the country depended upon how efficaciously national resources, including people, were utilized.[25]

By the time that Carl Megel served as president of the AFT from 1952 to 1964, the AFT had slowly converted this pervasive support and confidence into an effective strategy for resolving conflict between itself and boards of education. This was done through collective bargaining. During that time the AFT relied on it to achieve two objectives. The first was to minimize the reliance on strikes and to emphasize the principle of dialogue.

This strategy had the effect of taking away reasons used by the courts in the past to rule that, as civil servants, teachers could not resort to strikes. In 1974

---

23. From 1932 to 1936 Davis served as chairman of the Connecticut Legislative Commission on Jails, a position that gave him an opportunity to study and understand social issues.

24. Paul Douglas, "Why I Joined the AFT: Brief Statements by Individuals," 1957, AFT Files, Washington, D.C.

25. Ibid.

Megel recognized that while collective bargaining could still be improved upon it had become an acceptable means of settling disputes between teachers and school boards.At that time Megel reflected on the existing conditions and what the AFT was seeking to accomplish:

> On the issue of collective bargaining there is no agreement among public employee unions upon a common approach. The AFT, along with other AFL-CIO affiliates, seeks inclusion for public employees under the existing provisions of the National Labor Relations Act. The AFT opposes the creation of a separate agency for public employees. We feel that a separate agency would divide labor interests with the division of private employee unions from public employee unions. This would not be in the best interests of either private or public sector workers.[26]

The second objective was to initiate a political approach to its problems and agenda. Part of this approach was to alert AFT members to the voting records of the members of Congress. The AFT also took an active interest in the actions of President Richard Nixon and Gerald Ford. It concluded that both manifested political behavior that was anti-teacher in nature. Megel went on to state that the AFT concluded that "this can only be cured through effective political action for we believe that the American people understand what is at stake. All the scare tactics in the world will not save the political careers of those who constantly oppose the progress so much needed by our nation."[27]

During the period that Charles Cogen served as president of the AFT (from 1964 to 1967), critical events profoundly influenced the course of developments that were taking place. The enactment of the Civil Rights Act in 1964, the riots that took place in major cities, beginning with Watts in 1965, and the release of the Kerner Report in 1967 all compelled the AFT to adopt new strategies for seeking solutions to national problems. In 1967 when the AFT had 130,000 members, Charles Cogen expressed profound concern over the deteriorating conditions of education. He was compelled to write:

> There are too many children in the nation who are growing up without the basic skills necessary for future success as citizens. This nationwide crisis represents the emergence of the disadvantaged population in the slum areas, the lack of socioeconomic opportunity, the marginal cultural experiences, exposure to inadequate social and school environment which perpetuates a host of social evils. The schools are the only social agency to which all the children of our multi-ethnic populations are exposed. It is here where we should provide opportunities for intellectual challenge, integrated relationships, and cultural and emotional enrichment.[28]

---

26. Carl Megel, "The 93rd Congress: An AFT Report Card," *The American Teacher* (September 1974): 58: 15.

27. Ibid.

28. Charles Cogen, "Education in the United States Today," 1967, AFT Files, Washington, D.C.

Cogen went on to argue that in light of the economic affluence and the great resources of knowledge found in the people, the country was spending far less on education than other nations.[29] Cogen also emphasized that schools must demonstrate the commitment necessary to fulfill the basic educational needs of students. He called on teachers, the community, and local, state, and federal governments to do something before the situation reached the point of no return.

This call to action became a priority during David Selden's term of office as president of the AFT from 1967 to 1974. In January 1967, while still assistant to Cogen, Selden initiated an amendment to the AFT charter to strengthen the local affiliates, saying, "The AFT has historically been more active and effective at the local level than either at the national or state level. Because there are inadequacies such as the fact that there is no attempt to make sure that the executive council represents the spectrum of teacher interest, the time to take action to correct these inadequacies in the present AFT structure is now."[30]

Selden believed that the task of seeking improvement in education could not be successfully carried out without fundamental change in the structure and function of the AFT. This is why he suggested that authority and power must originate at the local level. Selden added, "We should strive to make the AFT structure stand in sharp contrast to the corporate structure of the NEA and the sooner this is done the better"[31] so that the AFT would be better prepared to launch its campaign for educational reform. Selden stated in a memo to Shanker, then president of the UFT, in January 1967, "In spite of our success in some areas, we are not properly set up to cope with the challenge which collective bargaining laws would present."[32]

ALBERT SHANKER OF THE AFT: SUMMARY

When circumstances forced Shanker to seek a teaching position in New York in 1952, he was unaware that he was launching a career that would make him a leading personality in American education. As the leader of a teachers' union he was so aggressive that he was arrested and sent to jail twice for leading what authorities considered to be illegal strikes. Shanker, however, regarded this as a legitimate action to improve the conditions under which teachers worked.

In 1989 Fletcher L. Byrom, the retired chairman of the Kappers Company which manufactured chemicals, said of Shanker, "At first I thought he was a reprehensible character. But now I think that Albert Shanker understands the

---

29. In Chapter 4 of this study Shanker cites some 1993 figures to reach this conclusion.

30. David Selden, "Reconstructing the AFT Executive Council" (memo to the Constitutional Amendment Committee of the AFT), January 17, 1967, AFT Files, Washington, D.C.

31. Ibid.

32. David Selden, to Albert Shanker, January 19, 1967, AFT Files, Washington, D.C.

problems facing public schools better than any other person in the country."[33] This author, who undertook this study with a preconceived bias against Albert Shanker's leadership, has experienced a 180-degree turn in his opinion of the man and strongly concurs with Byrom's statement.

The misconception about Shanker's intentions during the early years of his career as president of the UFT was quite common. In the 1973 movie *Sleeper*, Woody Allen, playing the main character, awakens from a deep sleep in 2173 to discover that the United States had been destroyed by a man named Shanker who never hesitated to use a nuclear warhead he acquired secretly.[34]

William Woodside, chairman of the board of Sky Chefs, Inc., confessed that he, too, was surprised to learn that Shanker was actually an open-minded and thoughtful leader. During a speech to the National Press Club in 1989, Shanker introduced the idea of a national proficiency test for teachers. Because the proposal was so controversial, Shanker's critics at first thought that he was pushing the idea to promote a personal agenda. But by 1992 most of those critics had changed their opinion of him.

Shanker's most outstanding contribution to American education has been his crusade to promote and entrench collective bargaining. He believed in this to the degree that during the early years of his presidency of the UFT he was prepared to lead strikes to compel school boards to implement it in good faith. Shanker has persistently argued that collective bargaining has two objectives. The first is to ensure the security of teachers, and the second is to promote their professional development. Each is critical to the success of the other. Those who have argued that Shanker has led the AFT only to demand more money do not understand his dedication to his mission. In May 1993 Eve Sacks, secretary to the AFT since 1967, told the author, "Mr. Shanker has had a profound impact on American education and society in ways few people have done. He understands the critical issues facing American society in a way that manifests his total dedication to the mission he believes must be carried out to strengthen the public schools."[35]

One can see evidence to suggest that Shanker had the potential to become a national leader as early as 1967 when he was defining the parameters of his leadership of the UFT. In May of that year he sent a letter to Charles Cogen, then president of the AFT, to make a proposal regarding the balloting procedure for electing members of the AFT executive council. His intended purpose was to strengthen it for the adoption of collective bargaining. The proposal read, "We will provide, no later than May 18, 1967, a critique of the article 'Collective Bargaining Contracts from the NEA and the AFT' by Peter Schnaufer, and that Mr. Schnaufer be authorized to prepare a revision of this article based on the critique and on any new material which becomes available. The revision will be submitted for public action in accordance with the guidelines adopted for the Research Department by the AFT executive council on April 2, 1967."[36]

33. Quoted by Edward B. Fiske, in "Where He Stands: Profile of Albert Shanker," 1980, AFT Files, Washington, D.C.

34. Ibid.

35. Eve Sacks, conversation with author, May 17, 1993.

36. Albert Shanker, to Charles Cogen, May 17, 1967, AFT Files, Washington, D.C.

Throughout his professional life Shanker has never ducked an involvement in controversial issues. In 1986, for example, Myron Lieberman, veteran educator and unsuccessful candidate for the presidency of the AFT, wrote an article that was critical of the union's tactics in carrying out its programs, saying, among other things, that teachers' unions were seeking more money and not vigorously promoting professional standards.[37] In September 1986 Shanker felt compelled to respond to Lieberman's charges, stating, "Every organized group is in the business of bettering the lot of its members."[38] Shanker went on to argue that Lieberman was making villain out of the AFT in order to find someone to blame for the poor condition of U.S. education.

Lieberman's major argument was that it was virtually impossible to achieve a leadership position in teacher organizations without supporting a single salary schedule covering all grades. What Lieberman was suggesting was that all teachers must be paid the same salary regardless of their qualifications and experience. This is needed in order to eliminate competition and rivalry, which, he said, often hurt the educational interests of the students and diminish the professional development of teachers. On this argument Shanker responded, "What Lieberman does not tell us it that single salary schedules became universal a decade and half before teacher unions achieved recognition of collective bargaining rights. In fact, it was not union but management that brought about the change in the early post-World War II period. The reason is that millions of children were entering elementary school in increasing numbers but there were not enough elementary schools teachers."[39]

In this response it is clear that Shanker wanted to know why, if Lieberman was correct that single salary was a policy imposed and maintained by teachers' unions, it was universally adopted before unions had any rights. As to Lieberman's claim that data were purposely left out because they would weaken union claims that teachers were underpaid, Shanker, following his characteristic practice, initiated an intense study of the claim and concluded that teachers' salaries were a matter of public record, adding, "The fact that teachers enjoy fringe benefits and pensions in addition to their salaries is a matter of public record."[40]

Concluding that Lieberman was living in the "fantasy land of comparable worth, an effort to determine teacher salaries by speculation about how they compare with others,"[41] Shanker outlined a story that Lieberman once told him. A dog food company brought together all of its department heads and consultants to make a presentation to the company. The dietitian demonstrated the superior nutritional value of their dog food relative to other brands. The advertising

37. Myron Lieberman, "Are Teachers Underpaid?" *The Public Interest* (Summer 1986): 5: 10. For further insights into Lieberman's earlier views of American education, see William van Til, *Education: A Beginning* (Boston: Houghton Mifflin, 1974), p. 484.

38. Albert Shanker, "Response to Myron Lieberman's, Are Teachers Underpaid?" September 4, 1986, AFT Files, Washington, D.C.

39. Ibid.

40. Ibid.

41. Ibid.

department compared its campaign with the advertisements of all other dog food companies and showed the superiority of its efforts. The packaging department compared all the cans and labels, and it was clear that none was better than its design. When all the presentations were made, the company executive officer asked, "If our product is superior in every way, then why are we doing so poorly?" A still, small voice was heard in the background: "because the dogs will not eat it."[42] Lieberman did not offer a rebuttal.

A letter that Edward J. McElroy, Jr., president of the Rhode Island Federation of Teachers, an affiliate of the AFT, wrote in January 1987 reveals the keen perceptiveness of Shanker's mind. McElroy was reflecting upon the substance of an AFT executive council meeting that Shanker had convened to discuss some issues that had been developing within the labor movement. That McElroy expressed the need to address these issues shows Shanker's ability to enable his associates to view the issues from his perspective. McElroy suggested that Shanker appoint a task force consisting of national, regional, state, and local representatives to conduct an in-depth analysis of "the continuing decline in organizational labor membership and the inability of many unions to successfully organize in their own areas as well as in less traditional areas."[43]

McElroy also suggested that the AFT pay serious attention to four issues that only it could resolve, existing the inclusive nature of Shanker's style of leadership. The first issue was that its governance should be restructured from a national perspective. The second was McElroy's view that the structure and functions of the AFT executive council should be reviewed to determines the need for regional representation. The third was the local and national national structures should be integrated. The fourth issue was that the AFT should be organized so as to increase membership. McElroy concluded, "Our union lives or dies by its ability to grow and to remain strong. Within the trade union movement there are many examples of unions which are unable to organize either in their traditional constituency or in new areas."[44]

McElroy put emphasis on the need to ensure that collective bargaining covered every teacher. This was an issue of great importance to Shanker as well. McElroy argued that despite having been initiated twenty-one years earlier, collective bargaining still did not cover every teacher. McElroy concluded, "Although we see surface kinds of data indicating relative salary scales of teachers in various states and regions of the country, we have not seen an in-depth analysis of the net effect of collective bargaining."[45] McElroy suggested designing a strategy of action to include all teachers in the process of collective bargaining. In arguing that the AFT needed organizational structure to bring in new leadership, McElroy called for the recognition that many of those in leadership positions at various organizational levels within the AFT had been in those positions for too long and that there was need for new blood.

---

42. Ibid.
43. Edward J. McElroy, Jr., to Albert Shanker, January 8, 1987, AFT Files, Washington, D.C.
44. Ibid.
45. Ibid.

McElroy challenged the AFT to recognize that development of an organization needed new faces and new ideas to make progress. He called for an amendment to the AFT charter to prohibit persons in high positions in the organization from seeking reelection after a term of six years. He concluded, "We seem to take for granted that the people who have led our unions for the past twenty years will always be there. This is not the case and we should make preparation for the next twenty years. We seem to have lost some of our sense of mission as we have succumbed to the comfort of business unionism. We should determine whether this is appropriate for us and beneficial to our members."[46] That McElroy and Shanker were in total agreement suggests their ability to grasp critical issues that were important to both education and the AFT itself.

The letter that J. Myron Atkin, professor of education at Stanford University, wrote to Shanker in March 1987 adds another example to substantiate the claim here that Shanker is a leader who has rightly earned the respect and gratitude of many. At that time the California legislature was trying to encourage educational institutions to initiate an effective international studies programs and asked Stanford University to coordinate the initiative. Atkin was appointed director. Sensing the potential that both he and Stanford could make a viable contribution to the development of a new educational venture, Atkin wrote a letter to inform Shanker about the program and to ask for his input, saying,

> The concern with the quality of international studies in California schools which guided the development of a program entitled "American Schools and the World," has now led to a major new development at Stanford. As a result of a bill passed by the California legislature, the state has formally established the California International Studies Project and has designated Stanford as the coordinating center for a state-wide network of university/school district partnerships devoted to the improvement of international and global education in California school.[47]

In characteristic fashion Shanker responded to give Atkin and the project his complete support and to indicate his willingness to assist in its development. From this new association between Stanford and Shanker a relationship developed between the AFT and educational institutions in California. This type of collaboration and research is fully rewarding for all involved. It has new educational objectives that are innovative in their content and fulfilling in their purpose.

This final section of the study must conclude with a discussion of the correspondence that Shanker had in March 1987 with Bruce R. Thomas, a resident of Chicago. Thomas wrote to him "to elicit as much advice and consultation as possible"[48] on what to do to solve the crisis that he saw in

---

46. Ibid.

47. J. Myron Atkin, to Albert Shanker, March 9, 1987, AFT Files, Washington, D.C.

48. Bruce R. Thomas, to Albert Shanker, March 11, 1987, AFT Files, Washington, D.C.

American education. He added, "Schools loom large as symbolic instruments of national purpose and policy. The resulting profusion of mandates, explicit and implicit, is more contradictory than consistent. We ask schools both to perpetuate and to alter the social order, to serve as both factory and filter, to mass produce education and to grade the relative quality of the product. We expect the schools to solve in one generation problems of racial and class conflict and division created by centuries and to preserve traditional social practices."[49] Thomas concluded that the result of this situation was a serious contradiction in school activity that meant that traditional schools were expected to meet the needs of rapidly changing society.

Thomas saw that in this contradiction schools become a transforming agency at the crossroads of conflicting and powerful political currents that require it to pursue irreconcilable objectives and so render it ineffective.[50] While Shanker recognized the essential nature of the elements of Thomas's perspective, he argued that the solution to the crisis lay in making an effort to bridge the gap between the charge placed on educational institutions and society's expectations of itself. Any other course of action, he concluded, would accentuate the crisis.

Shanker's ability to think issues through has enabled him to rise to the occasion numerous times to identify new directions that the organization he leads must take in seeking solutions to the problems it faces. This approach makes it possible for a new social order to emerge from the kind of educational system and development the AFT is seeking.

In 1994, Shanker's concern about quality education is no longer limited to his view that American society has a responsibility to improve the conditions of education. His chief concern now is what he perceives as a startling decline in the quality of teacher education. His current efforts toward reform began with the introduction of higher academic standards for teachers. More than ever he is worried about the caliber of American teachers. He expressed this concern to Thomas Toch, saying, "You always have to have the footnote that there are some very good people entering the profession, but overall I would say that we are in worse shape now than we were ten years ago. Every teacher in every other industrial country, in order to enter college, has to be literate and highly numerate. This country produces such a small number of high school and college graduates with that kind of education that it is impossible to put 2.7 million well-educated teachers in the classroom. It is very difficult for union leaders to push reform under these conditions."[51] But Shanker has not given up the struggle that has been his life's work.

---

49. Ibid.
50. Ibid.
51. Quoted in Thomas Toch, "Teacher Reform: Does Albert Shanker Still Believe," *America's Agenda* (Fall 1993): 63: 14.

CONCLUSIONS

The purpose of this study has been to present major developments that have taken place in the United States as a result of Albert Shanker's leadership of the AFT and the influence he has exerted since 1952. To enable the reader to appreciate Shanker's role, the study began by discussing the historical importance of events that began to unfold in Chicago in October 1902. It then moved to look at the leadership role that the AFT played in the development of both education and teachers in general. A discussion of major events that took place from when Shanker was born in 1928 to the present helped put this struggle into proper perspective.

Two questions present themselves. The first is, Who is Albert Shanker? The second, What has he accomplished? Answers to these questions present a picture of a national leader whose efforts have been directed at the transformation of his society. In 1986, twelve years after Shanker had assumed the presidency of the AFT, membership rose by 30 percent from 630,000 in 1974 to 820,000 in 1986.

In 1993, an increase of 23 percent over the membership of 1986 was realized. In addition to serving as president of the AFT, Shanker has served as vice-president of the AFL-CIO and has ranked fourth in seniority on its executive council. Shanker's national stature, especially in education and labor organizations, began to take on new dimensions when he was elected president of the UFT in 1964. That he held that position in conjunction with the AFT presidency until January 1986 evinces his total commitment to the organization.

In 1981 Shanker was elected president of the International Federation of Free Teachers Union (IFFTU), which has its headquarters in Brussels. In that position Shanker was committed to the development of teachers in three ways. The first was to enhance their position in their respective societies in terms of security and decent income, just as he had done in the United States. The second was to promote principles of democracy, even in countries that neither respect democracy nor practice it. The third was to promote professional competency for teachers as a distinctive component of elevating quality education so necessary for a rapidly changing world.

In addition to this, Shanker was a member of the Carnegie Forum on Education, serving on the Task Force on Teaching. A dedicated fighter for civil rights for all people, Shanker has also served as a member of the boards of trustees of the A. Philip Randolph Institute, the League of Industrial Democracy, the Population Institute, the Committee for Multilateral Trade Negotiations, and the Committee for the Free World. As a member of these organizations Shanker has traveled to a plethora of international conferences where he has met many influential individuals from whom he has learned a great deal. He told this author in May 1993, "This has forced me to constantly read more and to think of how to present an issue in a manner that is intelligent and logical."[52]

While Shanker's involvement in these organizations defines him as a visionary professional, it is also the reason why in May 1986 the New York

---

52. Albert Shanker, interview with author, Washington, D.C., May 17, 1993.

State Board of Regents presented him with the prestigious James E. Allen, Jr. Memorial Award for Distinguished Service to Education. This is the highest honor of its kind in the state of New York. This recognition heralded Shanker's role in promoting the position of teachers, especially the fight to institute collective bargaining. Shanker also worked for the improvement of teachers' salaries from an average of $2,500 in 1952, when he began his career as a teacher, to $38,000 in 1986.

In working for this improvement Shanker has sought to improve health care benefits and pension packages for the 60,000 teachers and the 10,000 classroom paraprofessionals in New York, most of whom are women. Since 1985 Shanker has played a prominent role in urging teachers to take seriously the various reports that have been critical of education in the United States and has urged them to play a leading role in initiating reform. He has urged them not to take things for granted. When combined, these activities answer the question of who Shanker is. There is no single activity, not even his serving as president of the AFT, that can define Shanker. He is a complex man who, like any system, is best described as a synergistic phenomenon.

The question of what Shanker has accomplished must be answered by individuals who have watched him closely over the years. As the AFT concluded in 1993, "Albert Shanker's conception of the role of the American teachers' organizations has opened new organizational frontiers and has revitalized the labor movement. He was the first teacher ever to become a member of the AFL-CIO executive council."[53] In February 1988, *U.S. News and World Report* stated, "Shanker is a statesman praised by politicians and executives alike for his foresight and leadership."[54] From his visits to countries under repressive governments, including Latin American and Eastern Bloc countries, Shanker has come to understand the need to organize teachers in order to generate a new level of public consciousness regarding the need to initiate a new struggle for their improvement.

In his involvement in these critical issues Shanker became controversial. In 1974 Edwin Newman, a veteran journalist, concluded, "Albert Shanker is one of the most powerful and controversial figures in public education in the United States today."[55] But Shanker appears to have made his greatest contribution to the understanding of issues in education and society in the United States through the series of articles entitled *Where We Stand*, which he intended to use as a means of educating Americans about the various problems the country has been experiencing. The success of the series and the impact it has had on the public perception of both him and the AFT can be measured best by the reaction he has had from people all across the English-speaking world.

Recognizing Shanker's contribution through this column, the *Wall Street Journal* concluded in 1987, "Shanker is a respected educational leader whose

---

53. The AFT, "Albert Shanker: President of the AFT," 1993, AFT Files, Washington, D. C.

54. *U.S. News and World Report*, February 8, 1988, p. 3.

55. Edwin Newman, "Meet the Press, " (Transcript), April 15, 1974, AFT Files, Washington, D. C.

vision of American school reform has shaken up the status quo."[56] In addition to these accomplishments Shanker has achieved remarkable success in three key areas of national importance. The first is the introduction of shared decision-making processes in public schools to allow for collective bargaining as a principle of democracy. The result has been that school boards have become more sensitive to the need to involve teachers or their representatives in the process of making decisions about the conditions under which they serve.

The second is the introduction of an awards system to encourage the professional development of outstanding teachers and schools. This not only encouraged the development of individual talent for the benefit of education, but also created an academic climate that facilitated better communication and the sharing of ideas. The third is the creation of an effective system of assessing student achievement in order to improve the system of standardized tests. This is why the *Christian Science Monitor* reported in 1985, "Albert Shanker is by far the leading thinker and strategist for teacher professionalism."[57]

Another of Shanker's outstanding qualities has been the strength of his belief that the integration in public schools of children from different racial and ethnic backgrounds is a key factor in making the United States successful as a country. He has persistently called for education to enhance cultural diversity as a means for national enrichment. About this aspect of Shanker's work, *The New Republic* observed in 1985, "Shanker's single-mindedness in the pursuit of this objective has certainly helped galvanize the movement for educational reform to achieve an integrated society."[58] These are only a few of Shanker's accomplishments, but they stand out as testimony to the efforts of a leader who has tried to serve his country well.

IMPLICATIONS

There is no question that during his term of office as president of the AFT Shanker has accomplished an impressive record. From the moment he decided to become a teacher in 1952 Shanker became fully committed to making an effort to make a difference in four areas of education that he saw as critical to its development. The first was to seek an improvement in the conditions under which teachers served, These conditions included salary, pension, and fringe benefits.

The second area was to initiate a process of dialogue for the purpose of introducing the principle of collective bargaining as an operative practice of democracy in order to ensure that school boards did not dictate conditions of service for teachers. The third was to seek improvement in professional competency for teachers as a prerequisite of seeking improvement of education.

---

56. "Albert Shanker's Vision of America," *Wall Street Journal*, November 24, 1987, p. 7.

57. "Strategists for Teacher Professionalism," *Christian Science Monitor*, December 9, 1985, p. 11.

58. "Albert Shanker on Social Integration Through Educational Reform," *The New Republic*, June 24, 1985, p. 3.

The fourth was to inform the public about the importance of maintaining public schools under the original objectives of the reform movement of the nineteenth century and to continue reform in order to meet the needs of a vastly changing society.

To accomplish his second objective Shanker has tirelessly worked in support of democratic practices as manifested in the principle of collective bargaining. But in his pursuit of this basic component of society Shanker has caused conflict in both American education and society. Although collective bargaining has been applied to contract negotiations in public schools, the principle has very little application to the operations and functions of institutions of higher education. It is a common practice for university officials, for example, to send a "contract" already drawn elsewhere, to instructors and ask them to sign and return it by a given date. There is usually no discussion with instructors or their representative group about any of the terms listed in the "contract." In August 1993 one new instructor at an institution of higher education told the author:

> Although I am pleased to have a position as a college instructor, I am not happy to receive a document called a contract already drawn up in the office of the president and be asked to sign it. I was never given an opportunity to discuss its terms. How can the college officials call this a contract? A contract is an agreement between two sides reached through negotiations. What has happened to the principle of collective bargaining that President John Kennedy initiated in his executive order in 1962? For unknown reasons the American Association of University Professors (AAUP) has chosen to cause its own death. Perhaps college instructors need to reevaluate this practice and seek the assistance of leaders of national organizations such as Albert E. Shanker of the American Federation of Teachers on how best to initiate it.[59]

For Shanker and the AFT the implementation of collective bargaining did not come easily. What this means is that nothing of lasting value or importance is free from resistance. But persistence must be supplemented by a combination of clear goals, strategies to accomplish them, patience, a knowledge of critical issues, an ability to articulate logical arguments, persuasion, and a unity of purpose among those who seek to accomplish a cause. From the very beginning of his crusade Shanker never lost sight of the direction and the objectives he sought to accomplish. He knew that ,without his vision as a leader, the members of the organization that he led would perish in the economic steel-trap jaws of the school board.

The success that Shanker has achieved since assuming the leadership of the AFT must not be considered an end in itself, but a means to an end: meeting

---

59. These comments were made by a new college instructor during a conversation with the author in Phoenix, Arizona, August 23, 1993. The instructor declined to be identified because, he said, "I do not wish to appear to criticize a system that has been in place in colleges and universities for quite some time, although, however, it certainly needs reform."

new challenges in seeking solutions to critical problems that education in the United States now faces. Among these challenges are the following: How can school personnel be trained to cope with the unprecedented wave of violence in schools? Should schools teach a new definition of morality? What initiatives can the AFT make to persuade state and federal governments to become more involved in making education relevant to the needs of students as a condition for making it relevant to the needs of society? What can be done to reduce the rapid change in the structure of the traditional family in order to create stable conditions for students? What can both education and society do to solve the problems of crime in schools and society? Who is best qualified to seek solutions to the epidemic of teenage pregnancy and drugs in schools? Should sexual abstinence be taught in order to minimize students' risk of being infected with the fatal HIV virus?

These and other questions must be answered in a forthright and complete manner if the future of both American education and society is to be ensured. But there are other questions that must be answered. In the face of rising costs and declining budgets, what are some methods of raising funds for education? What can educational institutions do to prepare teachers to motivate students? What are some possible alternative criteria to graduation from high school? Should the focus of education be liberal studies or technical training? To what extent does the law inhibit the ability of teachers to discharge their responsibility to their students? In 1993 the AFT concluded that these and many other relevant questions must be resolved as the country plans for the future.[60]

During the annual conference of the AFT, held in Washington, D.C., July 8-11, 1993, Shanker and the 3,000 delegates attempted to address these questions. During the keynote address Shanker himself recognized how important these questions were saying, "We in public education are paying a very heavy price for showing a lack of focus that school must have. In other countries it is very clear what school exists for. School is there for the purpose of teaching youngsters language, mathematics, history, geography, and science. I think that we need to start education with a clear understanding of what the problems of education and society are. We need to face these problems honestly because there is no way we are seriously going to address educational and social problems unless we first know what they are."[61]

Shanker then went on to argue that the United States now faces two choices. The first is to dismantle public schools in order to move toward a system of vouchers or some kind of competitive market system under the principle of private enterprise that would allow students and their parents to choose the school they attend. President George Bush outlined this proposal in *America 2000: An Education Strategy* in 1991, but it failed because many people, including Shanker, felt that its implementation would mean a return to

---

60. "Quality Educational Standards in Teaching," (abstract of a conference), AFT, Washington, D.C., June 21, 1993, July 9, 1993.

61. Albert Shanker, "Reforming the Academic Mission of the School," (keynote address to the Annual Conference of the AFT, held in Washington, D.C., July 8-11, 1993,) AFT Files, Washington, D.C.

conditions of education that existed prior to the reform movement of the nineteenth century. The problem that Shanker has persistently identified as arising from this system is that it would tend to produce elitist psychology. The reality of this outcome was addressed during the reform movement of the nineteenth century. That is why the common schools were introduced. If this system is adopted, it will mean a severe setback for education in the United States.

The second choice is to strengthen the public schools by reforming them so that they meet the needs of all students on the basis of equality. Arguing in favor of the second choice, Shanker went on to say, "President Bill Clinton was elected on an education platform that called for the establishment of standards of world class assessments, of a system that would deregulate and decentralize education so that people within schools would have greater empowerment to try different ways of reaching those standards. The public schools have done a good job for this country for over two hundred years."[62]

Shanker's view that "the whole game of education becomes public relations for school boards, petty politics at the local level unless you have a system that stands for something,"[63] presents the most serious challenge that the AFT faces in making efforts directed not only at maintaining public education, but also at reforming it so that it meets the challenges of building the future. Shanker argued that Clinton's approach to education, *Goals 2000: Educate America*, is based upon ideals and objectives that were established during the period of the reform movement in the days of Horace Mann and Henry Barnard and that must now be applied to meet conditions that exist in education and society today. For a man who has dedicated his life to seeking improvement of the public schools, the question of whether to maintain them is a troubling one.

Speaking at Georgetown University on February 15, 1994, to an audience of more than 700 students, parents, educators, and business, labor and community leaders, Richard Riley, Clinton's secretary of education, expressed similar concern when he said, "There is indeed a sense out there that this generation may be the first that has no great expectations of advancing the American Dream. Is a nation truly connected to its children and committed to their future when it allows one out of every five children to grow up in poverty and often with violence? When we see children killing children, can we say that we have listened to them with all due care? We must have a new ideal of American education grounded in the practical and hard-earned lessons of the last ten years."[64]

Shanker would argue that those who support the idea of vouchers under the principle of free enterprise do not seem to take all relevant factors into account. While free enterprise may be pertinent to economic activity, it may not apply to education because freedom of choice may lead to the economic inability of some

---

62. Ibid.

63. Ibid.

64. Richard Riley, "America's Moral Urgency to Reconnect Children and Schools," *Goals 2000: Educate America* (Washington, D.C., U.S. Printing Office, March 1994), 2: 1.

families to pay and so result in a discriminatory educational policy. The fact that minority groups are at the low end of the economic spectrum would mean that they would be unable to contribute to the cost of educating their children. As a result they would have to depend on other sources to finance the education their children need. Under private enterprise this may not be possible.

In arguing in favor of reforming the public schools Shanker went on to say, "It is important that we exercise intelligence in trying to deal with educational problems that we would exercise in making choices in any other field. The American people are trying very hard to preserve public education. Wherever they have had a chance to vote on funding public or private schools, they choose public schools. When they had a chance to make a statement in the election, they chose Bill Clinton who opposed vouchers over George Bush, who supported them. There is no evidence to show that there is a large rush on the part of the American people to abandon public education."[65] On December 17, 1993, Walter Annenberg adopted this line of thinking when he gave $500 million to improve public education, saying that if violence in schools did not stop, it will threaten the American way of life. Annenberg concluded that the problem with private education is that it does not extend the concept of equality to all students. This is what Shanker has always argued in favor of.

Shanker has placed his crusade to improve American education in the context of its global significance. In a letter dated July 1, 1993, and addressed to his friend Thomas T. Drysdale, director of the American Overseas Schools Archives at Northern Arizona University in Flagstaff, Shanker observed, "This important endeavor recognizes the unique and successful history of the schools that have educated the U.S. military personnel for more than 50 years. Since the Second World War more than two million American children have received all or part of their elementary and secondary education in military schools abroad. Through critical and turbulent years, these schools have not merely functioned efficiently, but they have also excelled at all of the things a school should do. The AFT supports the valuable and scholarly mission to which the Archives has committed itself."[66]

These are the words of a national leader whose knowledge of the issues that his nation faces has proven solid under any test. For him and the organization that he leads, these issues present a challenge that they must meet, a call that they must answer, and a task that they must accomplish. There is no room for failure because there is so much at stake. How this problem is addressed could well determine whether or nor United States remains a democracy. The words of Thomas Jefferson echo loud and clear--the foundation of any democracy is an educated citizenry. America, be well advised and be wise!

---

65. Ibid.

66. Albert Shanker, to Thomas T. Drysdale, July 1, 1993, (Courtesy of Thomas. T. Drysdale).

Selected Bibliography

BOOKS

Addams, Jane. *Twenty Years at Hull House*. New York: Macmillan, 1910.

Alberty, Harold B., and Boyd H. Bode (eds.). *Educational Freedom and Democracy*. New York: G. Appleton-Century, 1938.

Alexander, Carter. *Some Present Aspects of the Work of Teachers' Voluntary Associations in the United States*. New York: AMS Press, 1972.

Andrea, Robert G. *Collective Negotiations: A Guide to School Board-Teacher Relations*. Lexington, Mass.: D. C. Heath, Heath Lexington Books, 1970.

Axtelle, George E., and William W. Wattwenberg. *Teachers for Democracy*. New York: D. Appleton-Century, 1940.

Barness's Historical Series. *A Brief History of the United States*. New York: American Book Company, 1899.

Beale, Howard K. *Are American Teachers Free?* New York: Charles Scribner's Sons, 1936.

Bendiner, Robert. *The Politics of Schools: A Crisis of Self-Government*. New York: Harper and Row, 1969.

Berube, Maurice R., and Marilyn Gittell (eds.). *Confrontation at Ocean Hill-Brownsville: The New York School Strikes of 1968*. New York: Praeger, 1969.

Brameld, Theodore (ed.). *Workers' Education in the United States*. New York: Harper and Brothers, 1941.

Braun, Robert J. *Teachers and Power: The Story of the American Federation of Teachers*. New York: Simon and Schuster, 1972.

Brinkmeir, Oria A. *Inside the Organization Teacher: The Relationship Between Selected Characteristics of Teachers and Their Membership in Professional Organizations*. Danville, Ill.: Interstate Printers and Publishers, 1967.

Brooks, Thomas R. *Toil and Trouble: A History of American Labor*. New York: Delacorte Press, 1971.

Bush, George. *America 2000: An Education Strategy*. Washington, D.C.: U.S. Department of Education, 1991.

Callahan, Raymond E. *Education and the Cult of Efficiency*. Chicago: University of Chicago Press, 1962.

Campbell, Ronald F. *The Organization and Control of American Schools.* Columbus, Ohio: Charles E. Merrill, 1965.

____. and Donald Layton. *Policy Making for American Education.* Chicago: University of Chicago Press, 1969.

Carlton, Patrick W., and Harold I, Goodwin. *The Collective Dilemma: Negotiations in Education.* Worthington, Ohio: Charles A. Jones, 1969.

Carter, Barbara. *Pickets, Parents and Power: The Story Behind the New York City Teachers' Strike.* New York: Citation Press, 1971.

Chamberlain, Leo M., and Leslie W. Kindred. *The Teacher and School Organization.* Englewood Cliffs, N.J.: Prentice-Hall, 1958.

Childs, John L., and George S. Counts. *America, Russia and Communist Party in the Post-war World.* New York: John Day, 1943.

Clinton, Bill. *Putting People First: A National Economic Strategy for America.* Little Rock, Ark.: Bill Clinton for President Committee, 1992.

Cole, Stephen. *The Unionization of Teachers: A Case Study of the UFT.* New York: Praeger, 1969.

Counts, George. *School and Society in Chicago.* New York: Harcourt Brace, 1928.

____. *Dare Build a New School Order.* New York: John Day Company, 1932.

Cremin, Lawrence A. *The Transformation of the School: Progressivism in American Education, 1876-1957.* New York: Alfred A. Knopf, 1961.

Curle, Adam. *Education for Liberation.* New York: John Wiley and Sons, 1973.

Curoe, Philip R. V. *Educational Attitudes and Policies of Organized Labor in the United States.* New York: Columbia University, 1929.

Dewey, John. *Experience and Education.* New York: Macmillan Publishing Company, 1938.

____. *Education Today.* New York: G. P. Putman's Sons, 1940.

Doherty, Robert (ed.). *Employer-Employee Relations in the Public Schools.* Ithaca, N.Y.: Cornell University Press, 1967.

Duryea, E. E., and Robert Fisk. *Faculty Unions and Collective Bargaining.* San Francisco: Jossey-Bass, 1973.

Eaton, William Edward. *The American Federation of Teachers, 1916-1961: A History of the Movement.* Carbondale, Ill.: Southern Illinois University Press, 1975.

Elam, Stanley M. *Readings on Collective Negotiations in Public Education.* Chicago: Rand McNally, 1967.

Elsbree, Willard S. *The American Teacher: Evaluation of a Profession in a Democracy.* New York: American Books, 1939.

Fantini, Mario, and Marilyn R. Gittell. *Decentralization: Achieving Reform.* New York: Praeger, 1973.

Friedman, Leon (ed.). *Argument: The Oral Arguments Before the Supreme Court in Brown v. Board of Education of Topeka, 1952-1955.* New York: Chelsea House, 1969.

Goulden, Joseph C. *Jerry Wurf: Labor's Last Angry Man, A Biography.* New York: Atheneum, 1982.

Hampton, Henry, and Steve Fayer. *Voices of Freedom: An Oral History of the Civil Rights Movement from the 1950s Through the 1980s.* New York: Bantam Books, 1990.

Illich, Ivan. *Deschooling Society.* New York: Harper and Row, 1971.

Kliebard, Herbert. *The Struggle for the American Curriculum, 1893-1958.* New York: Routledge and Kegan Paul, 1987.

La Noue, George R., and Bruce L. R. Smith. *The Politics of School Decentralization.* Lexington, Mass.: D. C. Heath, 1973.

Lieberman, Myron. *Education as Profession.* Englewood Cliffs, N.J.: Prentice-Hall, 1956.

----. *The Future of Public Education.* Chicago: The University of Chicago Press, 1960.

Maslow, Abraham. *Motivation and Personality.* New York: Harper and Row, 1970.

Mayer, Martin. *The Teachers Strike: New York, 1968.* New York: Harper and Row, 1969.

Moreland, Willis D., and Erwin H. Goldenstein. *Pioneers in Adult Education.* Chicago: Nelson-Hall Publishers, 1985.

Morris, James O. *Conflict Within the AFL: A Case Study of Craft Versus Industrial Unionism, 1901-1938.* Ithaca, N.Y.: Cornell University Press, 1958.

Mungazi, Dickson A. *Educational Policy and National Character: Africa, Japan, the United States and the Soviet Union.* Westport, Conn.: Praeger Publishers, 1993.

Murphy, Marjorie. *Blackboard Unions The AFT and the NEA, 1900-1980.* Ithaca: Cornell University Press, 1990.

Myrdal, Gunnar. *An American Dilemma: The Negro Problem and Modern Democracy.* London: Harper and Brothers, 1944.

Newell, Barbara W. *Chicago and the Labor Movement: Metropolitan Unionism in the 1930s.* Urbana: University of Illinois Press, 1961.

Perry, Charles R., and Wesley A. Widman. *The Impact of Negotiations in Public Education: The Evidence from the Schools.* Worthington, Ohio: Charles A. Jones, 1970.

Potter, Robert. *The Stream of American Education.* New York: American Book Company, 1974.

Ravitch, Diane. *The Troubled Crusade: American Education, 1945-1980.* New York: Basic Books, 1983.

Robinson, Allen W. *A Critical Evaluation of the American Federation of Teachers.* Chicago: American Federation of Teachers, 1934.

Roosevelt, Franklin D. *State of the Union Message.* Washington, D.C: U.S. Government Printing Office, 1941.

Roosevelt, Franklin D., and Winston Churchill. *The Atlantic Charter.* Washington, D.C.: U.S. Government Printing Office, 1941.

Seeley, Levi. *History of Education.* New York: American Book Company, 1899.

Spring, Joel. *Conflict of Interest: The Politics of American Education.* New York: Longman, 1993.

Stinnett, Timothy M. *Turmoil in Teaching: A History of the Organizational Struggle for America's Teachers.* New York: Macmillan, 1968.

Taft, Phillip. *United They Teach: The Story of the United Federation of Teachers.* Los Angeles: Nash Publishing, 1974.

Talbott, Strobe, Edward Crankshaw, Jerrald Schecter. *Khrushchev Remembers: The Last Testament.* Boston: Little, Brown and Company, 1974.

van Til, William. *Education: A Beginning.* Boston: Houghton Mifflin Company, 1974.

GOVERNMENT DOCUMENTS

City Board of Education, Chicago. *School Records*, 1902.

Virginia Board of Education. Rules of Conduct for Female Teachers. Williamsburg, Va.: 1902.

City Board of Education, Chicago. Annual Report, 1903.

State of New York. *Report and Recommendations of the Joint Legislative Committee Investigating Seditious Activities:,* Legislative Document no. 52 (Clayton R. Lusk, chairman). Albany: Government Printer, 1920.

Department of the Interior. *Biennial Survey of Education*, 1920-24.vol. 2, no. 44. Washington, D.C.: U.S. Government Printing Office, 1925.

Brown v. Board of Education of Topeka, 347 U.S. 483, 1954.

National Defense Education Act. U.S. Public Law 85-864, 85th Congress. Washington, D.C.: U.S. Government Printing Office, 1958.

Economic Opportunity Act. U.S. Public Law 88-482. Washington, D.C.: U.S Government Printing Office, 1964.

U.S. Senate. Committee on Labor and Public Welfare. *Enactment by the 89th Congress Concerning Education and Training*. Washington, D.C.: U.S. Government Printing Office, 1966.

Chicago Division of Illinois Education Association v. the Board of Education of the City of Chicago, 222, NE., 2nd. 43 (1967).

Finot v. Pasadena City Board of Education 58 Cal. 520 (1967).

Tinker v. Des Moines Independent School District, U.S. Supreme Court, 393 U.S. 503 1969.

Perry v. Sindermann 408, U.S. 593 (1972).

Roth v. Board of Regents of California, 408 U.S. 564 (1972).

La Fleure v. Cleveland Board of Education. Washington (1974).

U.S. Senate. *The Challenge in the Third Century: Education in a Safe Environment* (Birch Bayh, chairman). Washington, D.C.U.S. Government Printing Office, 1977.

National Commission on Excellence in Education. *A Nation at Risk*. Washington, D.C.: U.S. Department of Education, 1983.

AFT MATERIALS

Adler, Mortimer, to Albert Shanker, AFT Files, Walter Reuther Archives of Labor and Urban Affairs, Wayne State University, Detroit, Mich., May 22, 1986

Aexlrod, Donald. "How 'Red' Is the Teacher' Union? Fellow Travelers Lose Control But Liberalism Remains Unshaken." *Common Sense* (February 1940).

Alexander, Lamar. "A Message from the U.S. Secretary of Education," Introduction to George Bush, *America 2000: An Education Strategy*, Washington, D.C.: U.S. Government Printing Office, 1992.

Arts and Entertainment. *Five Rings Under the Swastika: Olympic Games in Berlin, 1936,* (a documentary film), 1988.

Atkin, Myron J. Letter to Albert Shanker, March 9, 1987, AFT Files, Washington, D.C.

Barker, Mary C. "Address of President Mary C. Barker.*" The American Teacher* (October, 1930).

_____. Presidential Address, July 2, 1929. AFT Files: Walter Reuther Archives of Labor and Urban Affairs, Wayne State University, Detroit, Mich.

_____. "Address of the President." *The American Teacher* (September 1927).

_____. "Federation of Teachers Issues Program of Action." *American Federation of Teachers Monthly Bulletin* 5 (September 1925): 1.

_____. Letter to Florence Hanson, June 23, 1929. The AFT Files: Walter Reuther Archives of Labor, Wayne State University, Detroit, Mich.

_____. "Presidential Address," June 30, 1930. AFT Files, Walter Reuther Archives of Labor and Urban Affairs, Wayne State University, Detroit, Mich.

_____. "President's Address to the Thirteenth Convention of the American Federation of Teachers," *American Teacher* (October 1929).

_____. "President's Address." *The American Teacher* (September 1926).

_____. "President's Address to the Thirteenth Convention of the American Federation of Teachers," *American Teacher* (October 1929).

_____. "President's Address." *The American Teacher* (September 1926).

_____. "The Atlanta Public School Teaches Association." *American Teacher* (March 1928).

_____. "Presidential Address," June 26, 1928. The AFT Files: Walter Reuther Archives of Labor:, Wayne State University, Detroit, Mich.

Botel, Morten. Letter to Albert Shanker, March 19, 1986. AFT Files, Walter Reuther Archives of Labor and Urban Affairs Wayne State University, Detroit, Mich.

Bowen, John J. "Better Working Conditions, Better Education."*The American Teacher* (February 1961).

Clinton, Bill. *Goals 200: Educate America*. Washington, D.C.: U.S. Government Printing Office, 1994.

_____. "Committee on Commercial Education of the New York Chamber of Commerce." *The American Teacher*, vol. 6, no. 6., June 1916.

_____. "The Dismissal of Chicago Teachers." *School and Society*, 4: 94 (July 15, 1916).

"Chicago Teachers Federation and the Board of Education." *School and Society* 5, (May 5, 1917): 5.

_____. "The Marvelous Revolutionist," (editorial) *The American Teacher* 6, no. 6 (June 1917).

_____. "Through the Fluoroscope." An Editorial, *The American Teacher* 6, no. 6 (June 1917).

Twelfth Annual Convention held in Chicago, June 1928. The AFT Files. Washington, D.C.

"Annual Convention Proceedings," 1937. AFT Files, Washington, D.C.

Baltimore Teachers Union. "Resolution on Tenure Rights for Teachers," August 1935. AFT Files, Walter Reuther Archives of Labor and Urban Affairs, Wayne State University, Detroit, Mich.

_____. "Resolution on the Position of Teachers," October 10, 1935. AFT Files, Walter Reuther Archives of Labor and Urban Affairs, Wayne State University, Detroit, Mich.

_____. "Resolution on Denial of Academic and Political Rights to Teachers," August 10, 1935. AFT Files, Walter Reuther Archives of Labor and Urban Affairs, Wayne State University, Detroit, Mich.

The AFT. "Annual Convention Proceedings, Chicago," 1939. The AFT Files, Washington, D.C.

_____. "The Need for the AFT to Be Inclusive." *The American Teacher* 23 (March 1939): 5-7.

_____. "Report of the Resolutions Committee of the Twenty-Third Annual Convention of the AFT," August 1939. AFT Files, Washington, D.C.

The New York Teachers Union. "Statement on Collective Bargaining," April 12, 1962. AFT Files: Washington, D.C.

_____. "Shanker Meets the Press." *The American Teacher* (September 1974): 51.

_____. "Shanker Urges Affirmative Action Through Better Training and More Jobs," in *The American Teacher* (October 1974): 51.

"Early Childhood Education: A National Program," December 17, 1974. AFT Files, Washington, D.C.

_____. "Teacher Wins $40,000 Award for Fighting Firing Since 1968," *The American Teacher* (June 1975): 6.

The AFT. "Carter on Education." *The American Teacher* (October 1976).

_____. "Teacher Wins $40,000 Award for Fighting Firing Since 1968," *The American Teacher* (June 1975): 6.

_____. "Human Rights and Community Relations." *The American Teacher* (September 1975): 54.

_____. "Tribute to Margaret A. Haley and Catherine Goggin." *The American Teacher* (November 1975): 58.

The AFT. "The Big Question for 1976: More Vetoes or a Pro-education President" (editorial) *The American Teacher* (April 1976): 52.

"Early Childhood Education: A National Program," October 20, 1976. AFT Files, Washington, D.C.

The AFT. Ida Fursman's CTF Collection. AFT Files, Walter Reuther Archives of Labor and Urban Affairs, Wayne State University, Detroit, Mich.

_____. "Profile of Carl Megel." *The American Teacher* (February 1977): 52.

_____. "Shanker on Student Seminar." *The American Teacher* (March 1977): 53.

"Albert Shanker, President of the American Federation of Teachers," October 1990, AFT Files, Washington, D.C.

_____. Linville Collection. AFT Files, Walter Reuther Archives of Labor and Urban Affairs, Wayne State University, Detroit, Mich.

_____. "Quality Educational Standards in Teaching" (abstract of a conference held in Washington, D.C.), July 9, 1993.

_____. "Study of Teachers, Pay," The United States Compared With Other Countries. July 1993. AFT Files: Washington, D. C.

MATERIALS BY SHANKER

_____. "A Citizens' Review Board for Teachers?" *The American Teacher* (December 1966).

_____. Memo to Charles Cogen, the AFT President. May 17, 1967. The AFT Files: Washington, D.C.

Shanker, Albert. "The Real Meaning of the New York Teachers Strike." *Phi Delta Kappan* (April 1969).

_____. "Schools and the Union." *New Republic* (November 15, 1969).

_____. "What's Wrong with Compensatory Education." *Saturday Review* (January 11, 1969).

_____. "Where We Stand: For Teachers and Unions, A New High in Political Action and a New Need for Diligence." *New York Times* (October 22, 1972).

_____. "Why Teachers Need the Right to Strike." *Monthly Labor Review* September, 1973.

_____. "Where We Stand: The Public's View of the Public Schools." *New York Times*, September 16, 1973.

_____. "Where We Stand: Teacher Unionism: A Quiet Revolution Now Enters a Wider Arena." *New York Times* October 28, 1973.

_____. "Where We Stand: Teachers' Rights: Good Progress, but the Fight is Far from Won." *New York Times* December 23, 1973.

_____. "Where We Stand: Teacher Unity: Present Hopes Dashed, but the Need Persists." *New York Times* March 3, 1974.

_____. "Where We Stand: Now, More Than Ever, Teachers Need Unity-And Labor Support." *New York Times*, May 12, 1974.

_____. "Where We Stand: The Public Schools as Doing Better than Some Would Have Us Believe." July 7, 1974. AFT Files, Washington, D.C.

____. "An AFT Program for Lifelong Education." *The American Teacher* (October, 1974).

____. "Response to President Gerald Ford's Statement of October 9, 1974," *The American Teacher* (October 1974).

____. "Where We Stand: The Ford Administration's Policies." September 22, 1974. AFT Files, Washington,D.C.

____. "Where We Stand: Federal Aid to Cities." December 1974. AFT Files: Washington, D.C.

____. "Where We Stand: Strong Voice Against Ethnic Hiring." January 12, 1975. AFT Files: Washington, D.C.

____. "Why Teachers Are Angry." *American School Board Journal*, January, 1975.

____. "Where We Stand: Little Rock, 1959, Boston, 1974." January 26, 1975. AFT Files, Washington, D.C.

____. "Where We Stand: Why the Idea of Merit Lacks Merit." March 2, 1975. AFT Files: Washington, D.C.

____. "Where We Stand: Much More Than a Tax Rebate is Needed." March 30, 1975. AFT Files: Washington, D.C.

____. "Where We Stand: Dangers in the Concept of Educational Malpractice." April 20, 1975. AFT Files, Washington, D.C.

____. "Where We Stand: Federal Protection for Public Pension Funds is Needed." December 14, 1975. AFT Files: Washington, D.C.

____. "Financial Crisis in Public Schools," 1975. The AFT Files: Washington, D. C.

____. "Where We Stand: Decline in Test Scores, a Cause for Concern." March 14,

____. "Where We Stand: The Teachers Are Learning Labor's Lessons." *New York Times* February 2, 1975.

____. "Public Schools and Preschool Programs: A Natural Connection," (testimony presented to a Congressional Committee on Education) June 5, 1975. AFT Files: Washington, D.C.

____. "Where We Stand: The School Board as Sovereign: An Outmoded Idea." *New York Times* April 13, 1975.

____. "Power is Good." *Time*, September 22, 1975.

____. "Where We Stand: Teachers Save City, but Rescue Is Temporary." *New York Times* October 19, 1975.

____. "Ford vs. New York City: A Reckless Gamble." *The American Teacher* (November 1975).

____. "Where We Stand: How Safe Are Public Employee Pensions?" *New York Times*, February 22, 1976.

____. "Where We Stand: Supreme Court Upholds Residency Lay But City Would Be Unwise to Adopt It." *New York Times* April 25, 1976.

____. "Where We Stand: High Court Limits Public Employee Rights." *New York Times*, June 27, 1976.

____. "Teachers in Politics: The American Heritage" (a Report), September 1976. The AFT Files: Washington, D.C.

____. "Teacher Unity in Perspective." *The American Teacher* (September 1976).

____. "Tribute to Carl Megel," *The American Teacher* (February 1977).

____. "Where We Stand: Most Can Learn Under Right Conditions." *New York Times*, April 17, 1977.

____. "Were We Stand: HEW Threatens to Make Children Pay." *New York Times*, September 11, 1977.

____. "Herndon Debate On School Discipline, Testing." *The American Teacher* September 1977

_____. "Massive Action Needed to Stop Tuition Tax Credit Bill." *The American Teacher* (April 1978).

_____. "Where We Stand: Bilingual Education Must Be Expanded." *New York Times* (May 28, 1978).

_____. "Where We Stand: Is Tax Cut Fever Sweeping the Country?" *New York Times*, June 18,1978.

_____. "Where We Stand: Proposition 13: What Does It Mean?" *The American Teacher*, September 1978.

_____. "Where We Stand: Why Does NEA Resist Full Disclosure?" *American Teacher* February 1979.

_____. "Where We Stand: Speaking Out Against a Separate Department of Education." *American Teacher* April 1979.

_____. "Where We Stand: Day Care-We Lag Far Behind Europe." *New York Times* (June 10, 1979).

_____. "Meeting the Challenge," (position paper on education) September 1979. AFT Files: Washington, D. C.

_____. "Annual Report of the AFT: The State of the Union, 1980-1." AFT Files; Washington, D.C.

_____. "Where We Stand: A Sharp Look Inside Reagan's Tax Plan." May 15, 1982. AFT Files: Washington, D.C.

_____. "Where We Stand: School Priorities Need Balance." August 2, 1986. AFT Files: Washington, D.C.

_____. "Response to Myron Lieberman's Are Teachers Underpaid?" September 4, 1986. AFT Files, Washington, D.C.

_____. "Bush's 2000 Plan: A Feast or Private Schools," *The American Teacher*, November 1991.

_____. "Where We Stand: Reagan Takes Cuts to Disaster." April 28, 1982. AFT Files Washington, D.C.

_____, to Thomas T. Drysdale, director of American Overseas Schools Archives, Northern Arizona University, Flagstaff, July 1, 1993.

_____. "Reforming the Academic Mission of the School," (keynote address to the Annual Conference of the AFT), July 1993. AFT Files, Washington, D C.

Shanker, Albert, and Robert Porter. Tribute to George Counts. The AFT Files: Washington, D.C.

NEWSPAPERS AND PERIODICALS

Bernstein, Harry. "No Backing for Reagan: Shanker Says," July 6, 1983.

_____. "Teacher Union Leader Assails Reagan Stand," July 5, 1983.

Boyer, Ernest. "On Shanker," *U.S.A. Today* (January 9, 1990).

Bremfoerder, Alice. "Toledo Wins Full Restoration." *American Teacher* (January 1943).

Brewer, John M. "The Question of Unions in the Teachers' Profession." *School and Society,* January 14, 1922.

Bruce, William C. "An Illegal Strike." *American School Board Journal* (June 1962).

Byrnes, Mary. "Teacher Tenure: Report of the Permanent Committee to the A.F.T. 1929 Convention." *The American Teacher* (December 1929).

Callahan, Ray. Letter to Albert Shanker, July 14, 1985. AFT Files, Washington, D.C.

Callis, H. A. "The Negro Teacher and the AFT." *Journal of Negro Education* (April 1937).

Callahan, Ray. Letter to Albert Shanker, July 14, 1985. AFT Files, Washington, D.C.

Callis, H. A. "The Negro Teacher and the AFT." *Journal of Negro Education* (April 1937).

Capen, Samuel P. "The Teaching Profession and Labor Unions." *Journal of General Education* (July 1947).

Carr, William G. "Response to the AFT Memo," 1962. NEA Files, Washington, D.C.

_____. "The Education of William G. Carr," 1962. NEA Files, Washington, D.C.

Christian Science Monitor, "Statistics for Teacher Professionalism," December 9, 1985.

Counts, George. "Communists in the AFT." *New York Times* (December 15, 1939).

_____+. "Farewell Address," *The American Teacher* (October 1942).

_____."Is Our Union Controlled by Communists?" *The American Teacher* (December 1939).

_____. "The Teacher's Responsibilities." *The American Teacher* (October 1939).

Chambers, M. M. "Teachers' Union and the Law." *National Schools* (November 1938).

Chenery, William L. "Adulterated Education," *The New Republic* (October 23, 1915).

Clarke, James Earl. "The American Federation of Teachers: Origins and History from 1870 to 1952," Ph.D. diss., Cornell University, 1966.

Clohesy, Agnes B. "Some Objectives of the Elementary Teachers Union." *The American Teacher* (May 1928).

Coaldigger, Adam. "What the American Federation of Teachers Is Doing and Attempting to Do." *The American Teacher* (September 1929).

Coffman, Lotus D. Address to the NEA, February 1920. NEA Files: Washington, D.C.

_____. "Teachers' Associations." *M.S.T.A. Quarterly Review* (March 1920).

Cogen, Charles. "Education in the United States Today," 1967. AFT Files: Washington, D.C.

Collette, Earnest B. Letter to Freeland B. Stecker, June 19, 1921. AFT Files,Washington, D.C.

Cook, Cara. "Annual Conference of Teachers in Workers' Education." *The American Teacher* (May, 1931).

Cook, William A. "Rise and Significance of the American Federation of Teachers," *Elementary School Journal* (February 1921).

Corey, Arthur M. "Strikes or Sanctions?" *NEA Journal*, October, 1962.

Counts, George. "Dare Progressive Education Be Progressive." *Progressive Education* (April 1932).

Dawson, George G. "Doctoral Studies on the Relationship between the Labor Movement and Public Education." *Journal of Educational Sociology* (February 1961).

Davis, Jerome. "America's Educational Retreat." *Christian Century* (July 1937)

DeLacy, Hugh. "Retreat to the Mountain." *Social Frontier* (March 1937).

Dewey, John. "The Bearings of Pragmatism upon Education," *Progressive Journal of Education* (December 1, 1908).

Diamant, Gertrude. "The Teachers' Union." *The American Mercury* (September 1934).

Dorr, Rheta Childe. "What's the Matter with the Public Schools?" *Delineator* (January 1909).

Douglas, Paul. "Why I Joined the AFT: Brief Statements by Individuals." AFT Files: Washington,.D.C.

Elam, Stanley M. "NEA-AFT Merger-And Related Matters." *Phi Delta Kappan* (February 1966).

Fisher, Lyman B. "Buffalo Industrial Teachers' Association; Local, 39." *The American Teacher* (February 1931).

Fiske, Edward B. "Where He Stands: Profile of Albert Shanker, 1980." AFT Files: Washington, D.C.

Fordyce, Wellington G. "The American Federation of Teachers-Its History and Organization." *American School Board Journal* (June 1946).

Frank, Glenn. "Should Teachers Unionize?" *Century Magazine* (February 1921).

Frayne, Hugh. "Public School Teachers in Affiliation with the American Federation of Labor." *The American Teacher* (February 1916).

Frohlich, May T. "New Orleans Teachers Organize." *The American Teacher* (April 1919).

Fuller, Edward H. "Educational Associations and Organizations in the United States." *Educational Review* (April 1918).

Furdycee, Wellington G. "The Historical Background of American Teacher Union." *American School Board Journal* (May 1946).

Fursman, Ida L. M. "Freedom, Ignorance, and Poverty." *The American Teacher* (October 1916).

Gaines, W. W. "The Atlanta Public School Teachers Association and the Board of Education." *The American Teacher* (March 12, 1928).

Gilman, Charlotte Perkins. "Education and Social Progress." *The American Teacher* (December 1912).

Glassberg, Benjamin. "The Organization of Teachers in the United States." *Dial* (September 20, 1919).

Gogen, Charles. "Blueprint for Democracy in Teacher Bargaining." *The American Teacher* (September 15, 1965).

_____. "Inaugural Address." *Chicago Teacher and School Board Journal* (June 1899).

Goggin, Catherine. Letter to Cynthia Leet, October 15, 1905. AFT Files: Washington, D.C.

Goldberg, Kalman. Letter to Albert Shanker, April 1, 1986. AFT Files: Walter Reuther Archives of Labor and Urban Affairs, Wayne State University, Detroit, Mich.

Gompers, Samuel. "The American School and the Working Man." *Addresses and Proceedings of the National Education Association* (July 1916).

Gregg, Russell T. and Roland A. Koyen. "Teacher Association, Organization, and Unions." *Review of Educational Research* (June 1949).

Haley, Margaret A. Letter to Florence C. Hanson, May 23, 1934. AFT Files, Walter Reuther Archives of Labor and Urban Affairs, Wayne State University, Detroit, Mich.

_____. "Tribute to Catherine Goggin," January 1916. AFT Files, Washington, D.C.

_____. "Why Teachers Should Organize." *Addresses and Proceedings of the National Education Association*, Washington, D.C., NEA, August 1904.

Hall, G. Stanley. "Certain Degenerative Tendencies Among Teachers." *Pedagogical Seminary* (December 1905).

Hanson, Florence C. Letter to Mary Barker, June 19, 1929. AFT Files, Washington, D.C.

_____. "The American Federation of Teachers and Strikes." *School and Society* (January 8, 1927).

Hard, William. "Chicago's Five Maiden Aunts." *American Magazine* (September 1906).

Healy, Robert. "Tribute to Carl Megel," *The American Teacher* (February 1977).

Hibbard, Walter H. "Courage and Co-Operation: Providence, R.I., Local 197." *The American Teacher* (January 13, 1929).

Jackman, Wilbur S. "Teachers' Federation and Labor Unionism." *Elementary School Teacher* (March 1905).

Jones, Jerome. "The Relation of the Atlanta Public School Teachers Association to Organized Labor." *The American Teacher* (March 12, 1928).

Kelly, Florence, et al. "A Symposium on Teachers' Unions." *The American Teacher* (February 1919).

Kennedy, John C. "Labor Unions and the Schools." *The American Teacher* (October 1915).

Kerchen, J. L. "Mutual Aid of American Federation of Teachers and Workers' Education." *The American Teacher* (June 1927).

Kimball, Hattie. "Federation of Teachers." *Journal of Education* (September 1919).

Lefkowitz, Abraham. "Affiliation with Labor." *The American Teacher* (January 1928).

____. "Letting the Professor." *Survey* (May 1919).

____. "The Teachers' Union: Past, Present, Future." *The American Teacher* (June 1917).

Lieberman, Myron. "Are Teachers Underpaid?" *The Public Interests* (Summer 1986).

Linville, Henry R. Letter to Members of the AFT Executive Council, April 23, 1934. AFT Files Walter Reuther Archives of Labor and Urban Affairs, Wayne State University, Detroit, Mich.

____. "Plans for the Development of the Teachers Union." *The American Teacher* (April 1919).

____. "Program of Action of the Teachers' Union of New York City for the Year 1921-1922." *School and Society* (October 22, 1921).

____. "Through the Fluoroscope, " *The American Teacher* (June 1917).

Little, Mary V. and Elizabeth E. Dix. "Present and Future Objectives of Local No. 52." *The American Teacher* (March 1, 1928).

Lloyd, Ralph. "New York Teachers Don't Want War with the NEA." *The American Teacher* (April 1975).

Loeb, Jacob. "Stenographic Report: the Chicago Teachers Federation," (presented to the Chicago Board of Education) (February 2, 1917). AFT Files, Washington, D.C.

Loeb, Max. "The Radical Movement in Education." *Survey,* December 1916.

____. "The Teacher and the Union." *The American Teacher* (February 1917).

Lovett, John L. "Fighting for Chicago Public Schools." *Chamberlain's* (June 1917).

Lowry, Raymond F. "United for Democracy in Education and the Nation." *The American Teacher* September-October 1935.

"Governor George Deukmejian on Education," July 6, 1983.

Milwaukee Evening Wisconsian, December 30, 1915.

MacKenzie, Stewart. "Teachers' Strikes, a Professional Disgrace." *Nation's Schools* (July 1947).

Mayer, Milton S. "When Teachers Strike: Chicago Learns Another Lesson." *Forum and Century* (August 1974).

Mayman, J. Edward. "Business and Education," *The American Teacher* (June 1917).

McAndrew, William. "The Control of the Teacher's Job." *The American Teacher* (September 1916).

McCoy, W. T. "What We Have Accomplished." *The American Teacher* (June 1919).

McElroy, Edward J. Letter to Albert Shanker, January 8, 1987. AFT Files: Washington, D.C.

Meany, George. "For a People's Congress: Now More than Ever." *The American Teacher* (September 1974).

Megel, Carl J., et al. "Goals of the American Federation of Teachers: A Symposium by Executive Council Members Sums Up Our Objectives for Teachers of America." *The American Teacher* (April 4, 1956).

———. "Economic Conditions for Teachers." *The American Teacher* (October 1952).

———. "The 93rd Congress: An AFT Report Card." *The American Teacher* (September 1974).

Meyers, Ellen. Letter to Albert Shanker, March 11, 1986. AFT Files: Walter Reuther Archives of Labor and Urban Affairs, Wayne State University, Detroit, Mich.

"Milk Drivers and Professors." *Literary Digest* (July 19, 1919).

Miller, Frederick. "Teachers' Unions at Work." *The American Teacher* (February, 1916).

———. "What a Teacher's Union is Not." *The American Teacher* (April 1916).

Minton, Bruce. "The Plot against the Teachers." *New Masses* (November 12, 1940).

"Miss Margaret A. Haley." *Current Literature* (June 1904).

Morrison, Benjamin. "The Cleveland School Board and the Teachers Union." *The American Teacher* (September 1914).

Mortimer, Florence C. "The Value of Labor Unions." *The American Teacher* (December 1919).

Mungazi, Dickson A. Interview with Albert Shanker. Washington, D.C., May 17, 1993.

Myers, C. E. "Should Teachers' Organizations Affiliate with the American Federation of Labor?" *School and Society*, November 22, 1919.

NEA, "NEA and AFT Continue Merger Talks" (minutes), Washington, D.C., November 4, 1993.

The New Republic, "Albert Shanker on Social Integration Through Educational Reform," June 24, 1985.

New York Times . "The AFL-CIO and Shanker," February 16, 1976.

———. "Bilingual Education," November 5-6, 1974.

———. "Inauguration of Jimmy Carter and Shanker," December 6, 1976.

———. "New York City Board of Education and Shanker," March 24, 1976.

———. "Shanker on Equal Educational Opportunity," January 19, 1978.

———. "Shanker on Grading Students," November 20, 1977.

———. "Shanker and the Position of Teachers," January 5, 1979.

———. "Shanker on Reagan's Policy," September 27, 1982.

———. "Shanker on Special Education," February 3, 1980.

———. "The Rise of Albert Shanker," January 15, September 14, 1975.

U.S. News and World Report February 8, 1988.

Savage, David. "Teacher Union Leader: Shanker Out Front Again in Push for School Reform," July 2, 1983.

Wall Street Journal, "Albert Shanker's Vision of America," November 24, 1987.

Nearing, Scott. "The New Education." *The American Teacher* (January 1916).

Neuman, Joseph Whutworth. "A History of the Atlanta School Teachers' Association: Local 89 of the American Federation of Teachers, 1919-1956," Ph.D. diss., Georgia State University, 1978.

Newman, Edwin. "Meet the Press," April 15, 1974. AFT Files: Washington, D.C.

Noah, Timothy. "The Fiery Unionist as Educational Leader: Albert Shanker." *The New Republic* (June 24, 1993).

O'Hanlon, John M. "Why Organized Labor Welcomes the Teachers." *The American Teacher* (December 1928).

O'Hare, Kate Richards. "Who Said Jurisdiction?" *The American Teacher* (October 13, 1928).

O'Hanlon, John M. "Why Organized Labor Welcomes the Teachers." *The American Teacher* (December 1928).

O'Hare, Kate Richards. "Who Said Jurisdiction?" *The American Teacher* (October 13, 1928).

O'Reilly, Mary. "What Organization of the Teachers Means to Labor." *Life and Labor* (November 1915).

Overstreet, Harry A. and Davis Sneden. "Should Teachers Affiliate with Organized Labor?" *Survey* (March 13, 1920).

Persons, Warren M. "The Chicago Teachers Federation." *Commons* (August 1905).

Peterson, Ester, et al. "A Symposium on Organization." *The American Teacher* (March-April 1937).

Pifer, Alan. "When Fashionable Rhetoric Fails" *The Education Week* (February 23, 1983).

Price, Richard R. "Should Teachers Unionize under the American Federation of Labor?" *School and Society* (April 3, 1920).

Ramsay, Charles Cornell. "Impressions of the NEA Convention for 13." *Education* (September 1903).

Rankin, Jeanette. "Unionism among Teachers." *The American Teacher* (May-June 1918).

Reese, Arthur. "Freedom Schools: 1965 and 1966." *The American Teacher* (April 1966).

Reeves, Floyd. "Current Educational Problems and the Work of the AFT Commission on Educational Reconstruction." *The American Teacher* (October 1946).

Roach, Stephen F. "School Boards and Teacher Strikes." *American School Board Journal* (November 1957).

Rood, Florence. "A New Type of City School Administration." *The American Teacher* (June 1914).

_____. "It's the First Step that Counts." *The American Teacher* (October 1928).

Rosenfeld, Stephen. "Bilingualism." The *Washington Post* (September 27, 1974).

Roth, Herrick S. "Colorado Fights Faceless Informers."*The American Teacher* (December 1954).

Ruediger, W. C. "Unionism among Teachers." *School and Society* (November 1918).

Russell, James E. "Organization of Teachers." *Educational Review* (September 1920).

Sacks, Eve, "Shanker's Impact on American Education and Society," interview conducted by Dickson A. Mungazi. Washington, D.C., May 17, 1993.

Satterthwaite, W. B. "What Seattle Has Been Doing." *The American Teacher* (April 13, 1929).

Schnaufer, Pete. "Collective Bargaining Contracts." *The American Teacher* (March 1967).

Schwanke, Marie L. and Sylvia J. Solomon. "How Local 250 Became a Majority Union." *American Teacher* (December 1954).

Selden, David. Memo to Albert Shanker, January 19, 1967. AFT Files: Washington, D. C.

_____. "Parent's Role as AFT Sees It." *Senior Scholastic* (teacher supplement) (November 1, 1968).

_____. "Reconstructing the AFT Executive Council" (memo to the Constitutional Amendment Committee of the AFT), January 17, 1967. AFT Files: Washington, D.C.

_____. "Evaluate Teachers?" QuEST Papers Series, #4. Washington, D.C., 1969. Available from ERIC, Document #ED 032 271.

_____. "The Professional Improvement of Teachers and Teaching through Organization." *School and Society* (November 8, 1919).

Shukotoff, Arnold. "A Program of Defense." *The American Teacher* (November-December, 1937).

Sibelman. "A Philosophy of Splendid Isolation: The NEA v. the AFL-CIO" *The American Teacher* (October 1974).

Smith, H. P. "How Far Can Teachers' Organizations Go and Be Professional?" *Midland Schools* (April 1920).

Smith, William D. "Teaching: Not Just a Job, But a Profession," (draft article sent to Albert Shanker with letter dated March 11, 1986). AFT Files: Washington, D.C.

Snodgrass, Margaret. "The American Federation of Teachers." *American Federalist* (September 1916).

Stair, Bird. "The Unionizing of Teachers." *School and Society* 10 (December 13, 1919): 699-703.

Stecker, Freeland G. "Report of the Financial Secretary of the American Federation of Teachers." *American Teacher* (September 1918).

_____. Letter to Earnest B. Collette, June 17, 1921. AFT Files: Washington, D.C.

_____. Letter to Florine E. Francis, president of the Gary, Indiana, Teachers Federation, December 11, 1924. AFT Files: Washington, D.C.

Stillman, Charles B. and C. C. Willard. "The Teachers' Outlook." *Public* (March 1918).

_____. "Educational Recommendations of the Atlantic City Convention of the American Federation of Labor." *The American Teacher* (September 1919).

_____. "Four Months of Progress." *The American Teacher* (January 1919).

_____. Response to a Strike by Teachers in Seattle, March 20, 1919. *The American Teacher* (February 1919).

Sutton, Willis A. "Relation of Superintendent to Teachers Association, Atlanta, Georgia, Public Schools." *The American Teacher* (March 1928).

"The Maid of Chicago." *Journal of Education* (August 15, 1901).

The NEA. "Teachers Salaries and Cost of Living, 1918." NEA Files, Washington. D.C.

Toch, Thomas. "Teacher Reform: Does Albert Shanker Still Believe? *America's Agenda*, 1993.

Thomas, Bruce R. Letter to Albert Shanker (March 11, 1987).

"Toward Better Race Relations in Detroit." *The American Teacher* (February 1948).

Turley, Ira S. "Full Salary Restored to Chicago after Ten Years." *The American Teacher* (February 1943).

Varnum, Walter C. "ETV Messiah or Minister?" *The American Teacher* (October 1958). Bloom, Arnold M. "A More Militant Profession." *American School and University* (October 1964).

Wattenberg, William W. *On the Educational Front: The Reactions of Teachers Associations in New York and Chicago.* New York: Columbia University Press, 1936.

Wayne, Edward A. Letter to Albert Shanker (January 16, 1986). AFT Files: Washington, D.C.

Whitfield, Stephen J. *Scott Nearing: Apostle of American Radicalism.* New York: Columbia University Press, 1974.

Wood, Charles W. "Professor John Dewey on the Hysteria Which Holds Teaching in a Check." *American Federation of Teachers Semi-Monthly Bulletin* (November 5, 1922).

Woodring, Paul. *The Persistent Problems of Education.* Bloomington, Ind.: Phi Delta Kappan, 1983.

DISSERTATIONS AND THESES

Browder, Lesley Hughes, Jr. "Teacher Unionism in America: A Descriptive Analysis of the Structure, Force, and Membership of the American Federation of Teachers." Ed.D. diss., Cornell University, 1965.

Christensen, John Edward. "A History of Teacher Unions." M.A. thesis, Arizona State Teachers College, 1940.

Clarke, James Earl. "The American Federation of Teachers: Origins and History from 1870 to 1952." Ph.D. diss., Cornell University, 1966.

Close, William Edward. "An Historical Study of the American Federation of Labor-Congress of Industrial Organizations Involvement in Higher Education with an Emphasis on the Period 1960-1969." Ph.D. diss., Catholic University of America, 1972.

Dewing, Rolland Lloyd. "Teacher Organizations and Desegregation, 1959-1964." Ph.D. diss., Ball State University, 1967.

Eaton, William Edward. "The Social and Educational Position of the American Federation of Teachers, 1929-1941." Ph.D. diss., Washington University, 1971.

Gilmer, Mary Fant. "History, Activities, and Present Status of the Atlanta Public School Teachers' Association." M.A. thesis, Emory University, 1939.

Goulding, Joel Arthur. "The History of Unionism in American Higher Education." Ed.D. diss., Wayne State University, 1970.

Graybiel, John M. "The American Federation of Teachers, 1916-1928." M.A. thesis, University of California, 1928.

Hobbs, Edward Henry. "The American Federation of Teachers: A Study in Politics and Administration." M.A. Thesis, University of Alabama, 1947.

Lester, Jeanette. "The American Federation of Teachers in Higher Education: A History of Union Organization of Faculty Members in Colleges and Universities, 1946-1966." Ed.D. dissertation, University of Toledo, 1968.

Levitan, Sar A. "A Study of the American Federation of Teachers." M.A. thesis, Columbia University, 1939

Lowman, Fern Elizabeth. "The Rise, Objectives, and Mode of Operation of the American Federation of Teachers." M.A. thesis, State University of Iowa, 1945.

McLaughlin, Samuel J. "The Educational Policies and Activities of the American Federation of Labor During the Present Century." Ph.D. diss., New York University, 1936.

Miller, Charles William. "Democracy in Education: A Study of How the American Federation of Teachers Met the Threat of Communist Subversion Through the Democratic Process." Ed.D. diss., Northwestern University, 1967.

Miller, Oscar Edward. "A Comparative Study, as to Organization and Functions, of the San Antonio Teachers Council with Local Teacher Associations of Cities of the United States, of 100,000 Population or More." M.A. thesis, University of Texas, 1936.

Newman, Joseph Whitworth. "A History of the Atlanta Public Teachers' Association: Local 89 of the American Federation of Teachers, 1919-1956." Ph.D. diss., Georgia State University, 1978.

Nottenburg, Robert A. "The Relationship of Organized Labor to Public School Legislation in Illinois, 1880-1948." Ph.D. diss., University of Chicago, 1950.

Pearse, Robert Francis. "Studies in White Collar Unionism; The Development of a Teachers Union." Ph.D. diss., University of Chicago, 1950.

Pootishman, Nancy. "Jane Addams and Education." M.A, thesis, Columbia University, 1960.

Pearse, Robert Francis. "Studies in White Collar Unionism; The Development of a Teachers Union." Ph.D. diss., University of Chicago, 1950.

Pootishman, Nancy. "Jane Addams and Education." M.A, thesis, Columbia University, 1960.

Reid, Robert Louis. "The Professionalization of Public School Teachers: The Chicago Experience 1895-1920." Ph.D. diss., Northwestern University, 1968.

Salerno, Michael Philip. "A Study of Various Aspects of Teacher Unionism in the United States." Ph.D. diss., University of Wyoming, 1967.

Schiff, Albert. "A Study and Evaluation of Teachers' Strikes in the United States." Ed.D. diss., Wayne State University, 1952.

Tomlinson, James L. "Teacher Organization and Labor Affiliation With the Educational Activities of the American Federation of Labor." M.A. thesis, Cornell University, 1944.

Tostberg, Robert Dugene. "Educational Ferment in Chicago, 1883-1904." Ph.D. diss., University of Wisconsin, 1960.

Waskiewicz, Leon S. "Organized Labor and Public Education in Michigan From 1880 to 1938." Ph.D. diss., University of Michigan, 1939.

Welsh, James W. "A Brief History of the Union Movement Among Teachers in the Public Schools of the United States." M.A. thesis, University of Michigan, 1930.

Index

About the Author

DICKSON A. MUNGAZI is Regents Professor of Educational Foundations and History at Northern Arizona University in Flagstaff.

ISBN 0-275-94929-X

EAN

9 780275 949297

90000>

HARDCOVER BAR CODE